5/26/98

Dave —
Hope you enjoy this
book! It is ~~in~~ a particular
appreciation for a great friend,
a great pilot & a tireless
worker for all airline pilots!
(never said I was a great
inscriber!!) I'm one who
is lucky to have whacked
a ball or two with you

Al Mumford

THE PILOT'S BURDEN

THE
PILOT'S
BURDEN

Flight Safety and the Roots of Pilot Error

CAPTAIN **ROBERT N. BUCK**

 Iowa State University / Ames

CAPTAIN ROBERT N. BUCK retired from TWA after 37 years, beginning with the Douglas DC-2 and ending with the Boeing 747. He served as TWA's chief pilot, was director of thunderstorm research, and flew over 2000 Atlantic crossings. During World War II he was engaged in weather research for the U.S. Air Corps, flying a B-17 and a Black Widow P-61; for this he was awarded, as a civilian, the Air Medal by President Harry Truman. In 1930, at age 16, he flew alone across the United States, breaking the junior transcontinental speed record. More recently, Buck has been an air safety consultant to the FAA and various airlines and has worked with the International Civil Aviation Organization—the UN part of aviation—to develop a new plan of world airspace. Other books written by Robert Buck include *Weather Flying, Flying Know-How,* and *The Art of Flying.*

Authorization to photocopy items for internal or personal use, or the internal or personal use of specific clients, is granted by Iowa State University Press, provided that the base fee of $.10 per copy is paid directly to the Copyright Clearance Center, 27 Congress Street, Salem, MA 01970. For those organizations that have been granted a photocopy license by CCC, a separate system of payments has been arranged. The fee codes for users of the Transactional Reporting Service are 0-8138-2357-9/94 $.10.

⊛ Printed on acid-free paper in the United States of America

First edition, 1994

IOWA STATE UNIVERSITY PRESS
2121 South State Avenue
Ames, Iowa 50014

Orders: 1-800-862-6657
Office: 1-514-292-00140
Fax: 1-515-292-3348

Library of Congress Cataloging-in-Publication Data

Buck, Robert N.
    The pilot's burden: flight safety and the roots of pilot error / Robert N. Buck.—1st ed.
        p.   cm.
    Includes bibliographical references.
    ISBN 0-8138-2357-9 (acid-free paper)
    1. Aeronautics—Safety measures.   2. Airplanes—Piloting—Safety measures.   3. Aircraft accidents—Human factors.   I. Title.
    TL553.5.B78   1994
    363.12'414—dc20   93-27824

Last digit is the print number: 9   8   7   6   5   4

**DEDICATED
TO PILOTS EVERYWHERE**

*WHETHER AIRLINE, GENERAL AVIATION,
OR MILITARY, THEY ALL CARRY
ELEMENTS OF THE BURDEN.*

CONTENTS

PREFACE

Let's get something clear in our minds about airplanes: they are free souls. They are not on tracks to be directed without an operator on board; they are not on a road where you can pull over if there's a mechanical problem or the gas tank runs dry.

Airplanes go up, down, and sideways; they stay in the air only if the pilot maintains flying speed. Without attention to that the airplane will fall; if it is allowed to go too fast, however, the wings can come off.

The wind can blow the plane sideways, help it along, or hold it back. The only track to follow is an invisible one that comes via compass and map, satellites, radio, or sophisticated internal equipment. The pilot must understand how these things work and be skilled in their use, or the airplane can wander off course and get lost.

In many ways, flying an airplane is a balancing act: do not go too fast or too slow; don't go too high or too low; don't wander without keeping careful track of where you're going; keep a safe place to land within range of fuel and weather because once the airplane is in the air it cannot return to earth unless there's a suitable place to do it. It's kind of like swimming across a deep lake—you must keep swimming until a shore is reached because it is impossible to stop and stand in water that's over your head.

Always lurking as a potential adversary is weather, tormentingly capricious and served only by an inexact science. This pilots must judge and act upon because they are the final authority.

Keeping all this together depends on the pilot's knowledge and skill, procedures, and training. But training and procedures only tell the pilot how, where, and when; still necessary is a certain awareness, when breaking ground and climbing into the sky, that keeping everything under control, staying within the constraints, is the pilot's task and responsibility, and no matter what computers are on board it's the pilot's job to keep a suspicious eye on their action because they cannot do the total job and they occasionally make mistakes.

Pilot abilities did not mature quickly but over a period of time, in step with technological growth as well as regulatory and operational intricacies.

We relate here that history and evolution to the present time in order to reveal the probability that pilots are being asked to perform flawlessly in an environment that generates manifold opportunity for error—and that often strips them of the autonomy to use the very judgment we require them to have.

I imposed on a lot of people for information and confirmation. First I'd have to thank Captain Paul A. Soderlind of Northwest, retired, who read the manuscript cover to cover and confirmed its technical accuracy and made valuable suggestions; my son, Captain Robert O. Buck, who was a solid source for what's really out there now, and I ask his forgiveness for the many questions I asked him—although they led to stimulating conversations; my daughter, Ferris Urbanowski, M.A. and a faculty member at Antioch/New England in the departments of Applied Psychology and Environmental Studies, as well as instructor, Stress Reduction Program, University of Massachusetts Medical Center; my ever-faithful wife, Jean Pearsall Buck, who helped in a myriad of ways, especially with her spelling expertise. Thanks also go to the famous guru of all air safety, Jerry Lederer, who always had the numbers and facts; all of aviation's friend, George Haddaway, Dallas, Texas; Captain Clarke Billie, TWA; Captain Ed Betts, TWA, retired; Captain Jon Ertzgaard, SAS and Saab test pilot; James Grambart, FAA-ATC, retired; C. W. Harper, NASA-Ames, retired; Charles Hynes, NASA-Ames; Pat Malone, Delta Air Lines; Captain Ruben Black, Delta Air Lines; Richard Masters, M.D., M.S.P.H., and Ruth Masters, B.S.N., M.S.P.H.; Captain Dick Roberti, Continental Airlines; Captain Charles Simpson, executive vice-president, Operations, Air Canada, retired; William F. Smith, test pilot, Lockheed, retired; Bernard Dowd, TWA, maintenance supervisor, retired; Dan Sowa, chief meteorologist, Northwest, retired; William Donavan; Dr. Sam Seideman, Montpelier, Vermont; Archie Trammel, AJT, Inc., Trinidad, Texas; Jim Cook; Captain Robert A. Wittke, TWA, retired; Captain Claude Girard, vice-president of

Flight Operations International, TWA, retired, Paris, France; Alex DeGrimm, TWA, Paris; Captain Randall Larivee; Captain Bob Mudge, Cockpit Management Resources; William Paris, C.M., Ottawa, Canada; John Downs, former U.S. representative to ICAO; Leighton Collins; and special appreciation to my editor, Alexia Dorszynski, whose help has been invaluable.

ACRONYMS

AAS	advanced automation system
ACARS	Airinc communications addressing and reporting system
ADI	attitude direction indicator
AF	autofeather
ALPA	Air Line Pilots Association
APU	auxiliary power unit
AQP	advanced qualification program
ARSA	Airport Radar Service Area
ASDE	airport surface detection equipment
ASRS	Aviation Safety Reporting System
ATA	Air Transport Association
ATC	air traffic control
ATIS	automatic terminal information service
AVTECH	advanced technology
CAA	Civil Aeronautics Authority
CAB	Civil Aeronautics Board
CADC	central air data computer
CAT	clear air turbulence
CDU	central display unit
CG	center of gravity
CRM	cockpit resource management
CRT	cathode-ray tube
CVR	cockpit voice recorder
CWSU	Center Weather Service Unit
DME	distance-measuring equipment
ECAC	European Civil Aviation Conference
EGT	exhaust gas temperature
EICAS	engine indication and crew alerting system
FAA	Federal Aviation Administration
FARs	Federal Aviation Regulations
F/D	flight director
FDR	flight data recorder

F/E	flight engineer
FMS	flight management system
F/O	first officer
FPD	freezing point depressant
FSDO	Flight Standards District Office
GCA	ground-controlled approach
GPS	global positioning system
GPWS	ground proximity warning system
IATA	International Air Transport Association
ICAO	International Civil Aviation Organization
IFF	identification friend or foe
ILS	instrument landing system
INS	inertial navigation system
IRS	inertial reference system
ITWAS	integrated terminal weather system
IWS	instrument warning system
LLWSA	low-level wind shear alert
LOFT	line-oriented flight training
LOP	line of position
Loran	long-range navigation
MCA	minimum control speed in the air
MEL	minimum equipment list
METO	maximum except takeoff
NASA	National Aeronautics and Space Administration
NIH	not invented here
NRA	National Recovery Act
NTSB	National Transportation Safety Board
NWS	National Weather Service
OBI	omnibearing indicator
PRT	power recovery turbine
QDM	magnetic bearing to station
RA	resolution advisory
RAF	Royal Air Force
RTCA	Radio Technical Commission for Aeronautics
SELCAL	selective calling
S/O	second officer
TCAS	traffic alert and collision avoidance system
TDWR	terminal Doppler weather radar
TP	turbulence pilot
UTC	universal time coordinated; same as Greenwich Time (Z)
VFR	visual flight rule
VHF	very high frequency
VIP	video integrator processor
VOR	very high frequency omnidirectional range

THE PILOT'S BURDEN

1 | WHEN FLYING WAS AN ART

A DC-9-87 tears down runway 3 at Detroit. In unsteady fashion it rises into the air but doesn't stay there because it hasn't enough lift to keep going. It hits a light pole, and the roof of a rental car facility, and then skids across the ground, breaking up and catching fire. One hundred fifty-six people are killed, including two on the ground unassociated with the airplane.

The National Transportation Safety Board (NTSB), the official U.S. accident investigation agency, said the airplane didn't fly because the wing flaps for takeoff had not been extended. NTSB determined that the probable cause was the flight crew's failure to read the checklist to ensure the flaps and slats were extended. In other words, pilot error.

"Pilot error" refers to error by the pilot up front in command of the airplane. In recent years it has been recognized that other people also contribute to airplane accidents, so the appellation "human error" is coming to replace the term "pilot error." Of course, when an accident is labeled human error—and 60 percent to 90 percent are, depending on who you're listening to—the thoughts and focus go right to the cockpit, and pilots still collect the major blame.

Human error is seldom accounted for in its entirety. This flying business is a big, complicated arena with many humans involved, most of whom are seldom if ever mentioned. To point out a few: the people who design and manufacture the airplane who may have made a serious error in stability and control; the test pilots who may not have been firm enough in condemning the fault; the company disregarding the pilot's warning; the Federal Aviation Administration (FAA), who makes the rules and puts its stamp of approval on the aircraft by granting its license; the air traffic control (ATC) system, whose employees are made to work with the concept that they must attempt to shove two pounds in a one-pound bag on a daily basis; the U.S. Congress for legislation passed in the heat of emotions or for funding unprovided; even the president of the United States, who upset the ATC system by firing experienced air traffic controllers who were impossible to replace for years, thereby screwing up an already overburdened system. There are also passengers, who add pressure unknowingly with their gripes and demands to make schedules for their connections, as well as their unspoken demands for a smooth ride, which pressure the pilot to request and at times argue with ATC for a better altitude where the air is smooth; the flight instruction system that taught the pilot to fly but missed on teaching judgment; the mechanic who didn't secure an oil drain plug; the people behind the weather dissemination system who didn't alert the pilot to a severe and growing thunderstorm at the airport of destination; the people responsible for airport design and construction who create a mishmash of taxi strips difficult to follow or runways located so aircraft must cross them while taxiing, which in turn strains the babble of communication to the point where misinterpreted instructions can put an airplane on an active runway in position for collision; the members of the local planning commissions who allow schools to be built almost on the end of a runway and then demand that the pilot follow hazardous noise reduction procedures; and the executives of the airlines who pressure the ATC system with more flights than the system can handle. Actually there are even more involved, since almost any human connected with the system can have an effect that contributes to the chain of events that finally leads to an accident, that creates an unbearable load that results in human error. Yes, the pilots may have forgotten to read the checklist and put the flaps down before takeoff, but why? In the 90 years since the Wright brothers' first flight, an intricate pattern has been woven, crossing the threads of technical advances with those of error, omission, self-interest, and simple stupidity, so that today we have a complicated tapestry that allows a pilot to forget the flaps.

This situation is not unique to aviation; in our society, these same threads have created patterns that result in suffering, unnecessary dislocation, potential environmental ruin, and even degradation of our way of life. But we are slow to see these snarls as calamitous and even slower to act to unravel them. With rare exception, little is done until catastrophe strikes. An airline accident is a sudden, dramatic disaster, one that gets immediate media attention; before the smoke has cleared, the hounding questions heard from all quarters are: "What happened? Who's at fault?"

This book attempts to identify the extent of the fault—not for the sake of sensationalism or to point fingers or to provide alibis but rather to understand why the present system demands faultless pilot performance 24 hours a day, often under severe stress, in order to make air travel safe.

Airplane accidents are indeed dramatic. One might theorize on the ironic possibility that aviation's courtship of the media for banner headlines to reward its great feats plays a part in the lurid response to accidents by newspapers and TV. But by any reasonable standard, air travel is the safest mode of transportation—the chance of being killed in an automobile is 20 times greater than in an airline accident. We don't get off lightly, however, because the system is potentially dangerous, as the occasional accident demonstrates.

Airline industry people wince at the possibility of a series of accidents occurring at once, at the potential for danger becoming reality—as happened when a KLM Royal Dutch 747 aircraft collided with a Pan Am 747 on the ground at Tenerife, Canary Islands, March 27, 1977, with the loss of 642 lives. On that day, circumstances—a runway shrouded in fog that made it impossible for the aircraft taking off to see the other taxiing down the same runway—combined with human frailties and previously ignored problems in a formula for disaster: an inadequate airport; improper communication and procedures; personnel of three different nationalities, with the cultural differences and gaps inherent in language interpretation; a crew member, probably affected by these difficulties, failing to be assertive enough; the rules limiting pilot duty time that may have pressured the KLM captain to be in a hurry; and the lack of technical aid, such as radar in the airplane that would show the pilot if the foggy runway ahead was clear. The Tenerife crash was an appalling example of errors of commission and omission combining in diabolic fashion to create tragedy. The official Spanish report of the accident said:

> The fundamental cause of the accident was the fact that the KLM Captain:
>
> 1. Took off without clearance.
> 2. Did not obey the "stand by for takeoff" from the tower.
> 3. Did not interrupt takeoff when Pan Am reported they were still on the runway.
> 4. In reply to the Flight Engineer's query as to whether the Pan Am had already left the runway, replied emphatically in the affirmative.

The fourth conclusion clearly reveals the breakdown in communications; obviously the KLM captain thought, through the mishmash of confused radio transmissions, that the runway was clear. No pilot would attempt to take off knowing another aircraft was on the same runway.

While the Tenerife tragedy was in 1977, and this is 1993, most factors that influenced this accident are still in place: the burden on people, this dependency, this disregard for human weakness. The potential for accidents *can* be reduced, but first we have to look at where we've been and then examine where we have to go, studying the whole without prejudice, emotion, or greed. Then, perhaps, we can define and make progress toward a better way.

Let's start in 1931, on a personal note. I was in a Pitcairn Mail-wing—an open biplane, 225 horsepower, no radio or fancy instruments, only a simple gyro instrument called a turn-and-bank indicator, which had a broad needlelike vertical hand that swung left or right with the airplane's nose, and a curved carpenter's level with a steel ball instead of a bubble to show slip and skid. Airspeed and rate of climb instruments (the rate of climb is now called a "vertical speed") made up the complement of blind-flying instruments. Doing it this way was called "flying by needle, ball, and airspeed."

The airport was Westfield, New Jersey, where the weather was bad: rain, low ceiling, and poor visibility. I wanted to get to New Hampshire. There the weather was high overcast with good visibility; the Weather Bureau over at Newark said so. I didn't know it then—I do now—but a warm front was south of New Jersey, slowly spreading its bad weather northeast-ward, as such fronts do. But the bad weather wouldn't get to New Hampshire before I did—if I got going.

The question was how to sneak through the rain, low ceiling, and poor visibility, past hills, obstructions, and New York City. This wasn't a situation for contact flying—that is, staying in sight of the ground. With the bad weather I soon wouldn't be able to *see* the ground. But although only a few pilots knew how to fly by instruments at the time, I was one of them. I'd taught myself to "fly blind," as it was called, by making a hood to cover the rear cockpit of the Pitcairn; I sat under the hood using only instruments to fly while a pilot friend, Bill Mumford, rode the front cockpit equipped with dual controls, where he could see, to keep me from running into another airplane. He could also right the Pitcairn when I got into weird maneuvers as part of the learning process. Now, I had this ability, so why not use it? The idea was to take off, climb to a safe terrain clearing altitude over New York City and the Connecticut hills—about 3000 feet—and fly northeast until I flew out of the bad weather.

I sat there and aimed the plane's nose down the grass strip we called a runway. To my left, beyond the airport boundary where the ground sloped up toward a farmhouse and barn with a nearby stand of elm trees, the scene looked misty and gloomy. Rain blew back from the propeller blast and

PITCAIRN PA-6 MAILWING being flown by the author. This is the airplane flown in the early blind flight described in the text. This type aircraft was used for flying the mail by Pitcairn Aviation, which later became Eastern Airlines, between Newark, New Jersey, and Atlanta, Georgia.

collected in a small swirling puddle on the orange wing fabric behind the inter-plane struts. I hesitated a moment after running up the engine and testing the magnetos, not quite sure about it all, but determined, and with the expression pilots often mumble to themselves—"Here goes nuthin'"—opened the throttle, raced down the field, and lifted into the wet sky. At first I stayed low, afraid to let go of the visible earth, but it was obvious I couldn't see enough to spook along by contact, so I lifted the nose and in an instant was in cloud. A quick look outside revealed nothing but white. Back inside I kept my eyes clamped on the turn-and-bank indicator. As I watched, it slipped off center, and the ball slid the other way. For an instant panic seared through me, but I knew I had to get the needle centered, the ball back where it belonged, to survive. I concentrated as never before, and the airplane tracked true as the altimeter hand crawled upward.

At 3000 feet I leveled off, set cruise RPM, and moved back a bit from the edge of the seat. Then a strange thing happened. The tenseness subsided, and I felt quite at ease, with an unexpected feeling of security. I wasn't down there ducking obstructions, trying to see through poor visibility, sticking my face out into the stinging rain, straining for vision; no, I was flying high, relaxed, and feeling protected. With each minute that ticked by, I felt more at ease and could handle the instruments with less strain.

A bit over an hour out of Westfield fright returned as my surroundings changed from white to gray, then dark gray. What was this? Some sort of storm? I looked ahead, above, and then down. Through thinning clouds, way below, I saw, intermittently as the cloud wisped past, the ribbon of a road lined by trees and fields. I shoved the nose down and quickly broke out beneath the clouds; there was long visibility ahead and much ceiling. I'd flown out of the weather! What an exhilarating feeling! I did a loop and at the top went into the clouds for an instant and then rushed down the backside into clear air again. I was between Hartford, Connecticut, and Boston.

Imagine flying across New York City through the northeast corridor with no traffic, no ATC, no two-way radio, not a thing to think about except those key basics: fly the airplane, navigate, and avoid the terrain. It was a beautiful, simple life.

The statistics as to who cracked up airplanes in that era look different from today's. The Aeronautics Branch of the Department of Commerce listed 43.29 percent of all accidents as pilot error, 16.59 percent as engine failure, 10.23 percent as due to weather, and 8.72 percent as due to terrain. They didn't account for the other 21 percent. Today, mechanical failure accounts for the cause less than 10 percent of the time, putting human failure at 90 percent, plus or minus a few decimal points.

It's clear that our advances in airplanes and engines have been wonderful, but what has happened to the human element? At first glance, it seems obvious that the airplane has become so reliable that the only thing remaining to cause an accident is human error—so the human error gets pride of place. Logical? Of course, but have we looked at the problem thoroughly and honestly? Have we weighed the human factor properly against the complexity of the system and aircraft? Has the opportunity for the human to err become greater? What happened to the uncluttered, uncomplicated task of using only a few instruments to fly an open biplane through clouds and rain? It's clear that advances in technology and training and the growth of the airline industry have changed flying, but have we also lost sight of some essential simplicity along the way? Was it necessary to create intricacies that demand so much of the human being? Let us search for that answer.

2 | THE TECHNICAL AGE COMMENCES

In the 1930s I, like most pilots, was watchful around the local airport but didn't think about running into other airplanes in the wide open, uncluttered sky. Then one day at Newark Airport, the serious idea that airplanes could collide became part of my flying intellect.

I was approached by Larry Pabst, an Eastern Air Transport airmail pilot who flew the mail in a Pitcairn like mine. He pointed out that I was one of the few private pilots who flew at night and that I could be a hazard to the mail pilots because the position lights on my airplane—white on the tail, green on the right wing tip, and red on the left—were an old type, made of some sort of plastic that clouded up with age, making the light dull. The airmail airplanes had been modified with glass-covered navigation lights that stayed clear and allowed maximum brilliance. The mail planes had been modified because they'd had some close encounters. How about installing the new glass lights on my airplane?

I saw the point and got the new lights. As a pilot, I'd had one bad scare at night, enough to want my lights as bright as possible. This philosophy—action after experience—lives with ATC today, and unfortunately action to create methods for expeditiously moving the constantly growing mass of traffic never catches up with demand.

In the early 1930s the airlines worried about aircraft flying blind in clouds and converging on an airport with no control or priorities. There were no traffic cops in the sky, no rules. Pilots often worked these things out themselves by knowing each other's schedules and talking between planes to decide who would land first. I can remember doing this myself on a routine basis over the airport in Columbus, Ohio, in 1937.

In December 1935 the first airway traffic control center came into being at Newark, New Jersey. It wasn't operated by the government, however; so urgent was the problem and so slow the government's response that the airline companies organized and manned it themselves. The next year, the airlines opened control centers at Chicago and Cleveland. Finally, in July 1936, the government (under the authority of the Bureau of Air Commerce) took over these centers. The entire country wasn't covered by a long shot, only key busy terminals; all other areas were still on a lucky-miss basis.

How did these control centers relate to pilot error? The first order of business was communication, so two-way radio became part of the airplane's equipment—two-way so that the pilot could receive traffic advisories and ask for weather and dispatch information as well. This added radio to the simple cockpit of needle, ball, and airspeed. The radio is, of course, helpful, but it is a diversion as well from the basic job of flying the airplane. And unfortunately even a mandated diversion doesn't relieve the pilot of keeping tabs on the airplane's flying and control. In reality the radio isn't only a diversion but also added work. The pilot is like a juggler who starts with two balls and then has a third added. It's necessary to keep all the balls in motion, and as we'll show, additional balls are frequently thrown into the pilot's juggling job, so there are many more than three in the air all the time.

Early radio was not a crisp, clear channel of communication but rather a noisy, ear-shattering mess of static necessitating much repeating, shouting, and even whistling dots and dashes to transmit code to get the message through. Because various frequencies were used, reception would skip and take long hops. Frequently an inbound pilot calling the La Guardia, New York, tower from over Coney Island might only hear garbled garbage from La Guardia but receive strong, clear instructions being given by the Chicago tower to someone landing there—a skip to New York that overpowered La Guardia's signals, making a mess of instructions and creating a hazardous situation.

The single pilot mail planes were gradually phased out in the early 1930s as technology created airplanes that could carry passengers as well as mail and express; Ford and Fokker trimotors were the popular ones. In 1932 the first low-wing, twin-engine all-metal airliner was developed: the Boeing 247. Close behind it, in 1933, the Douglas DC-2 came on the scene, followed a few years later by the famous DC-3. The new airplanes provided for two pilots, and the captain-copilot team was born, the copilot to help with the workload, especially radio contacts. But the copilot wasn't a perfect answer to the radio diversion; the captain still listened in on the mishmash to help with interpretation through the static to be certain the message was without error, which wasn't always possible by any means.

Nor was the copilot always a helpful addition. It wasn't simply a matter

THE BOEING 247D, which lead the industry into the modern age of low-wing, all-metal transports. The basic configuration still holds in almost all modern airliners. (*University of Texas History of Aviation Collection*)

of the copilot's inexperience but of the captain's new role as a commander. There wasn't necessarily a smooth flow of cooperation. Pilots who had flown alone in mail planes, doing things their own way, anyway they pleased, tended to go right on flying that way, leaving the copilots baffled as to what their roles were and what they should be doing. Procedures and crew coordination had not been introduced, or even considered seriously. Thus the mechanics of radio communication added to the pilot's distractions, and so did the copilot. This situation, in various degrees—sometimes serious—is present today.

The advent of traffic control didn't involve communication alone but also additional planning and thinking. If the pilot was told to hold until other aircraft landed, the pilot then had to decide how much delay doing so would cause and how much reserve fuel would be used. Using reserves meant, and still means, that the possibility of going to an alternate airport, should the original destination become unlandable because of weather, might be a serious problem. So while the pilot was tending the task of flying the airplane—and that could be in turbulence, ice, or other weather—the pilot's mind was also busy doing sums and worrying how the weather was acting at two airports, or perhaps three or even more if the weather at the first alternate was shaky. It's the same today, and it's a more pressing problem.

In the early days, the air traffic control (ATC) instructions were simple, but the poor radio reception, with repeated calls and half-heard messages, made them difficult. The pilots didn't talk to the air traffic controllers but to their company radio operator, who then contacted the air traffic control by telephone, got any instructions for the pilot, and relayed them to the pilot via company radio—a slow procedure.

With landing delays, the infamous holding maneuver—grinding around in the sky in a racetrack-shaped path—came into being. At first, holding patterns were pretty much the pilot's choice, but as traffic became heavier, the patterns had to be spelled out precisely. Today, the pattern is not only a very tight and specific one, with exact location and headings, but is part of a complicated procedure that specifies how to enter the pattern, depending on the direction the airplane is coming from. The pattern leg (one side of the racetrack) is to be flown for 1 minute before turning 180° and returning on the opposite side if below 14,000 feet, 1.5 minutes if flying above that. Speeds have been stipulated for entering and holding in patterns since a Trans World Airlines (TWA) and United Air Lines collision near Staten Island, New York, December 12, 1960, when the United DC-8 entered a holding pattern area at a high rate of speed, causing that airplane to overshoot the pattern boundary and enter TWA's air space. All 128 occupants of both airplanes were killed.

The industry's manner of curing ailments has generally been to create a new rule, unworkable though it may be. The problems of ATC were handled this way extensively. The cure then, and now, is to squeeze the air space to make room for more airplanes; invariably, the result is to make the protective air space around the airplane smaller, which offers less protection and adds to pilot and controller workload and stress. Such action creates more rules that are difficult to understand and comply with. Thus with the development of the ATC system, pilots had a new factor injected into the task of flying: worrying whether or not their flying was legal. These problems of legality, new and additional flying techniques, plus the added burdens caused by delays have not gone away through the years, but actually have been exacerbated.

From almost the first day of commercial air travel, passengers and airlines have pressed for faster traffic movement, but the development of air traffic control actually added delay in flying from point A to point B. There was no radar at the time, so each airplane was held in the sky until the one ahead was in view of the control tower or on the ground. In the early days, spacing between landing aircraft in bad weather was often 15 minutes; today it's a few minutes or less.

To speed things up, ATC demanded that pilots in a holding pattern be back over the station at a designated time. This was an attempt to have the airplane close to the station and ready for approach when its turn came rather than way out on the end of the holding pattern, which meant that no time would be wasted turning around and flying back to the station. The mental and physical gymnastics the pilot had to perform to accomplish this—which had nothing to do with flying an airplane—were bits and pieces added to a pilot's chores. (Such timing is rarely used today.) This goes on in rain or snow, with turbulence and possibly ice to fret about, and in the back of the pilot's mind must still be a concern about fuel reserves, landing alternates, and local weather—as well as keeping an eye on engine icing. Flying had to be and has to be exact in an up-and-down sense, because there is another airplane 1000 feet above and another 1000 feet below in the holding pattern that you don't want to get close to.

Rule-making was not confined to ATC but covered the entire flying spectrum. How low the airplane let down (descended) through the clouds to land became strictly regulated, for example. To descend, the pilot followed a beam. The beam was an audio path in the sky. If on the beam—on course—the pilot heard a steady tone. If the pilot went off to one side, the steady tone began to be interrupted and became the signal for the letter A: dot-dash. Going off course to the other side, the letter was an N: dash-dot. The beam wasn't always crisp and clear because static affected it, and flying in heavy snow and other precipitation could wipe out reception totally. In addition, the beam wandered and had false on-course areas. So beam riding required a lot of skill and cunning.

The procedure for making a descent through clouds was a careful, time-consuming maneuver called a let down or, more commonly today, an instrument approach. For example, an airplane coming from Philadelphia to Newark, New Jersey, where the ceiling might be 300 feet and visibility 1 mile, first flew at a safe terrain-clearing altitude of 2000 feet to the Newark radio range station; this established exact position. Then the aircraft turned around and flew out the beam leg away from the station for about 10 miles, made an exact turn around (called a "procedure turn"), descending to 1000 feet, then flew the beam back to the station, which was down in the Newark swamps near Elizabeth, New Jersey. On crossing the station the pilot descended to minimums—300 feet—toward the airport a mile and a half away and hoped it would show up.

To speed let-down procedures, a high-frequency fan marker was located on the beam leg some miles from the station. This, in vertical shape, was like an invisible fan placed on the beam leg; as the airplane flew through it, a bright white light flashed on the instrument panel and produced a loud, intermittent screech in the pilot's headphones as well. The fan marker was

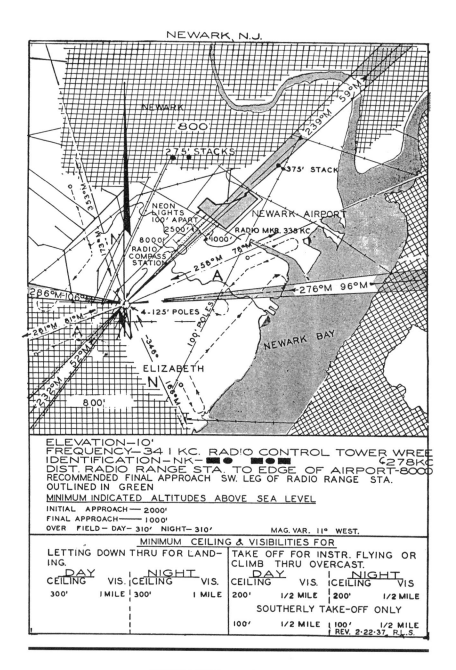

EARLY RADIO range instrument approach plate; Newark, New Jersey, February 1937. This was all it took for arrival and departure; on departure just turn to the necessary heading and go.

narrow and flight through it took less than a minute. This gave the pilot an exact location, which removed the time-consuming necessity of flying over a station and then going through the ritualistic maneuver of flying away for 10 miles and returning. By using the marker, the pilot could let down to final altitude for approach on the first arrival over the station, making what's called a straight-in approach.

The maneuver saved time but didn't solve the jam-up of aircraft pouring toward a destination at cruising speed while landing aircraft were slowing to half-speed or less. The ATC solution was, and is, like the bottleneck caused when high-speed highway traffic comes to a place where four lanes are squeezed into one. (Procedure turns still exist in some places, and fan markers are used extensively on instrument approach aids and en route.)[1]

By May 1939 there were 231 radio ranges—as the beam was called—and 21 fan markers. This federal airways system covered 25,000 miles, but this didn't mean there was traffic control over all these miles; instead, it was mostly confined to terminal areas. There was no control at all over the great spaces off the narrow airways.

The bad weather approach minimums—300 hundred feet and a mile visibility, in the case of Newark—were the minimums; going below that was breaking the rules.[2] Pilots cheated on occasion, depending on the airport and current weather. This was a time when it was permissible to attempt an

---

1. At one point, the story goes, a railroad man was called in to look at the air traffic problem in the hope that railroad experience might provide a few helpful tricks. After studying the problem, the railroad man laughed and said, "It's hopeless. You've got it all backwards. Railroads have one track en route and then spread out to many at the terminal. You have many tracks en route, but then squeeze them all down onto one at the terminal. It'll never work." He shook his head and departed.

2. "Minimums" is the common expression denoting how low an airplane can legally descend through clouds flying blind to an airport for landing. Minimums are expressed in ceiling and visibility. The minimums are approved by FAA after considering local terrain, airport size, lighting, obstructions, and electronic landing aids installed. Minimums are variable with airports; Wakefield, Virginia, with only a radio beacon for navigation has a relatively high minimum of a 727-foot ceiling and 2-mile visibility; Kennedy, New York, on runway 4R (R for right), with the best and latest instrument landing and lighting equipment, has the low minimum of 600-foot visibility with no ceiling specified. Airports have different approaches and minimums for different runways. There are about 15 various minimums and approaches at Kennedy, for example. These change when parts of the lighting or electronic aids are unserviceable. Pilots have to be aware of this and know it well or where to look it up quickly. The pilot descends through the clouds to minimums, and if the airport runway becomes visible at or before, it is okay to land. If, however, the runway doesn't come into sight at minimums the approach must be abandoned. Then the pilot faces decisions; hold for improving weather? Make another try? Go to an alternate airport? No one orders the pilot which to do; the pilot, the only person with all the facts, makes the decision—thank the Lord!

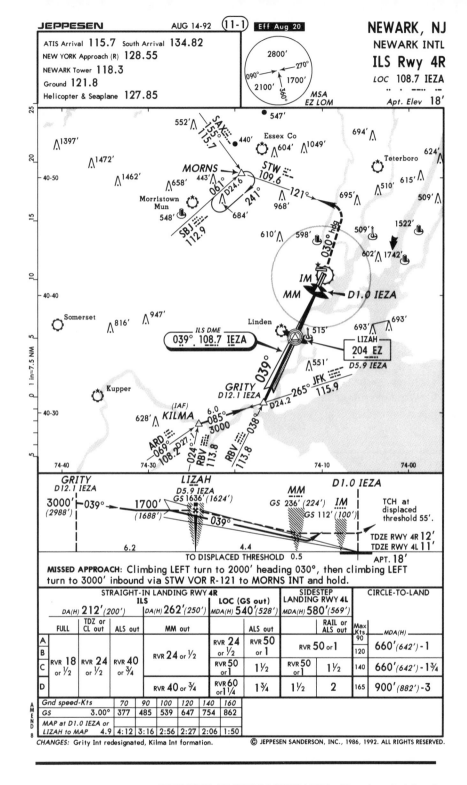

PRESENT-DAY APPROACH PLATE for Newark on the left and arrival routes on the right. There are three pages of arrival routes called Standard Terminal Arrival Routes (STAR) and six pages of departure routes called Standard Instrument Departure (SID).

JEPPESEN   16 JUL 93   (10-2B)   Eff 22 Jul

ATIS Arrival 115.7
South Arrival 134.82

 STAR

NEWARK, NJ
NEWARK INTL

WARRD FOUR (ENO.WARRD4)
(APPLICABLE TO TURBOJET AIRCRAFT ONLY)

**TURBOJET VERTICAL NAVIGATION
PLANNING INFORMATION**
Expect clearance to cross Ridgy Int at
FL 240. Expect clearance to cross Holey
Int at **11000'.** Expect clearance to cross
RBV VOR at **8000'.**
TRANSITIONS
**Agard (AGARD.WARRD4): From Agard Int
to ENO VOR:** Via SIE R-276 to
Speak Int, then via ENO R-235. Thence
**Patuxent (PXT.WARRD4): From PXT VOR
to ENO VOR:** Via PXT R-046 and
ENO R-226. Thence
ARRIVAL
From ENO VOR via ENO R-044 to Davys Int,
then via RBV R-238 to RBV VOR , then
from RBV VOR via RBV R-024 to Warrd Int.
Expect radar vectors to final approach
course after Warrd Int.

Direct distance from Warrd Int to:
    Newark Intl **24 NM**

WARRD
N40 21.7 W074 26.6
Expect radar vectors to
final approach course

SAX
115.7
185° D43

Newark Intl
18

083°

YARDLEY
D(L)108.2 ARD
N40 15.2 W074 54.5

024°
10
3000

249°
069°
R238°
238°

HOLEY
N39 58.3 W074 49.6
Expect clearance to
cross at **11000'**
3000
21

D
3000

D20
307°

Expect clearance
to cross
at **8000'**

ROBBINSVILLE
D(H)113.8 RBV
N40 12.1 W074 29.7

WOODSTOWN
D(L)112.8 OOD
N39 38.2 W075 18.2

DAVYS
N39 55.3 W074 53.8
D25
058° 4
3000
D22   296°

SKIPY
N39 30.4
W075 16.3
30
3000
D14   273°

COYLE
D(H)113.4 CYN
N39 49.0 W074 25.9

044°
3000
20

SMYRNA
D(L)111.4 ENO
N39 13.9 W075 31.0

R235°
R226°

CEDAR LAKE
D(L)115.2 VCN
N39 32.3 W074 58.0

AGARD
N39 02.6 W076 04.2

D50 235°

SPEAK
N39 03.5
W075 44.8
055°
3000
15
D
22
4000
D

SEA ISLE
D(H)114.8 SIE
N39 05.7 W074 48.0

AGARD
(AGARD.WARRD4)
096°   7000
15
D59

D44
R276°

RIDGY
N38 56.6 W075 47.4
Expect clearance to
cross at **FL 240**

101° D34
18
4000
GARED
N38 41.7 W076 01.4

NOTTINGHAM
D(L)113.7 OTT
N38 42.4 W076 44.7

D
(PXT.WARRD4)
PATUXENT
4000
30

046°

N
NOT TO SCALE

PATUXENT
D(L)117.6 PXT
N38 17.3 W076 24.0

approach even if the weather was reported below minimums—say 300 feet at Newark. Later the Civil Aeronautics Authority (CAA), FAA's predecessor, removed this permissiveness by passing a rule that said a pilot could not even try an approach if the airport was reported below minimums. This infuriated the pilots because what the weather report said and what the ceiling actually was were frequently different; an airport reporting 200 feet might actually have 300 or even 400 hundred when the pilot took a look. Observing ceilings was not an exact science then and isn't now, so the argument against strict minimum rules goes on.

Predictably, the business of minimums did not remain simple; instead, various "ifs" were added. If the wind is across the runway above a certain amount, the minimum is higher; if certain lights are not working, the minimums are higher. Today there is a plethora of rules about minimums. They are not easy to interpret, and of course, the pilot is flying, often in trying weather, and thinking about fuel, alternates, and all the rest while deciding if it's legal to let down or not. One night at Kennedy, 20 pilots from various domestic and foreign airlines had violations filed against them (later rescinded) because they had landed illegally—even though safely—due to their misinterpretation of the ambiguous rules on landing with a tail wind.[3]

From the beginning of instrument approaches the procedures have been mapped out on sheets of paper and placed in a loose-leaf notebook the pilots carry, along with books of rules and operating procedures and airplane technical manuals. This mass of stuff to carry, plus a required flashlight and in the early days a few tools, created a need for something to carry it all in. The black salesman's sample cases fitted the bill and were soon adapted to the task. One sees airline pilots lugging them, or trailing them on little wheel carts, through terminals. Complexity has added pounds of books to each black case.

By the late 1930s, ATC, two-way radio, and many rules were added to the simple job of moving controls and getting an airplane up and down. The pilot, then as now, must fly the airplane and battle the elements, but the addition of these other tasks started a trend that put distracting elements in a position to affect judgment and draw attention away from the primary task of flying—a situation that had a serious effect on safety and that continues to grow with malignancy today.

---

3. Violations are filed against a pilot by FAA, generally by letter, or in the case of immediate safety by an FAA inspector through various means. The penalties can range from a warning letter to fines, license revocation and grounding, even criminal action if indicated. A complicated legal process gives the pilot an opportunity to plead the case. This may take months, and during that time the pilot may not be able to fly or earn a living.

3 | TECHNOLOGY MEANS COMPLEXITY AND NEW PROBLEMS

Let's talk airplanes.

When you're talking commercial aviation, you have to start with the Douglas DC-3, which was the backbone of the airline industry. Far advanced from the simple open biplane with which we started, the DC-3 had two engines, retractable landing gear, wing flaps, and controllable pitch propellers. The Boeing 247 actually preceded the DC-3 and had many of the same advances, but it was smaller, and the DC-2 came along close behind and quickly developed into the DC-3. Both the 247 and the DC-3 represented advances in size and performance, but the Douglas aircraft, DC-2 and DC-3, soon took over the commercial skies.

Although the DC-3 is revered by old-timers who tend to get misty-eyed when talking of it, in many ways it wasn't a good airplane. Getting below the minimum speed for flight resulted in a stall that had nasty characteristics; one wing might duck down to start a spin, a fact that was vividly brought home to me while giving new copilots training at La Guardia in 1942. One heavy-handed student hauled the control wheel back hard while working steep turns, loading the wing and slowing it; in the flicker of an eye, we were in a tail-spin. We quickly recovered but only after a wild moment when the toilet door flew open and the "honey bucket" spilled its contents well over the cabin. (Normally the receptacle was removed for training flights, but it had been overlooked on this memorable flight.)

The DC-3 was a tail wheel type—a "tail dragger" in the parlance—and a pilot had to be careful when steering it on the ground or a ground loop spin around was possible. The plane's performance on one engine was marginal;

A DOZEN DC-3s lined up at Newark, New Jersey, airport in the late 1930s. (*Aviation Hall of Fame of New Jersey*)

it would never meet today's regulations for airliner engine outperformance.[1] The saving grace was the reliability of the engines. Early DC-3s had Wrights and the military C-47, still a DC-3, was equipped with Pratt and Whitneys. Both engines were highly reliable; if they hadn't been, the accident rate would have been much higher than it was, given the plane's lack of performance with an engine out and its squirreliness in certain areas of stability and control.

Then as now, the pilot had to remember the landing gear, although a horn sounded if it hadn't been extended for landing. (This didn't—and doesn't—always do the job. Recently, a Boeing 747 was down to 200 feet approaching London for landing with the wheels still retracted. Fortunately the tower, in its routine check of landing aircraft, noticed and warned the

---

1. "Engine outperformance" simply means how well an airplane can perform with one of its two engines not running; in the trade this is known as having an "engine out."

With four-engine airplanes it's one or two engines out. (Sometimes this is called "losing an engine"; that doesn't mean it fell off the airplane, just that it failed for some reason.) The regulations demand ability to clear terrain with engines out and to continue takeoff after a certain point and to clear obstacles. More on this later.

pilot. Why the horn warning was never heard hasn't been sorted out as of this time.)

The engines became more complicated as they became more efficient; the propeller pitch was controlled for maximum RPM during takeoff but had different settings for climb and cruise. The engines were supercharged, and if the throttles were opened wide, without the propeller controls set to match, severe engine damage and failure might occur. In addition the engine's carburetor iced up in conditions of rain, snow, and sometimes even clear air if the moisture content and temperature were just right. This required applying heat to deice. Putting on heat, in turn, disrupted the balance of fuel and air, so then it was necessary to readjust the mixture controls to fit the heat application—like learning the holding pattern, a juggling act that didn't have much to do with flying the airplane. Occasionally the pilot needed an extra eye to check the oil temperature, and if it wasn't where it should be, the pilot needed an extra pair of hands to move levers to get it right. Gill-like flaps on the engine cowl, called "cowl flaps," controlled engine cylinder head temperature and had to be opened for takeoff and climb, closed for cruising. The old biplane had none of this aside from mixture and carburetor heat controls we weren't quite certain what to do with. Early on I had asked a more-experienced pilot what I should do with the lever marked "carburetor heat." He didn't really know, he said, but expected you turned it on in the fall and off in the spring! This would have materially decreased engine performance, but fortunately the heater wasn't very effective and didn't do much, off or on.

The new engines created more work, as did the hydraulic system that moved landing gear and flaps. The pilot had to understand the system and be certain all was working properly—not a big job but another ball added to the juggling act.

By the mid 1930s we added radio, the developing ATC system, rules for the system and weather flying, and more complex airplane and engine systems. Pilots now were burdened with concern for requirements that don't have a thing to do with flying an airplane, requiring a different and removed thought process, so that while moving rudder pedals and wheel to respond to rough air, ice, the vagaries of weather, or the necessity to climb, descend, turn, or land, the pilot's mind also was off thinking about an ATC clearance, a delay, the airport weather, fuel reserves, and other things better thought about from behind a desk.

When the Boeing 247, the DC-2, and then the DC-3 came in, seat-of-the-pants flying went out. While there had always been thinking pilots, until then flying basically had primarily involved fine touch on the controls, a feel for the airplane's limits, and boldness. Flying was an art. The DC-3 made airline flying useful and economic; its ability to fly more weather with higher performance was achieved through technology that required the pilot to start down the road to being a technician, a direction that now takes precedence. Flying, however, periodically still needs the fine touch of the art of flying, although hard-nosed scientists believe technology can do it all. This split has created a conflict within aviation that is far from settled.

The DC-3 added a copilot and some instrument improvements; the turn-and-bank was still on the instrument panel because it could be used to recover from any unusual attitude, but it was replaced as a primary instrument by the artificial horizon and directional gyro.[2] While these made instrument flying easier and more precise, they still required concentration and attention from the pilot.

An autopilot was also added; crude by modern standards, it was useful in keeping the airplane straight and level—a work reliever for normal flight. If flight became abnormal, however, the pilot quickly turned the autopilot off and flew by hand.

The introduction of the autopilot was the beginning of a paradox that not only lives in today's aircraft but becomes more complex with each new airplane. When a structure like the autopilot is added, the pilot has to learn about its limitations and how to use it. The autopilot doesn't turn itself off and on or decide what mode it should be using or even if it should be used under present flight conditions. So its presence helps, but it adds to the pilot's task, requiring judgment and attention—another ball to juggle.

Now we must talk a bit about a basic philosophy of the aviation world—in one word, *redundancy*. It's the word used by the industry even though its connotation isn't quite correct. "Redundant" tends to mean the second thing is superfluous, but in flying it very often isn't. So we'll use the word "redundancy," or "redundant," to mean that we have two or more of anything necessary: electrical, hydraulic, and pneumatic systems, as well as two or more engines, instruments, radios, computers, and other things. The idea—the religion, actually, in flying—is that if one fails another can take over. A major part of airplane safety relies on this redundancy, but it doesn't come freely; the added systems and backups require attention,

---

2. The turn-and-bank and artificial horizon are both instruments that maintain a reference by a stable spinning gyroscope. The artificial horizon, however, could fail because the gyro would "spill" and become unusable if the airplane exceeded certain bank or pitch angles; the turn-and-bank is unspillable, which is part of the reason it's not as easy and natural to use as the artificial horizon developed to make blind flying less work. (Modern airplane artificial horizons do not spill.)

DOUGLAS DC-2 COCKPIT. Pilots unknown. (*National Air and Space Museum, Smithsonian Institution* [*SI Neg. No. 72-3707*])

too, some very little and some on a constant basis.

When the primary system fails, some heed must be paid to the second system's takeover to see if it is up to speed and functioning. (More of this later, when we talk about computers and automatic airplanes.) But the simple fact is that redundancy adds work and is, to a large or small degree, another demand on the captain and crew.

In addition to being a helper, the copilot is also part of the redundancy; if the captain falls over dead the F/O—"first officer," as copilots are now called—is there to take over. The redundancy of a working F/O, however, has its distraction in the simple fact that one crew member must check the work of the other to be certain it has been done correctly, another redundancy. So while the first officer is a work load reducer, his or her being there doesn't relieve the captain of the responsibility to check particular parts of the first officer's action. (The first officer should check certain aspects of the captain's work as well.) Thus more time is required as the price of aid; there is little added to airplanes and their operation that doesn't increase crew work load, which results in attention being diverted from something else, perhaps something very important. This interrelationship has not been lessened by the modern high-tech airplane—rather, it's been worsened.

All is not redundant, however, and one of the most important things that's not is the fuel on board. When the fuel is used up, there's no second load to turn to, and the airplane comes down. So fuel, its use as affected by weather, head winds, and ATC's circuitous clearances, is constantly in the captain's mind—often a worry demanding frequent computations and examination of "what if" factors. This worry goes on while the other side of the pilot's mind is tending to the multitudinous and diverse problems of getting an airplane safely from A to B.

The next major airplane advance in commercial aviation came when Boeing introduced the Stratoliner. This was a fat, four-engine, pressurized airplane—the first wide-body, actually. Its genesis was the B-17 bomber; it had the same wings, tail, landing gear, and many systems, the big difference being the fuselage, which could carry 33 passengers in ultracomfort, including berths for overnight travel. For the first time, pressurization gave lower-level breathing comfort to high-flying aircraft. Stratoliners flew at a modest 17,000 to 20,000 feet (today's airliners cruise up into the 40,000 foot range), but the passengers were living and breathing as though only at 8000.

In terms of pilot relationship, the Stratoliner brought a big addition, the F/E, or flight engineer. The Stratoliner's two additional engines, pressurization, and other systems added enough work for an extra hand.

In addition to the in-flight duties, the F/E also had ground duties, primarily inspecting the airplane before flight, "giving it a preflight" as the trade calls it. The original concept also called for the flight engineer to go to the hangar after flight and explain to maintenance what was wrong with the airplane that needed fixing; there was even the proposal that the engineer would stay in the hangar and make sure everything got done. But after flying all day or night, few F/Es found much charm in hanging around a hangar after-hours. The proposal quickly faded from the job duties.

The F/E position was not only helpful in flying the airplane but the F/E's presence gave the pilots a secure feeling about the airplane; the people put in this job were mostly mechanics taken from the hangar staff. If the F/E, a mechanic, inspected and checked the airplane and then came along on the flight, one felt the airplane's condition was bound to be near-perfect.

BOEING 307 STRATOLINER, the first pressurized, wide-body airliner. (TWA, courtesy of *National Air and Space Museum, Smithsonian Institution* [*SI Neg. No A 4470*])

The captain now had two crew members to deal with, and crew management responsibilities became more intense. Some pilots could mold the crew into a good team; others, however, created extra problems as they favored one crew member over the other or treated one as excess baggage. Often the first officer became the underdog because the airplane condition and the person who knew it well, the flight engineer, seemed to be more important than flying help. Recognizing some of the problems, the airlines established procedures as to who did what and when. About the same time, the checklist was introduced. Before the checklist, pilots had their own systems for checking the necessary items before and during the flight, generally in a systematic, across-the-cockpit manner, touching each item as it was inspected. But with added and more-complicated systems, missing an item became a real possibility. So one crew member, often the F/E, read

THE COCKPIT of a Boeing 307 Stratoliner shared by Captain M. C. Williams and First Officer Clarence Kulp. (*Ed Betts Collection*)

each item on the checklist, and the pilot responded after looking and often touching the object for confirmation. The military was first to use these checklists on the B-17, but the airlines quickly picked up the idea. The lists

THE FIRST FLIGHT ENGINEER'S STATION in the cockpit of a Boeing 307 Stratoliner is behind the copilot. (*Ed Betts Collection*)

differed from airplane to airplane and from airline to airline.

In later years a nasty, and to some, unreasonable union row caused a contract agreement that required all flight engineers to be pilots. The professional engineer, as we called the mechanic engineers, has gradually disappeared into retirement so that today almost all F/Es are pilots. Pilots are hired and first go to work as flight engineers. (The appellation "flight engineer" has just about disappeared, and now they are called S/Os—second officers.) From the S/O position they work up to first officer and eventually captain as seniority allows. So the second officer is a pilot champing at the bit to get in a pilot's seat and only suffering through the days of being a second officer. While many S/Os are conscientious, old pilots, like me, liked the original F/Es better—but that's another story.

The Stratoliner came in just before WW II. TWA purchased five from Boeing and Pan Am three. Howard Hughes bought one for himself for his usual mysterious reasons (many thought for a round-the-world flight, even nonstop, but it never happened), and the airplane sat out its life at the Hughes Airport in Culver City, California. The airplane had a few bursts of celebrity flying and was sold once, only to be repossessed by Hughes. Through uncharted vagaries the plane's fuselage finally became a boat, which a man uses as his home in Florida, while the wings simply disappeared, probably junked.

As World War II approached, this is how air transportation looked: the DC-3, blind weather flying, early air traffic control, a growing mass of regulations, and faintly showing on the horizon, the complex future in the form of the four-engine Stratoliner.

4 | WORLD WAR II CHANGES THE GAME

In 1941 war came—World War II—and the concept of minimum risk flying blew away like an autumn leaf before the wind. Our wings stretched, and we learned what the airplane could really do—and what we could as well. It was a shock; before the war regulations governed where and how we flew (down airways, along beam courses, to the specific airports a preflight inspection had qualified the pilot to use); the airplane's maximum allowed gross weight was spelled out and never exceeded. The late 1930s had just seen a battle royal between pilots and the airlines over raising the DC-3's gross weight from 24,400 pounds to 25,200 pounds; we feared this 800-pound increase would degrade safety, make performance marginal if one engine failed. How innocent we were.

The commercial, passenger-carrying part of the airlines held to conservative prewar rules, with the emphasis kept on safety; the only change came with Congress's passing a law that raised pilot maximum monthly flying hours from 85 to 100. The law was repealed in 1947, and commercial airline pilots were again restricted to 85 hours. (There's always been a great argument between management and pilots as to whether this is a safety matter or union job protectionism, but we talk about that later.)

Many airline pilots with reserve status were called back to service, but in addition, airline crews—captains, copilots, and flight engineers—were asked, as civilians, to fly military missions. In this service rules of hours per month and airplane gross weight were overlooked; one month, for example, I flew 126 hours in this type of operation. My first experience was assignment to an army air corps troop carrier outfit. Along with 10 other line crews, I was to fly C-47s out of Presque Isle, Maine, northeast to airports being constructed for a bridge across the North Atlantic. We'd haul cargo.

The assignment was vague, to say the least. How long would we do this? No answer. Were we in the army? No answer. What was our status if captured? No answer, although later we carried letters explaining that we were civilians flying for the military, to be treated as military prisoners of war rather than shot as spies. I never knew of anyone being captured, but that doesn't mean it never happened somewhere. It was a bastard status until the Air Transport Command created a uniform for the civilian pilots, and although it was more reminiscent of a uniform of a banana republic than of the U.S. Army Air Corps, it ended the question about our wearing various airline uniforms or civilian clothes while on military bases.

At Presque Isle, the routes and destinations were revealed: Goose Bay, Gander, Meeks Field. All strange names, but more important, where were they? Goose Bay in Labrador, Gander in Newfoundland, BW-1 in Greenland for gawd's sake, Meeks in Iceland. The maps handed to us had large white blank spaces, designating areas of unknown terrain heights. Radio ranges were located only at the destination, with none in between; we navigated by holding a compass heading until the destination range came within hearing, an operation that was somewhat disturbing because the radio ranges were operated by gasoline-powered generators and subject to shutdown. And, to add gnawing uneasiness, the DC-3s we'd fly—called C-47s in the military—would be flown at 32,000 pounds gross weight, no questions asked. And we had worried about that 25,200 pounds on the commercial DC-3!

My indoctrination came at 2:00 A.M. in Presque Isle. Russ Morris, my copilot, and I walked to the airplane, hunching over to try to stay dry in the pelting cold rain barely warm enough not to be snow, knowing it probably would be wet snow when we got to cruise altitude. The C-47 in army drab was austere and unfriendly, and the load of steel pipe and large boxes brought the gross weight to 30,800 pounds—5000 more than we'd ever flown. The cloud bases hung raggedly close to the ground; we weren't certain of the surrounding terrain because we didn't yet know the airport, a situation unheard of in commercial flying. The takeoff was nervous, the roll long, and the climb sluggish. In the air the clouds enveloped us immediately, shutting off all outside vision. Was our slow climb enough to skim over the local hills we couldn't see? My hands were tight on the control wheel straining upward as though trying to lift the airplane faster; when the altimeter crawled through 3000 feet, my hands relaxed, and I slid back from the edge of the seat relieved, knowing we were at least above the hills.

The arrival at Goose Bay was an instrument approach using the radio range for descent: low altitude in gray clouds and rain, then glimpses through breaks in the clouds of jack pine forest and a clean tumbling river close below, finally under all clouds at 200 feet, then landing on a gravel runway not yet completed—the rules already broken because legal minimums, laughed at then, were 800 feet. We were back to barnstorming.

That particular assignment lasted about two weeks and covered a lot of wilderness country and sections of ocean. We didn't have navigators, and the dead reckoning of prebeam days was inadequate for the job; instead, careful computations with untrustworthy weather data applied to magnetic courses gave a compass heading to hold as we sweated along, waiting for the destination beam to come within hearing range. Headings like that are subject to the capricious nature of winds aloft, so a precision track to destination was suspect. The magnetic variations in northern latitudes are big—36°W at Goose—so if you wanted to fly north, you followed a compass heading of 36°, which is considerably east of north, which made it seem a bit odd. Ironically, the army airplanes were fitted with a neat navigation station and the books, octants, and astro-compass needed for celestial navigation; the problem was none of us knew how to use it. After the first mission I collected the books, locked myself in a room, and came out a week later ready to navigate celestially.

The Japanese had bombed Dutch Harbor in the Aleutian Islands of Alaska, and at one time, rumors had them invading by the thousands! The national mood was frantic, if not downright panicky. We received new orders: to fly one of our own DC-3s from La Guardia to the Middletown, Pennsylvania, Army Depot, to pick up a load of cargo, and to head north.

The middle of the night—why did we always seem to fly in the night? Darkness everywhere as they loaded us, except for small floodlights that half-lighted the cargo door and airplane. Always the same smell around cargo areas of nothing particular and nothing appealing; if smell had color this one would have been dirty tan. With scuffles and bangs and blunt suggestions called out by men with heavy leather work gloves, the airplane was filled with big boxes, contents unknown—not because of security but simply because no one knew. I signed a batch of flimsy papers written in GI gobbledygook, utterly incomprehensible except for the destination typed on the top corner of one paper: Fairbanks, Alaska.

The load was tied down by a web of rope. We always took this tie-down seriously because in a thunderstorm or very rough air, loose cargo could be lethal, breaking the airplane or changing its center of gravity so it'd be uncontrollable; even a minor accident in landing could have the cargo tearing forward into the cockpit, doing us in. You looked it over carefully, pulling on a rope here and there, pushing against a box to make sure it was anchored. You were never satisfied because there were hidden elements—knots under things, questions of the rope's strength—but you accepted it and went.

Then off and across the night-shrouded country, with a long grind toward Great Falls, Montana, the jumping-off point for the Alaskan theater of operations. All theaters had airports to clear through, like big reinforced gates you dared not enter without approval: Great Falls for Alaska; Hamilton Field, California, for the Pacific; Presque Isle, Maine, for the North Atlantic. At these places you were briefed and given the dope—"gen," the British called it—on how to behave when you got in the territory of that piece of the war and its dangers.

We were given an emergency kit for the airplane, specifically Emergency Sustenance Kit Type E-2. It was alluring and harkened back to Boy Scout days except there was an adult seriousness to it. The possibility of using emergency equipment was real, so we dug out instruction books and studied them. There was a feeling of responsibility, also; you were the captain, and if the airplane was forced down or crash-landed in a remote, snow-covered area, the crew would look to you for leadership. You'd better have an idea how to cope with it.

Fort Nelson in British Columbia, Canada, is an airport cut out of a forest on a bluff above a river. Base leg over the bluff we took a quick look down at the trees and white water in the river—an unspoiled forest rich with moose, deer, bear, a river that must have been teaming with fish. Excitement is dulled by the frustration of flying, flying that takes one to isolated wilderness, exotic lands and cities, but only in a teasing way. See it on base leg to landing; glimpse a river like this one, called Fort Nelson, imagine casting a line into pristine waters, feel the solitude, smell the pine and forest, but have no chance to get in it, to live in and experience it. Tear your mind back to the landing, pick the landing spot on the runway, gauge the obstructions to miss, the winds that might be swirling around the surrounding trees, then touch down. After that, fuel up, make a flight plan, taxi out, glimpse the woods, swing around, pour on the coal and take off. Tantalizing, like passing a pretty woman you'll never know on the street.

Flying north there was high overcast, but unlimited visibility. The northern visibility is old style unlimited, like a brisk winter day in the United States when a cold front pushed by an Arctic air mass has blitzed through, blowing away pollution and giving us, briefly, before the pollution builds again, rare crisp air with the sharpness of a knife blade's edge.

With only a cabin full of boxes there were no queasy stomachs to make us hunt for smooth air, so we descended to the giddy height of a few hundred feet made giddy not by the height but by flying low and fast, looking down at details, into the trees at the earth, rocks, cuts and small valleys, and little streams, all rushing by, taking us back to days of no restrictions.

The course crisscrossed the Laird River tumbling through valleys and a canyon with red rocks that peered out from the wooded slopes, rivaling the

Grand Canyon for beauty. Not a person, town, or sign of habitation, only purity. We dove into a low place and pulled up over a climbing hillside— wild relief for airline pilots used to tight discipline and impeccable care for passengers.

It wasn't just a respite from the tight restrictions of line flying but also a return to using judgment that, in some areas, line flying took away. On the airline, courses were the same, terrain-clearing minimum altitudes were specifically spelled out, gas loads were decided in the dispatch office (although if you wanted more fuel you got it), radio navigation aids were many, and the law said you had to have one within range at all times. Down the airway to Pittsburgh 4000 feet cleared the highest terrain. But let loose in strange country, you carefully inspected maps for terrain height and decided for yourself what a safe minimum instrument altitude would be; distances were measured in detail, winds and weather judged to decide how much fuel was needed and how much extra to protect against the wiles of weather. On the line, an airplane's load was calculated by agents in an office; a slip was handed to you, stating what that load was, and your only task was to see that the numbers had been added accurately and agreed with the legal gross load. In this unusual military operation, you did your own computations and checked the pounds carefully; once in the air you dusted off your navigation skills for use when radio aids weren't available.

It may not have registered quite then, but the war gave back a sense of being a total pilot, of using skills and judgment that had become automatic or relinquished to others. Fortunately you had the skills, born in a time when there were no aids and few regulations. Judgment was still in the bag of tricks—learning and flying by rote had yet to infest the business.

5 | PILOTS ADD PSYCHOLOGY AND SCIENCE TO THEIR SKILLS

After the Alaskan junket the mission expanded. Those four-engine Stratoliners donned wartime camouflage and with extra fuel tanks and a 12,000-pound gross weight increase headed out over oceans.

The flight crew grew: a captain and two copilots, two flight engineers, a radio operator, a navigator, and a purser. The captain was suddenly at the head of a large group of people with no training or direction on how to manage this multiple crew. We learned the role demanded strong command, understanding, and an appreciation that the others had skills and brains worth using. The job of captain now included leadership—the skill to use all those people properly, keep them happy, and above all, try to make them respect you and feel you're a good enough pilot to keep them alive.

Today there's a big movement to make certain all crews receive psychological training to deliver the best; cockpit resource management (CRM) is the buzzword, and I have lots to say about that later on. But back then we grasped the need without the fancy psychological jargon because we knew that if we didn't achieve cooperation the cockpit could become a shambles.

As commander you had to size up crew members in order to work around any weak ones and double-check everything they did. Overly assertive crew members could be a problem, often going off on their own and doing something you weren't aware of. An instance of this occurred to me shortly after the end of the war when I was flying a Constellation nonstop from Boston to Paris. We'd taken off and were climbing through 15,000 feet over the Gulf of Maine when a fire alarm bell shattered the quiet cockpit and a red light flashed, warning of an engine fire. We went into action, performed the emergency checklist, and discharged a fire bottle, and as we did all this, I turned to head back for Boston. "Tell ATC," I told the first officer, "we have a fire indication and are descending, off course, and returning to Boston."

"The radios don't work," he said. "We have no radios!"[1]

My mind tore around as it tried to visualize the airplane's systems, wondering how in hell an engine fire would knock out the radios. Nothing logical occurred to me. We finally found the problem: the radio master switch was off. Questions revealed that the radio operator had turned it off when he heard the fire bell. He had decided, on his own, that if a fire occurred he was going to turn off all radios, on the premise the radios might have caused the fire, even though there was nothing in the carefully thought out procedures requiring him to do so. Once on the ground we had a firm chat about this. That's an example of what overly anxious, assertive crew members can do; a captain always has to keep in mind that he or she may have to "throw a net" over an unusually eager one.

The navigators, in general, came from worlds other than the sky; hired in desperation, sea people's most sought after skill was celestial navigation. The task of going from a 10-knot cargo ship to a 150-knot airplane wasn't easy for them. A handful of navigators were men who had rushed to attend school and obtain a skill that would land them a better war berth than the draft. They navigated, but we pilots looked carefully at their work because they came to us void of experience. I felt fortunate to know celestial because my appraisals could be more complete. On one westbound flight, for example, the navigator burst into the cockpit exclaiming, "Captain! We're standing still."

I knew there was a heavy head wind, but I didn't think we were actually standing still. I struggled out of my seat and went back to the navigation station. "Now, let's go back over all your figures," I said.

"I've checked everything three times—we're not moving," he insisted.

It was easy to spot the problem: he had used the wrong day page in the almanac for hour angle computation. Using the correct one, we showed progress, albeit slow. Anyone could make such an error. Some of the men were sharp and adapted quickly, a few were useless, one was an alcoholic, but all in all, each trip showed improvement.

The flights required bigger gas loads, higher gross weights, and greater

---

1. The radio setup involved radios in the cockpit with microphones for the captain and first officer to talk to towers, ATC, and such. Behind the captain was a radio station with a radio operator and equipment to communicate long-range using code—dots and dashes.

runway lengths than ever before needed. The vast expanse of sea we headed across had nothing to show the way; hence the importance of celestial navigation. Actually there's no big mystery to it; take a sextant, measure a star's angle above the celestial horizon, note the exact time and by some mumbo jumbo, plot a line on the chart called an LOP, for line of position. The only ability you really need is the intelligence to add and subtract and tell time. Do two more stars, and where the lines cross is a fix—that's where you were when you took the fix; actually it's historical data. The fixes on our missions weren't always textbook precise; shooting in rough air made an LOP inaccurate, maybe 10 miles wild. Three like that didn't give a neat place where all LOP's crossed but rather a figure like a big cocked hat; you were somewhere inside it, and part of the art of navigation was using an educated hunch to decide where. Now study the fix, look back to the last one, and see how the flight has progressed both in direction and speed; then think, look at the weather map, and contemplate its accuracy modified by what you've seen and learned by flying through it; then set a new course you hope will lead the airplane toward its destination. An hour later do another fix and go through the guessing, judging, and decision making again.

It wasn't always the navigator's decision alone; the captain, with worldly knowledge of sky, winds, and navigation, added thoughts and suggestions. Generally the interchange was unemotional, accomplished by discussion and exchange of ideas. It was cockpit resource management 40 years before it was "invented."

Of course, during daylight hours there are no visible stars, so an LOP is plotted from a shot of the sun, but this is only one line, only part of a fix—either an indication of how fast or slow, or an indication of how far left or right, but not both. And sometimes bad weather wrapped the airplane in clouds, and many anxious hours passed with no lines of any kind. If the sea was visible, a double drift could be taken, and the wind direction and velocity plotted. Wind is the key; without it, a straight and narrow course to a destination can be flown using an accurate compass alone, but wind carries the airplane sideways and affects its speed. The wind is invisible and not easy to forecast with great precision; you're always trying to find this invisible force that is close by, carrying you along, but never telling its strength and direction.

A double drift required a 45° right turn, the heading held while the navigator looked through a drift meter, a sort of downward-looking telescope poked through a hole in the floor. The navigator watched the white caps below drift across grid lines. Line them up, and you have the drift angle; then make a left turn of 90°, and do it again for another drift reading on this different heading; then return to the original heading. A little work with plotter and dividers and you have the wind direction and velocity.

In the early time of ocean flying, when we were still nervous, when the security of land seemed a long way off, you hated to change anything: don't fool with the engines, don't make big airplane maneuvers, don't make a move that might change the rhythm or the steadiness of flight. Don't risk disrupting something. One day is so indelibly etched in my mind that now, 50-odd years later, I can still see it like yesterday: middle of the ocean, bad weather, turbulence, rain, no celestial possible. Suddenly we flew into an area where the clouds were broken below, and we could see down 7000 feet to the sea. It was wild; hurricane-force winds spewed the white water in sheets off wave tops. The waves were tremendous, rising and falling, surging, crashing. In the middle of this, Ralph Alleman, navigator, came forward. "Skipper, let's do a double drift while we've got this hole." The old sea navigators always called you Skipper, and Ralph was one of the best.

I hated to turn and deviate from any course over the madness below, but we did, making the turns as I would without a qualm over land. Looking down at the wild disorder, though, I felt uneasy, realizing a forced landing in that fury would spell doom.

Radio operators were a new and mysterious breed. Sitting in a small corner, radios stacked behind them and the key for banging out dots and dashes at hand, they reported our positions and got weather and any message pertinent to the flight. With blackouts and jamming and radio frequencies difficult to use, they worked hard and did well even though there were occasionally big time gaps in communications; on certain routes such as Prestwick, Scotland, to Marrakech, Morocco, across the Bay of Biscay while the Nazis still held France, we maintained total radio silence.

Except for an oddball occurrence like the radio operator master switch incident, there was discipline in the cockpit. We developed the procedures and methods as we went along; flying oceans with sketchy navigation in overloaded airplanes was all new. The psychology of a crew working together wasn't spelled out as it is nowadays as a result of the quest for better cockpit management. We did it even though there wasn't a fancy acronym for it. Crew members' suggestions for better ways of doing things were adopted both when there was a quick need for action and in the long-term establishment of procedures for future operations. Captains, seeking better solutions, talked problems over with crew members. Listening to proponents of CRM today, you would think we operated in a way just short of bedlam before "modern" CRM came along. Not so. We had to work together in new and trying circumstances, and we did. Finding himself in a modern CRM class, a veteran of that era would scratch his head a bit and probably mutter, "So what's new?"

It was a big transition going from the New York to Kansas City run, with solid land below and a beam to guide the way, to an overloaded takeoff with a long run and the navigator passing up a piece of paper with 096°, or some appropriate heading, written on it. You crossed the coastline, and the airplane headed out over a wide sea. As a pilot you always kept in mind the possibility of engine failure; over land, you expected to find some safe place to set down or at least crack up gracefully, but over the sea this is impossible. We carried life vests and life rafts and emergency equipment, but no one really thought they'd work in the North Atlantic when the air temperature was near freezing and the waves were mountainous. The airplanes were not high-flying and pressurized as they are now. They flew at lower levels—7000 feet, plus or minus a few thousand, where clouds gather to confront you with ice or, in warmer climates, thunderstorms.

How hours were spent on the flight deck, in the dark: look at the air temperature that sits below 0°C; shine a flashlight outside the windshield corners to see how much ice is collecting; check the airspeed to see if it is falling off because of the ice's drag; talk over the carburetor heat situation with the flight engineer; study his computations of fuel remaining and check the notoriously inaccurate gauges to see how they compare; translate this into hours; try to make intelligent guesses about how many more it will take to reach the far shore and how much reserve fuel there will be, if any; talk it over with the navigator (his reply: "I haven't had a sight in three hours—how long we gonna be in this stuff?") and discuss what's on the weather folder they gave you that in words and picture told the meteorological prognostications for the flight; compare that with the weather you're actually in and see if it matches; wonder, always fret and wonder, about how slow you're going, how bad the head wind is because you don't know until the navigator gets a fix and he won't get one until you're out of this cloud mass; talk over the pressure changes he measured between barometric altitude and radio altitude, and both of you kick around the looks of it and possibilities; check the destination weather reports the radio operator has collected: "Gander: 800 feet, snow, visibility 1 mile, wind northwest 20 with gusts."

Plenty good enough for landing, but it tells a story of other things; the northwest wind means a cold front has gone through and passed over the ocean, moving slowly, and churning between you and Gander. Flying through it will bring ice, but more important, the area behind it, toward Gander, will have a deck of stratocumulus clouds—we call them "stratocu"—with tops of 12,000 to 14,000 feet and in them will be much ice. And 14,000 is high in a C-54 (civilian DC-4); if there are passengers, they'll require oxygen, but you don't have any provision for that.

All that's out ahead of you yet to combat; behind the front are strong head winds. Look again with the flashlight for ice, make another engine check with the flight engineer, darken all the cockpit lights, and stare out and up through the windshield, hoping to see a star. Seeing none, you turn on the landing lights to check if the beam has a fuzzy look that indicates you're in cloud, which means ice, or if the beam is sharp, which indicates you're probably between layers and at least are not getting ice. But all you see is a racing mass of sparkling streaks—snow.

The relief pilot comes forward from his nap in the bunk. It's your turn for a rest, but you pass it up. This is not the time you want to be sleeping; you couldn't fall asleep with all this going on. You don't think of the angry sea below or the chance of those pounding engines acting up, maybe one or more failing; it just wouldn't fit this situation, so you don't think about it. You trust the steady pounding to keep up its unbroken rhythm. The thought flashes through your mind, "I wish the son of a bitch who said pilots were just bus drivers was up here with me."

When land finally slides under the airplane, you seem to come back to reality. Out over the ocean, with all the problems and questions, there's an unreal sense. You're in a nether region where you don't belong to life, but back over land and security the fact of living becomes real again.

As more flights were flown, and experience gained, this feeling lessened for me, but way back in my psyche, when over the sea, bits of worry slipped in and out of my thinking if only for an instant. It wasn't until the arrival of the jet airplane and its modern navigation—the inertial system—that pilots' overocean minds were essentially cleared of worry. Of course, now that airlines cross the oceans with many two-engine airplanes, rather than four, I imagine pilots have, again, occasional disquieting thoughts.

Before and during the war, technical advances in navigation were in development; the war accelerated them. The low approach changed from the crudeness of flying a beam to a precision procedure made possible by radar. It was called GCA, ground-controlled approach.[2]

In the GCA system, two trucks equipped with radar parked on the airport in a specific spot; the approaching airplane was captured on radar, which gave both lateral and vertical direction. A highly trained operator concentrated on the radarscope and told the pilot to turn left or right and to descend faster or slower. The pilot was totally dependent on the GCA operator. GCA was a useful rig for wartime because the two trucks that housed the equipment could be moved to a new airport quickly and soon be

---

2. GCA is where the terminology "Talk the pilot down" came from. The expression, and lay public concept, should have ended with the demise of GCA because pilots, today, are not "talked down;" they are cleared by ATC to approach but then do the steering and make decisions themselves.

of help to airplanes arriving in bad weather there. It was good for an approach down to a 200-foot ceiling, although many operators bragged they could direct a pilot right to the ground in a blind landing. While such may have occurred on some desperate occasions, it wasn't routine by a long shot.

ILS—instrument landing system—was also developed in this period (actually before the war). In this system two beams are transmitted down the runway, one for left-right guidance and the other for descent; very high frequency fan markers along the path tell the pilot of the airplane's progress and location along the way. The beams are very precise because of the very high frequency they use. The ILS beams are not listened to; instead one "sees" them on an instrument with two needles, one for left-right, the other for up and down. The pilot's job is to keep them centered as airspeed, descent, and direction is maintained. The job demands a high order of concentration; descending on an ILS requires busy eyes that constantly scan and check many instruments, with the ILS indicator capturing center stage. As the plane approaches the runway, the beams narrow and become more difficult to follow; only tiny control corrections are needed, but they're needed quickly—overcontrolling at this stage ruins the approach, and it has to be abandoned.[3]

GCA demanded high concentration too, but was different in character from ILS and easier to fly, as the ground operator said things such as, "Three degrees right," and the pilot simply turned 3°. The pilot didn't have to judge the degrees needed; the ground controller did that, and the pilot simply carried out the order.

Any approach to any unseen runway is a precision task, and the quick corrections are needed as soon as you discover, either by instrument or ground controller's voice, that you're deviating from the straight and narrow. The quicker the deviation is spotted, the sooner the small correction is made and the chances for a good approach ensured. This, for one reason, is why GCA eventually went the way of the dodo bird.

GCA also added another human to the chain of possible error. Visualize an approach with the airplane sliding slightly off course to the right; the GCA operator sees this on the radarscope, decides how much correction the pilot should make, and then radios the information to the pilot, who has to absorb it and then react. Now imagine a landing the ILS way: the instant the airplane slides off to the right, the pilot sees the needle movement and immediately starts a correction, deciding how much correction to make as it's

---

3. The ILS indicator is a straight-line connection to the radio receivers and so is called "raw data." Later, sophistication and automatic pilots changed this. But keep in mind raw data as we come back to it later on.

GCA EQUIPMENT for talking pilots down to the runway during bad weather. The aircraft in flight is a Douglas C-54. The commercial version is known as the DC-4 and was the dominant aircraft first used on international routes. (*National Air and Space Museum, Smithsonian Institution.* [*SI Neg. No. 76-3182*])

done. There's a big difference in time, reaction, and therefore deviation from the beam. GCA would also be difficult to lock on and put in the autopilot electronics for an automatic approach in a completely blind landing.

GCA was used in Gander, Newfoundland, for some time after the war for commercial trans-Atlantic flying. I was enthusiastic about GCA and the Gander operators were superb, but one snowy night my enthusiasm was dashed as I approached Gander for landing under a moderate ceiling. As the operator announced that I should see the runway directly ahead, I broke out of the clouds, but instead of the runway I saw the roof of a hangar—we were well off course. I never felt comfortable with GCA again. GCA is still used by the military for certain of its operations, which differ, of course, from the civilian variety.

ILS was not handy for general war use because the system requires a good location for the shacks holding the transmitters and much adjusting to correct for local terrain, minerals in the earth, and the other variables that affect the system. One area where it was used, however, was the Aleutian Islands. The Air Corps there kept a very careful eye on the ILSs, and a pilot flew in and out of each station almost daily to check their accuracy. I used these ILSs a considerable amount during that period on the islands of Shemya and Adak while doing weather research. They made possible a lot of bad weather flying that couldn't have been done with the old radio beam. Still, for all its strengths, ILS is another addition to the pilot's many tasks. The old beam that pounded in the pilot's ears and required a certain technique to use gradually disappeared, but the chatter of ATC, company radio, necessary intracockpit communication, markers, navigation aid identification and bells, buzzers, clackers, and such for system failure warnings soon moved in to fill the space that dit, dahs, and steady tones vacated. ILS also added an instrument to the panel; since the beam and GCA came in their ears, the pilots only had to respond visually to a group of instruments that were mainly heading, attitude, air, and vertical speed—along, of course, with power setting and occasional glances at engine condition. The ILS demands close attention so that the pilot's cockpit scan has to be faster; the key job is to watch the instruments that keep the airplane under control and move it where and to the degree desired. The technique is to clamp on the heading and descent rate but to keep one eye on the ILS for any needle movement off center, which is simply information; any fixing is done using those other instruments. The ILS indicator is, in a way, like adding a fourth ball to the juggling act. The amount of concentration necessary, especially as the airplane gets lower and closer to the runway, is so great that it's almost mesmerizing; it's easy to overlook an occasional check to other instruments, which is why the copilot has work to do also—calling out airspeed, altitudes, large rate of descent changes, and big ILS needle deviations. An ILS landing is a real team effort.

Originally, if the ILS failed, a red marker, referred to as a flag, came into view on the instrument face—a small, subtle flag popped up in a corner of the instrument. The needles, in this event, didn't do anything special; they simply stayed on center as though the airplane was right smack on perfect course. Time and again, while giving pilot check rides, the check pilot would pull the circuit breaker on the ILS, simulating a failure, but the pilot flying was concentrating so intensely, so mesmerized by the tight task of flying the ILS, that the red flag was rarely noticed. The airplane continued, inevitably wandering off course while the pilot thought everything fine. The check pilot, of course, took over before things became dangerous. Today this checking is done in a simulator, and the check pilot doesn't take over but lets the airplane "crash," which the simulator does with jerks and loud noises. In modern airliners the indicating needles now disappear from view when there's a failure in the instrument system. There are many older airliners flying, however, the instrument needles of which still remain centered when there's a failure.

The wartime operation made everything bolder. Instead of Newark to Chicago nonstop, it was Gander to Prestwick, Scotland, across the North Atlantic; where before we'd been flying with emergency airports always within 50 miles or less, we now had nothing but the cold sea below and the first landing spot likely to be 1000 miles away. On the airliner, when an engine missed a beat, it was, "Oh damn it—what's going on?" Over the ocean, it was translated to dry lips and a lump in one's stomach.

We renewed old feelings and skills in dealing with the uncertainty: the unfamiliar airports, sketchy weather information, navigation, limp signals from far-off radio stations that had to be balanced against other flight information, and bearings, referred to in the "Q" code as QDMs, sent to us by land direction finder when requested by our radio operator. Between Scotland and Iceland, the Germans in Norway would send us phony signals in an attempt to suck us off course, but the signals were crude and easy to recognize and avoid. Information came in codes, like the important altimeter setting, and codes can be misinterpreted or sent wrong, as happened the day we shot a 200-foot ceiling in Adak in the Aleutians and broke out of the clouds almost on the ground—the ceiling was 100 feet or less—because of a wrong altimeter setting.

Official ceiling and minimums were not strictly enforced, and most times the minimum was what the pilots thought they could manage—often very low indeed. Interestingly the accidents were so few on these "use your own judgment" approaches that I cannot recall any. The worry of en route weather lessened, however, because the destination was far off and one could more easily zigzag to avoid bad weather on these long jaunts through the empty sky than when trying to duck weather on a short flight like Pittsburgh, Pennsylvania, to Columbus, Ohio.

Wartime flying was a maturing experience, speeding the development of overocean international flight. Without the war, we would have progressed in smaller, slower steps, but the war's desperate requirements pushed us to the far horizon. When it ended, we went back to flying the line, our skills and perspectives vastly expanded. With the start of commercial international aviation, there was relief from the anxieties of war, but commercial, international flying was almost the same as wartime overocean flying; we simply changed uniforms, repainted the airplanes, added cabin attendants—guys and gals—and were off.

The regulatory agencies of the United States and other countries hadn't yet gotten organized to put down or enforce rules, so the operation retained that freewheeling feel of wartime, and we did well. The International Civil Aviation Organization (ICAO) was formed in 1944 and was still stumbling along to get organized and create rules and methods.

The radio navigation aids were spotty and old-fashioned; we used radio beacons interpreted by an instrument that is a needle on a compass rose face. You tuned into a station and followed the needle, although it wasn't quite that easy because it was necessary to track toward or away from the station, correcting for wind, which requires some mental gymnastics to make it come out right. These beacons were also on radio frequencies subject to interference from other stations and affected by atmospheric conditions. A lot of dexterity was needed to sort that out. Instrument approaches were made using the radio beacons. An old European system used at some airports required your radio operator to request a QDM, a magnetic bearing to the station; the station took a bearing on your radio signal, then sent it to the radio operator who passed it along to you, the pilot. This was a crude form of GCA but without vertical guidance. You judged that by altimeter. The minimums had to be higher because of this. The entire process was cumbersome and required three people to make it work, which gave lots of chance for error. Europeans had been accustomed to the system, and some did a magnificent job; Geneva, Switzerland, comes to mind as a place that could put you right down the runway. Interpreting the QDMs and deciding which way to turn and how much was a high-concentration job for the pilot, demanding thought and visualization; by today's standards, however, it was primitive.

Air traffic control was not well developed, and it was important to listen to others and keep informed as to where they were in relation to you and to check that ATC hadn't made an error, as it did the night I reported over Mount Ceneri beacon near Locarno, Switzerland, only to hear another aircraft report over at the same time and altitude! We slipped past each other in the cloud-shrouded night, not seeing, never knowing how close our miss had been. When the ground was somewhat hysterically told of this, the response was, "You'd better watch out."

As time went on, regulations were put in place piecemeal, and the unsettling question of "Am I legal?" moved in. The war had reminded us that pilots depending on their skills worked very well; we felt as though a flight was always under the pilot's command. But as regulations built toward a bureaucratic "bookful," and enforcement methods increased, the discouraging feeling that others were trying to take over command, or at least part of it, crept in. Split command creates confusion as well as questions that may cause a Milquetoast pilot to waver in making a decision—a dangerous situation. The years have exacerbated this problem, and it is a serious factor in our quest for safety today.

6

POSTWAR AIRPLANES AND REGULATIONS: THE BURDEN GROWS

With the war's end, the era of complexity began in earnest. New aircraft entered service: the Constellation, DC-6, Boeing Stratocruiser, Martin, and Convair. These were complicated planes, their cockpits confusing places of levers, switches, valves, and instruments. Much of this had to do with the engines of the time, which were internal combustion engines pumped up to put out maximum horsepower with minimum weight and fuel consumption and slinging big propellers. Despite their size and power, these engines demanded precise, delicate management if damage was to be avoided. Superchargers resulted in high pressures within the engine; in order to adjust fuel mixture controls precisely, the flight engineer scrutinized the readings of a special analyzer. The temperature of the cylinder heads had strict tolerances, and flaps on the back of the cowling were opened and shut as more or less cooling was required. One engine even had a spark advance control lever like some automobiles of the 1920s. Whatever the airplane, engine management was a big part of its operation.

The fuel systems, too, became more involved as wing tanks were supplemented with tanks in the fuselage. One didn't just turn on the fuel and then forget about it; rather the fuel had to be used from the tanks in a certain order to maintain the airplane's structural integrity. The new fuel systems, in turn, had implications for landing, as landing weight is different from takeoff weight; landing weight is required to be less than on takeoff because designers and engineers reason that the structure may have to take a bigger clout during landing than it would during takeoff. An added performance factor, too complicated to deal with here, also plays a part.

A Lockheed Constellation 749A was allowed a takeoff weight of 107,000

DOUGLAS DC-6 in Swiss Air markings. The DC-6 was pressurized and was a competitor of the Constellation. The Douglas DC-7, a subsequent model, was made bigger and faster to compete with late model Constellations. (*Swiss Air, courtesy of National Air and Space Museum, Smithsonian Institution.* [*SI Neg. No. 93-13156*])

pounds but was restricted to a maximum landing weight of 89,500 pounds. Well, suppose you had to return and land shortly after takeoff? The answer was to dump fuel until the weight was legal, a procedure that introduced a special reference speed—"max fuel dumping speed"—into aeronautical parlance. This was in the late 1940s and early 1950s, but weight difference and fuel dumping exists today as an important part of modern airline airplane operation—the Boeing 767-200, for example, has a takeoff weight of 300,000 pounds and a landing weight of 270,000 pounds.

The new electrical systems had four generators, in the case of four-engine airplanes, and a spaghettilike mess of wires and gadgets, with many, many circuit breakers (a Boeing 707 had 430 in the cockpit area) to make it all flow as needed. The electrical system too required attention.

Hydraulics powered the flaps, brakes, and retractable landing gear and provided steering for the nosewheel on the ground. The hydraulic system, with fluid, pumps, check valves, accumulators, and reservoir, was another system that needed a watchful eye.

The Constellation, Stratocruiser, and DC-6 had pressurization systems that allowed pilots to fly as high as 20,000 feet, although normal cruise altitude was closer to 17,000, and yet keep the passengers as comfortable as they might be around 8000 feet. The airplane's ability to fly higher helped the pilot escape much of the en route weather but not all of it by a long shot. The price for pressurization was another complication added to the flight crew's work load, not only in the sense of systems management but flight management too. When the airplane climbed and descended, the pilot had to be certain airplane climb and descent rates would match the cabin's pressurization rates too and not get out of proper phase.

With all these systems the flight engineer on the four-engine airplanes was an important part of the crew, monitoring and operating systems and relieving the pilots from the work. Of course, flight engineers didn't run off to make major decisions on their own but worked with the pilots, telling them what the problems were and their effect on the airplane. The flight engineers kept a close eye on the amount of fuel available and being used and could report the amounts to the pilot at any time the pilot would ask for it; the pilot then quickly did rough math to "feel" if the figures were "in the ball park." Other chores piled on engineers included some radio communication and gathering weather reports. A good flight engineer was a very useful adjunct to the crew, allowing the pilots to concentrate on matters of flying, navigation, and weather.

The range of the most-used airplane, the DC-4, at the start of international operations in 1946 was limited. We had to stop at Gander, Newfoundland, and Shannon, Ireland, when going from New York to Paris. The fuel reserves were tight, and some westbound flights against head winds were difficult. One winter night I departed Shannon for Gander with a flight plan against strong winter winds for over 10 hours. Our progress was slow and tedious, and routine position plots on the howgozit fell in the danger zone. Over Ocean Vessel Charlie, a Coast Guard boat that was stationed a little past halfway across the ocean to provide weather and navigation information (and that night the first good, solid fix we'd had), the howgozit said, in effect, "You ain't gonna make it."

We refigured, looked at the poor weather Gander reported, checked again, and then looked at each other in some surprise. "We have to turn around and go back to Shannon!" So I did a 180° turn in the middle of the North Atlantic and, with the fierce wind behind us, "blew" back to Shannon in no time.

The early Constellations that came soon after the DC-4 gave more range, and we were generally able to pass up Gander or Shannon. The last model

EARLY LOCKHEED CONSTELLATION COCKPIT. The floor-boards have been removed on the copilot's side. (*Ed Betts Collection*)

Constellation, the 1649, which came on the scene in 1957, had long wings and big engines and could carry lots of fuel, allowing us to maintain a Los Angeles–London service. We made it nonstop most of the time eastbound and one-stop westbound. Flights of over 20 hours in the air were not infrequent in that airplane.

The twin-engine airplanes didn't have flight engineers, and the pilots had to carry the work load, which wasn't much less than that on the bigger airplanes; the systems were all there in the pressurized Martin 404s and the Convair 240, the only difference being that there were two fewer engines. The pilots were busy people. The confusion of gadgets, instruments, levers, and such were not always well placed in accordance with scientific, human factor design. The cockpit design may have started out that way, but space was critical—after all, there's only so much room on an instrument panel or in the cockpit.

These airplanes forced the development of procedures to cope with their intricacy; the task of each crew member was spelled out as well as when and how that person was to do his or her duties. Checklists were long, and since they took time and patience to complete, some pilots tended to rush through them or pass over items. Regulations and company policies came down hard on such pilots, and finally the use of checklists became de rigueur. But their length meant long waiting times at the end of the runway, so they were

FLIGHT ENGINEER'S STATION in an early Lockheed Constellation (*Ed Betts Collection*)

THE LAST MODEL LOCKHEED CONSTELLATION—the 1649 Jetstream. It was truly a long-range airplane and TWA operated them from Los Angeles, California, to London, England, nonstop. The schedule was about 18 hours. (*National Air and Space Museum, Smithsonian Institution. [SI Neg. No. A 533 B]*)

constantly being redesigned to reduce them to essentials. Basic philosophical differences emerged regarding their use: Do you read the checklist item by item, with the crew member answering and performing the check then? Or do crew members take care of things as time allows, with the checklist then read shortly before takeoff to make certain all has been done? This controversy hasn't been settled yet, and tense arguments along such lines can be found in many pilot's bull sessions. I attended a conference in December 1990 on modern cockpit management during which a psychologist said he'd looked through all the literature and could find nothing on the philosophy behind or efficacy of checklist use. A research project was subsequently set up to make a study—52 years after checklists first came into use!

Airplane regulation was developing as well. In 1946 the Civil Aeronautics Authority (CAA) demanded compliance with a new set of regulations regarding airplane performance, today's FAR, Part 25, "Airworthiness Standards: Transport Category." The industry simply uses "T category" as the day-to-day reference.

The regulations spelled out the requirements for the airplane's structure, performance, stability, control, gadgets, and operational limitations, with divisions and subdivisions of details. One of the most talked about and obvious bundles of rules was, and continues to be, those pertaining to the airplane's gross weight and its performance when an engine fails, or other troubles develop, during takeoff. This set of rules stipulates what length runway would be required for specific conditions of weight, altitude, temperature, obstructions, and runway slope.

The section also directs the manner in which the airplane is to be flown. Prior to the issuance of these regulations, an aircraft was certified by the CAA to a certain gross weight; generally speaking, pilot grit decided if the airport and runway were long enough. Safety margins on takeoff should an engine fail were swept under the rug. Not so when the T category became law. The T category rules today are basically the same as originally developed, although they have been modified and polished through the years.

In simple form, T category rules say runway length has to be enough for the airplane to start a takeoff, have a serious emergency such as an engine failure during takeoff, and then either stop within the confines of the runway or continue the takeoff and clear a 50-foot obstacle at the end of the runway—and be able to climb at a certain minimum slope angle after that.

These requirements dictated a batch of speeds for the pilot to remember that prodded him or her to react or fly. The speeds are signified as V—for the airplane's velocity—with a subscript defining the specific condition it applies to. The paramount speeds during takeoff are V_1, V_r, V_2.[1] There are lots of other V speeds for pilots to worry about, but they pertain to other areas. V_{le}, for example, is the maximum speed for extending the landing gear, and V_{lo} is the maximum allowed speed after the landing gear is extended. V_{mca} stands for minimum control speed in the air, meaning that if you are going slower than that and an engine fails there will not be enough

---

1. Because of different runway lengths, airplane weight, temperatures, and other factors, these speeds are essentially different with each takeoff. For reference, the speeds are written on a card after the first officer looks them up in charts or graphs. The card is placed on the control pedestal where the pilots can see it. Markers, referred to as bugs, are set on the airspeed indicator for additional reference. The speeds are sometimes computed by the airline and given to the pilot by radio or paperwork before departure. Conscientious pilots always double-check the figures because they're important stuff.

air flowing over the controls to keep the airplane from turning off on its own and you'll be helpless until you react to correct the condition. These are only a few examples; we could fill pages with speeds the pilot has to know and be able to respond to.

V_1 is commonly known as the decision, or go/no go, speed. It describes a speed, indicated on the airspeed indicator, to help the pilot decide whether to stop the airplane on the runway remaining or take off and limp around the airport if an emergency such as an engine failure occurs during the takeoff. The speed has been established so that if an engine fails before the aircraft reaches that speed in its roll down the runway there will be sufficient pavement ahead to stop—provided, of course, the pilot quickly cuts back on the good engine or engines, raises the spoilers, and slams on the wheel brakes. If the airplane is going faster than V_1 when an engine fails, the plane has enough "performance" to continue the takeoff and clear that 50-foot obstacle; when the jets came along, the height of the imaginary obstacle was reduced to 35 feet, which may not seem to have been a prudent change, but it's acceptable because jets are different from prop planes in having more reserve thrust—power.

The V_1 decision is a dicey one, and pilots were quick to point out that a slippery runway, whether caused by rain, snow or ice, or worn brakes, makes any standard V_1 invalid. The latest concept suggests that decision speed be thought of as being a few knots short of V_1 and the actual V_1 as the point by which the stopping action—cutting other engines, raising the spoilers, and slamming on brakes—has been initiated. To a pilot rushing down a runway dry or wet, a V_1 decision is a near-desperate determination about whether to try to stop or to keep going. It is one of the few decisions an airline pilot faces that demands fast action; although it's an aeronautical axiom that more accidents occur because a pilot moves too fast than too slow, but the pilot has to act on the V_1, go-no-go, decision fast! All of which puts more pressure on the V_1 decision.

If the airplane is going faster than V_1, you *must* keep going. This requires staying on the ground until the plane reaches a specific speed called V_r—for rotation—and then lifting the nose and attempting to fly at the next speed, V_2, which is called the takeoff-climb speed. This speed must be held very precisely because if the airplane gets slower the possibility of stall becomes serious, and if it's flown too fast, the climb path will not be as steep as it needs to be to clear that theoretical 35-foot height, which might be a real obstacle at the runway's end. Generally speaking, continuing takeoff, if properly done, turns out successfully.

There's a point before V_1, while still on the ground, where it's possible to have an engine failure and still keep going, to take off and clear that thirty-five-foot theoretical obstacle—although you may only clear it by 15 feet, which in the mumbo jumbo of the regulation is okay. The industry, in general, says keep going—that doing so is better than trying to stop—and the accident record tends to substantiate this as most aborts, as stopping takeoffs are called, end up in a crash of some sort. (However, there are lots of aborted takeoffs that originate at speeds far below V_1 that are successful. I mention this so that airline passengers will not go into shock anytime a pilot cuts the power and stops early in the takeoff run.)

The problem, however, is that there isn't any information in the cockpit, in training, or even in the manuals that precisely tells the pilot where, before V_1, it's safe to keep going. So the judgment as to whether or not it's safe to continue a takeoff with a failure before V_1, as pilots are being urged to do, is dumped on the pilot, who has to make the call without adequate factual information as to what speed *below* V_1 it is possible to keep going and fly. The decision has to be made quickly when things happen suddenly. Noise, vibration, and unusual airplane actions are typical of the perplexing clues the pilot must use to analyze the problem and decide whether to go or not. The decision is called a WAG when pilots swap stories—a wild ass guess.

The tendency is to think of the V_1 decision as a neat, clear-cut proposition, but it isn't because other things can occur. The sudden vibration may be a tire disintegrating; it's estimated that tire failures cause more V_1 decisions than engine failure. What about an engine fire warning with or without engine failure? Should the takeoff be continued so you get into the air with a fire, or is the situation desperate enough to stop? Manuals tend to say, "Keep going, don't touch anything until you're in the air, and then put out the fire." The manufacturer feels confident that fires can be handled in flight better than risking a stop with a fire, and that's probably correct, but suppose you feel a loud bang and vibration an instant before the fire bell sounds? Now you want to know if there's been airplane structural damage. How bad is the situation? It is pretty well recognized that there have been more false fire warnings than actual fires. Judgment is made by assumptions, background, experience, and guesswork. Or suppose an instrument fails and falsely indicates an engine failure. The time to analyze the situation would put the airplane well beyond the stopping point. We could go on with a lot of different circumstances that might face a pilot; the point is that the V_1 decision isn't all clear-cut and tidy. The pilot is taught about V_1 in its theoretical sense; he or she can stop before and keep going after, but then the industry says, "Don't stop if you can help it—keep going." Clearly, a pilot can easily be blamed for an accident due to a V_1 problem. The investigators can as easily say that the pilot was wrong to keep going as they can say that the pilot was wrong if he or she tried to stop. The pilot is likely to be sandbagged on this one.

Braking studies demonstrate the lack of reliability of V_1. Also, it's widely suspected that one of the reasons more people have been hurt in trying to stop than in continuing takeoff is that abnormal skills are required to stop; flights to demonstrate an airplane's stopping ability—and hence its V_1 determination for FAA certification—are done with experienced test pilots, although the regulation says no exceptional pilot skill should be required. In addition the test pilot knows what's going to happen; the demonstrations are done on a dry runway with a friction coefficient of about 0.8 (1.0 is perfect). The airplane roars down the runway, and an engine is cut at V_1, and the test pilot waits about 3 seconds (that's a time "delay" that is supposed to simulate the time a normal pilot discovers the problem, analyzes it, and performs the necessary stopping action). The test pilot then slams on the brakes until the airplane stops; this action is so violent that the brakes and tires generally catch fire.

In actual day-to-day flying the runway friction coefficient is much less due to runway contamination from the rubber left by landing aircraft—that squeak you hear on touchdown is rubber burning off the tires onto the runway—the presence of slight moisture, which degrades the coefficient, and/or brake wear after many airline landings (the test airplane, of course, has new brakes in perfect condition). One canny engineer who did the math revealed if an engine was cut at V_1 and the pilot did all the right things the airplane would slide off the end of the runway going about half V_1 speed if the braking coefficient was 0.6—which is close to realistic in day-to-day flying. If, for example, V_1 was 140 knots, the airplane would run off the runway, crashing into light poles and whatever at 70 knots and, possibly, doing harm to those aboard.

V_1 is part of the allowable-gross-weight-and-runway-length criteria, which determine how much weight will be allowed for a certain runway, but no consideration is given to what's at the end of the runway—whether it is a clear area of fairly level ground that an airplane could bounce or slide across with reasonable chance for less than fatal damage or a mass of rocks that is part of a seawall where an airplane would crash and break apart, as USAir flight 405 did in March 1992 at New York's La Guardia. There are many runways with sure disaster off their ends. Given that most V_1 rejected takeoffs wind up running off the runway, why isn't the surrounding terrain taken into consideration? The answer is economics because runways that end in rocks or some other hostile terrain might require appreciable reduction in payload to make V_1 less dicey and more realistic.

Given the variations in braking coefficient, time needed to analyze a problem with different and confused clues, runway conditions, weather, darkness, pilot fatigue, and all the other conditions that separate the real world from tests made on a sunny day, and computer analyses that confirm V_1's accuracy, perhaps it's no surprise that the industry tries to convince pilots it's better to keep going when the speed is near V_1. Even as we write (November 1993) new V_1 flight procedures are being taught to pilots. And the Boeing Company has a major effort in progress to teach pilots "proper" ways of dealing with V_1.[2]

V_1 has always bothered the airlines, manufacturers, pilots, and FAA— something that is quite evident in the fact that since its inception in the late 1940s the understanding of what it is and how it's to be used has been reviewed and changed periodically and most recently in Boeing's effort. One would think that after 34 years of jet operation V_1 training, its use and limitations, would be well established.

This controversy developed because of an attempt to protect against something that's a rare occurrence. I flew airliners for 37 years and never had an engine failure or problem close to the "nervous" area of V_1. Nevertheless, during thousands of takeoffs, V_1 was right up front in my thinking as I watched the airspeed build during the ground run. Flight after flight, I sat waiting for the first signs of a problem, relaxing only when the first officer called out, "Vee one," and I saw the airspeed increase beyond it. Visualize rushing along the ground at 170 MPH with 700,000 pounds of airplane attached to you on a runway you've used a lot of already and suddenly feeling a vibration followed by a firebell ringing that says, "What'cha gonna do, Buster? Decide right now!"

Make no mistake, however; T category creates safer flying on takeoff, where it's most visible, and everywhere else as well. When passengers look down a cabin full of people and wonder how the airplane can get off the ground with that load, they should realize that the T category has it all measured out, with adjustments made for airplane and runway. There isn't any doubt about whether or not the airplane can carry the load. It can.

But the introduction of the T category regulations increased demands on the pilot—to understand them and to know the speeds and how to use them, along with what dangers lurk in the package. The problem really stems from the fact the decision to stop or go is a difficult judgment call when a pilot is

---

2. Boeing claims that 80 percent of accidents that happen while attempting to stop, called RTO (rejected takeoff) are potentially avoidable—55 percent by continuing takeoff, 16 percent by correct accelerate-stop techniques, and 9 percent by correct preflight planning. (Letter in *Aviation Week and Space Technology* from Boeing's flight training director, Boeing Commercial Airplane Group, April 20, 1992.)

thundering down a runway at high speed with tons of airplane quickly building a mass of kinetic energy. It all centers around the V_1 speed critical in probably only a 20-knot range that is rushed through in seconds, a tiny segment of the airplane's range of speed. It is a tough area and one that always may, but rarely does, spawn accidents. Pilots certainly understand this; the V_1 decision is one of the many things pilots categorize as, "What I get paid for."

7

DEMANDS ON PILOTS INCREASE AS TECHNOLOGY EXPANDS

Speed is the lifeblood of flying, and all flying is done between a speed that's too slow and one that's too fast. In between these speeds, V_s, and V_{ne} (never exceed), are a host of others that pilots must know. The glossary of the Federal Aviation Regulations (FARs) has a long list of them.

V_s, the velocity of stall, is a slow speed that doesn't produce enough airflow over the wing to keep the plane flying and maintain altitude and control; below V_s the airplane falls out of the sky. V_s isn't one simple number but varies with the plane's weight and flap setting and is different for each angle of bank when the airplane is turning. There are a multitude of stall speeds, so the pilot has to think of stall in regard to the condition of the airplane and the maneuver the pilot is performing.

There's a basic speed, specified as V_{ref}, but spoken of by pilots as "vee reff," or simply "reff." It is a speed 30 percent above an airplane's stall for its weight in landing condition. It's the speed FAA uses on landing distance certification, the speed an airplane should have when crossing the runway boundary on approach to landing—controlled, of course, by the pilot. V_{ref} became the speed to add to for all sorts of conditions and maneuvers; V_{ref} + 5 knots, for example, is the speed one should maintain during a descent on the ILS glide path until 50 feet off the ground, and it is then reduced to V_{ref}. Speeds are added to V_{ref} for flap positions that relate back to stall. With flaps up, on a Boeing 767-200, the pilot must carry V_{ref} + at least 80 knots; with 1° of flap, it's V_{ref} + 60; at flaps 15° it's V_{ref} + 20 knots; and for 30° flaps, it is exactly V_{ref}. On top of these additives are those for wind conditions; you add half the reported wind velocity at the airport, plus half the speed of any gusts reported—that is, if you're not using autothrottle. If you are using it, then you may add the wind factors, provided you disconnect the autothrottle prior to touching down and if the autothrottle activity is complicating manual pitch control. A lot for the pilot to remember. To aid memory, various bugs are set on the airspeed indicator at V_{ref} and flap additive speeds. Either the airplane's computer comes up with these numbers, when asked to do so, or a pilot looks them up in a book. V_{ref} is not a number to memorize because it differs with landing weight, which, in turn, differs for each landing.

V_{ref} is used during landing, but for takeoff and its additives, V_2 is used—the takeoff safety speed we talked about. So there is one reference for landing and a different one for takeoff.

Takeoff isn't simple: for a 747-100 you roll down the runway past the go-no-go V_1 speed we've talked about; then at V_r (rotation speed) pull back the wheel, which pushes the tail down and nose up, which "rotates" the fuselage (hence the V_r appellation); then climb at V_2 plus 10 knots (or if an engine fails, fly at V_2). After 1000 feet the flaps are retracted using the $V_2 + 40$ knots for first retraction of flaps to 5°, then $V_2 + 60$ knots for flaps retracted to 1°, and then all retracted at $V_2 + 80$ knots. It's important not to go *below* these speeds because to do so brings us too close to V_s or stall.

All the V_{ref} and V_2 speed additives could be reduced to one setting of the bugs on the airspeed indicator without the need for memorizing any numbers, with or without an engine failure, and at the same time operating the airplane more efficiently if a system developed by Captain Paul Soderlind, and used by Northwest Airlines, was used universally. But the idea that Soderlind, rather than the manufacturers or other airlines, invented it may have kept it out of airline use—the old "not invented here" (NIH) factor at work. Many corporate jet aircraft have adopted the system, however.

There are maximum speeds—speeds not to exceed—for flying with flaps down because if one goes faster than these speeds there's danger of damaging the flaps or, worst case, blowing them off. These speeds, V_{fe}, pilots have to remember.

The too slow speed, V_s, and the too high, V_{ne}, are so important that warning signals go off in the cockpit if the pilot approaches either one; come close to V_s, and you hear a clacking noise and feel the control wheel shake—the trade calls this warning the "stick shaker." On some airplanes with critical stall characteristics, the control wheel is automatically given a push forward to get the nose down and help the airplane gain speed and get away from the stall.

Early airplanes had no stall warning devices because the airplanes had a built-in warning; as the airspeed slowed toward stall, the turbulent air bouncing over the structure made it shake and shiver with a violence the pilot couldn't ignore. Today's sleek jets don't have this kind of feel—oh, there may be a nibble just before stall or even considerable shaking in stall, but by then the condition has gone too far to be corrected quickly. Hence the need for warnings.

On the too fast end of the speed spectrum, a bell or other such warning device tells the pilot when the maximum operating speed is being approached. In making a fast descent, pilots will often be very close to the max speed warning bell (in the jargon of the trade that's known as "just tickling the bell"). If you exceed V_{ne}, the wings won't immediately fall off—the speed has a cushion built in—but at that speed you want to avoid turbulent air or abrupt maneuvers.

In an old open biplane a pilot recognized high speed by the feel of everything tightening up; the controls became stiffer, the wires sang, and seat-of-the-pants told you the speed was getting high. The jet doesn't have this kind of feel; in particular, noise inside doesn't increase with speed. The controls stiffen up some because an artificial feel is put in the system, but the sensation is a bit phony. Air noise doesn't build up because the streamlined "clean" airplane keeps the airflow so smooth you don't hear it. And, also, the airplane is well soundproofed.

The modern airline cockpit provides the comfort of a shirtsleeve environment, with living room temperatures. There are no leaking windshields, and the lack of noise can make the pilot feel almost detached from the airplane. Thus changes of speed and altitude go unnoticed as busy pilots perform chores more typical of the office than cockpit: programming the flight management system (FMS), checking a malfunction, looking up an unusual routing on charts, studying the weather, and others. Hence the need for warning devices and the danger they bring when one fails to warn the pilot who is working on technical matters while the airplane goes off on its own.

Buried in the T category—FAR, Part 25—along with other factors of landing runway length is the airplane's ability to abort the landing and go up again for another try. Passengers tend to be a little uptight during landing and are very happy when the airplane thumps on the ground and the noise of reversing and feel of brakes take over, but if, on the other hand, the pilot opens the throttles and climbs away from the ground just before touchdown, passengers grip their armrests and go white-knuckle scared. Actually they shouldn't, because "going around," as we call it, is a maneuver that's planned for and approved in the FAA's airplane certification to ensure there's enough performance available to climb safely away from the

THE COCKPIT of a Boeing 707 showing captain and first officer positions. The flight engineer would be behind the first officer on the right. (*Ed Betts Collection*)

earth. The airplane can easily climb because a landing aircraft weighs less than when it took off because of the fuel used, so it has an abundance of power available to climb. A go around is generally caused because the runway wasn't clear—perhaps the aircraft that landed just ahead didn't clear the runway quickly enough and the pilot decided to abandon the landing, or the tower may have told the pilot to go around because of traffic, a gusty wind, or some other reason generally having to do with squeezing traffic in too tight. Go arounds don't happen very often, and a pilot probably only has one every year or so. Even more scary to passengers is the go around when the airplane is still in clouds with no visibility; this is probably a case of the pilot making an instrument approach and finding the ceiling too low to land—below minimums—and then pulling up. When the pilot opens the throttle and the engines roar, the passenger should feel relieved and relax because the airplane is going up and away from tree-scraping low level to higher, safer altitude. The pilot will either make another attempt because the ceiling is variable or elect to go to an alternate; it's the pilot's decision, but the passenger's safety is ensured because of T category requirements.

The original T category spelled out what an airplane had to accomplish for runway length requirements, but the sharp pencil boys soon found a way to finagle the rules and allow greater loads for the same runway with propeller-type aircraft. This pleased the manufacturers because it made their product easier to sell and pleased the airline because it could carry more payload. This was possible because of a gadget called "autofeathering," which appeared about 1947 and was immediately proclaimed a safety device.

Feathering relates only to propeller airplanes; if an engine fails, the propeller continues to turn—"windmilling," we call it—because the airplane's forward motion is like a kid slinging a pinwheel on a stick to make it spin. This windmilling propeller has enormous drag, which affects that important climb segment of the T category. To do away with the drag, propellers are feathered, which means when an engine fails the pilot pushes a button that, through electric and hydraulics, twists the propeller blades so they are streamlined, edge forward into the wind almost totally removing the windmilling drag and improving the plane's performance, especially in the critical area of climb at takeoff with an engine out.

The gimmick engineers found was tied to the few seconds it takes a pilot to discover which engine has failed and then to feather it. If this time span, tiny though it is, could be reduced, the airplane would be able to carry a greater load and still climb out within the regulation's requirements. So a system was designed to sense the engine failure and automatically detect which engine it was and feather it immediately, faster than any pilot could. Obviously, the system was complicated.

After due testing the FAA approved the autofeather device, although the Air Line Pilots Association (ALPA) said it was dangerous and shouldn't be used; pilots are automatically suspicious of new safety devices because many of them cure one problem, only to add others. The pilots were overruled as they are in most matters that have financial implications. In fact, the auto-feather did what pilots worried about: it malfunctioned on a few occasions, causing a surprise engine shutdown when there was no need for it. I myself know of two cases, one which caused a serious accident. The vagaries of the system were demonstrated in a strange experience my friend Captain Paul Soderlind had with a Martin 404. He and his copilot had finished flying for the day and, after unloading the passengers, taxied the airplane to a parking area and shut it down for the night; they turned off all switches, cut the electrical power, and departed. As they walked toward a hangar, backs to the empty airplane sitting alone, they heard a strange noise behind them and turned to look at the airplane just in time to see both propellers go into full feather position all by themselves! No, it wasn't Halloween.

All pilots had a spooky feeling about the autofeather. We had it on certain model Constellations. There was also an off-on switch to turn it off after takeoff. The manual for the 1049H Constellation said the gross weight allowable was 140,000 pounds with autofeathering (AF) on but was reduced to 134,500 pounds with it off, which gives you an idea of the gross weight gain from AF.

There was no way to recoup from an inadvertent autofeather because the device acted in seconds, which would never be enough time to overrule its action. Many pilots kept it turned off—illegally—even when the plane was loaded to 140,000 pounds because it gave them one less thing to worry about on takeoff. The risk of engine failure within a time period measured in seconds against the chance of malfunctioning of the complicated system was well worth taking, and we were still there to do the feathering manually, albeit about 4 seconds slower. Flying four-engine aircraft, as I was, gave an added safety factor in that I had a flight engineer whose eyes were glued to the engines on takeoff, ready to instantly spot trouble and go into action. I've never heard of accidents happening because the pilot had the autofeather off, but I've heard of them when it was on.

A plus for autofeathering is that it removes the chance of the pilot misidentifying the problem engine and perhaps feathering the good engine, resulting in no power in a twin-engine airplane, or only half the power in a four-engine aircraft—the wrongly feathered *good* engine plus the other one that actually had failed. But other systems exist that simply show which engine is malfunctioning and depend on the pilot to do the feathering. I've flown such a system on a twin-engine airplane and found it both excellent and uncomplicated. Another factor relating to pilot judgment comes into play here: in some conditions, such as intermittent or partial power loss, it might be better not to feather, but the autofeather, robotlike, overrules the pilot's judgment and may feather when a pilot knows from experience it would be best not to.

Fortunately, pure jet airplanes don't have propellers, so there's no feathering problem. However, jets with propellers, called turboprops—and most commuter airlines fly these—are autofeather equipped. Of course, technological advances in the 40 years since it was created has made AF very reliable, and its safety advantages now outweigh the potential for trouble, slim though it might be. No matter how safe, however, AF is another system for pilots to know, check on, and be aware of on every takeoff.

Before putting aside the internal combustion propeller airplane in favor of jets, we should mention a few more additions, like reversing propellers. These were a big gain in the problem of stopping the airplane, especially on slippery runways. By reversing the propellers and taking advantage of their function to move air, the thrust can be directed backward to counter the airplane's forward motion, thus slowing it. Jets use this idea, but reversing the jet stream flow isn't nearly as complete or effective as a reverse propeller.

Stopping an airplane on a slick surface is a ticklish business because the airplane, even though below stall speed and incapable of flying, is still getting some lift as it speeds across the runway pavement in the course of gradually slowing down. This lift, of an amount depending on the plane's speed at that moment, means all the weight isn't on the wheels and that the airplane is tiptoeing along, making it easy for wheels to slide on the wet or icy surface. The landing wing flaps hanging down add aerodynamic drag that helps slow the airplane, but they can also add lift and keep the wheels from being firmly planted on the ground where brakes can do the most good. So, at times, the pilot is between the famous rock and hard place. There's little braking action; should the flaps be left down for drag? Or should they be quickly retracted to get weight on the wheels? Generally the answer is to raise the flaps, but not always. The pilot doesn't have a lot of time to consult others or put it to a vote, and there are no hard, fast rules or numbers to go by. On jet wings there are spoilers—panels that come up out of the top of the wing on demand of the pilot. As they stick into the air flowing over the wing, they make the air turbulent and destroy the smooth flow that gives lift. Passengers can see spoilers pop up just after the airplane lands; actually, they come up automatically as soon as the airplane touches the ground. Then, on pilot demand, flaps under and at the rear of the wing are raised, if pilot judgment deems it best under current conditions. Quickly following in this landing sequence, the engines are put in reverse and the power increased.

How much braking action there is on the runway itself is often unknown. In the United States there's no standard system to measure a runway's braking capacity; the best system consists of a special measuring vehicle that runs down the runway to check its condition. A Saab automobile, like the ones we're all familiar with, is outfitted especially for this task and does an excellent job. It has a fifth wheel that's lowered to the ground and tracks along with a certain friction in its rotation, causing the wheel to slip an amount that depends on the runway's friction. A computer digests the information and spills out a silver tape with a profile of the runway's coefficient of friction for the entire length, reported in mu (μ), the Greek letter used for braking coefficient. I was given a demonstration ride in one of these test cars on an icy runway in Sweden. My interest in the tape read-out was high, but more intense was my increasing terror as we sped along the icy surface at 90 MPH with the runway's end coming up—could the car be stopped before plunging off the runway, which ended in a sharp drop? It could.

But FAA doesn't report a runway's mu value; instead it reports braking action either nil, poor, fair, or good. This nonspecific type report doesn't give pilots a solid idea of what's going to happen when they apply the brakes—"braking action poor" means one thing to a small commuter airplane but quite another to a big one. Reported braking action says nothing to indicate that a Boeing 767 at landing weight will take x distance to stop in reported poor braking conditions. In using the mu value, by contrast, a pilot has a more accurate idea of stopping ability. Mu is used extensively in Europe.

In fact, mu is used in many countries. SAS, the Scandinavian Airline System, has a very extensive educational program for pilots that clearly informs them of all the variables involved in braking and what mu numbers mean. The SAS program also spells out certain restrictions to use under various conditions. One might argue that SAS needs the efficiency of mu numbers because it operates in areas of severe and changeable weather, but the United States, with its great variations of climate, can duplicate any bad conditions found in Scandinavia. And with the speed and range of jet operations, a pilot based in Florida may routinely battle winter weather in Minnesota, Idaho, or even Stockholm if the airline is international; Boston-based pilots on a major airline go all the way to Anchorage, Alaska, routinely, so pilots see and must handle a large variety of situations.

A few airports in the United States are getting vehicles to measure mu, but it isn't reported as such; they still fall back on the nil, poor, fair, good system, which is vague and inconclusive. Airports that don't have mu measuring vehicles use a wide and sometimes bizarre diversity of methods in reporting braking action. One is airplane reports, but of course the airplane reporting braking action on landing may be a 2000-pound Cessna 172, whose report doesn't have much relevance for a 630,000-pound Boeing 747. Even similar airplaness can find differences in braking action, depending on where the airplanes touched down and applied the brakes, simply because one part of a runway may be better or worse than another under patchy ice conditions. A remarkably crude method regularly used by some airport authorities to determine braking conditions is to run a car or truck down the runway, slam on the brakes, and see how much the vehicle skids. Sometimes the determination is made using a lunch box perched on the edge of a pick up truck's seat. If the box falls off the seat when the brakes are slammed on, the braking action is reported as good; if the box doesn't fall off, braking action is poor.

Obviously the aviation community needs to pay realistic and serious attention to the reporting of braking action if it is to provide a clear picture that allows pilots to make precise decisions. At present it's another one of the many indistinct elements of aviation that put unfair demands on pilot judgment and lead to "pilot error."

Sometimes braking conditions come as a surprise. Landing at Orly Field, Paris, very early one morning in a 747, we had just touched down and were going into reverse when the tower called. "Oh, yes," the man said, "The braking action is nil!" Too late to go around again. We used reverse to the limit, with the spoilers up and the antiskid brake system doing its best, but we kept on sliding. This early 747 could only reverse down to 100 knots; below that there was danger of compressor stall and engine damage amounting to about $250,000 per engine. So racing through my mind were the choices of keeping the engines roaring in reverse and ruining them or trying to curve off the runway into the ground area, taking out runway lights in the process (although with no traction for nosewheel steering, it would be difficult to make the airplane turn), all the while visualizing what was beyond the end of the runway should we slide off and imagining what kind of damage we'd do there. Well, the antiskid braking started to take hold, and we finally stopped at the very end of the runway, still on the pavement and without ruining the engines—but no thanks to the late alert from the tower.

Antiskid braking came in with jets. The system automatically releases the wheels when they start to slide, then reapplies pressure when they aren't skidding; the pilots simply push their feet down on the brake pedals, and antiskid does the rest automatically. In early installations you could feel the off-and-on action, which is frequent and fast. This braking action makes it possible to stop in difficult situations, in some cases in half the normal distance. The antiskid brake is an excellent device—and the principle is not bad to remember in an automobile that slides on ice. Instead of keeping your foot clamped down to the floor, let up on it and do an on-off-on sequence every couple of seconds or so to help give traction.

The latest jets have automatic braking systems. Before landing, the pilot selects the amplitude of braking desired: four different levels plus an all-out maximum position. As soon as the airplane touches down and the throttles are full idle, the brakes come on and slow the airplane to a stop without the pilot doing anything further.

Accidents have occurred because of braking conditions; a World Airways flight went off a runway's end at Boston's Logan Airport, January 23, 1982, and finished up in the bay; the airplane broke apart, and there were two fatalities and numerous injuries among the 210 people aboard. The official National Transportation Safety Board report cited among other things,

> the pilot landed the airplane without sufficient information as to runway conditions on a slippery, ice covered runway . . . the lack of adequate information with respect to the runway was due to the fact the FAA regulations did not provide guidance to airport management regarding the measurement of runway slipperiness under adverse conditions . . . the FAA regulations did not provide the flight crew and other personnel with the means to correlate contaminated surfaces with airplane stopping distances . . . tower controllers failed to transmit available breaking information to the pilot of Flight 30H.

The report continued, "Contributing to the accident was the failure of pilot reports on braking to convey the severity of the hazard to following pilots." This accident and report of the investigation that followed provided proof of the problems with braking that a pilot contends with—the lack of specific, clear-cut information with which to make a critical judgment. It's another situation ready to sandbag pilots, to set them up for unreasonable blame.

Little has been done to change the situation; each winter we face the same chances of an airplane sliding off a runway.

Engine reliability in late Constellations and DC-7s was poor in comparison to that of past engines. The quest for greater range, load-carrying ability, and speed demanded an engine of high power and low weight. The turbo-compound was the result—an 18-cylinder monster that used, along with normal piston engine action, the exhaust gas flow to turn turbines that spun shafts connected to the crankshaft, giving added power to the engine. They were called "power recovery turbines" (PRTs); they also came with mechanically driven superchargers of two stages. As the plane climbed to higher altitude where the air is thinner, the flight engineer "shifted gears" so the supercharger twirled faster to compact more air. This was a tricky operation that involved reducing the power on the two outboard engines, then pulling two levers to change the supercharger stage. The action produced a shuddering thud through the airplane that raised passengers' eyebrows and had them looking around quizzically. Then the power on the engines was brought back up slowly and carefully. The operation was repeated with the two inboard engines.

We had more engine failures with these complicated bundles of machinery than we'd had before; crews generally referred to them as "parts recovery turbines," in sarcastic reference to their many failures. I had one tear up just after liftoff in 1956 at Frankfurt, Germany, causing a fire and power loss. I made an immediate turn around the field as we went through the fire drill, and we landed, although not without some discussion with the tower. My F/O called and told them we had a fire and were returning immediately. The tower responded with an order to go toward a certain radio beacon until an approaching aircraft had landed. My F/O was fast on the draw and firmly told the tower, "We have a fire; we're returning immediately. Get the other traffic the hell out of the way!" They did, and we landed. The fire was put out using the airplane's fire-extinguishing system shortly before we landed.

Another failure occurred on a black night between Bombay, India, and what was then Colombo, Ceylon. There was no fire, but we spent an hour or so flying on three engines and had a long wait for a new engine in Colombo. The failure rate of the turbo-compound engines was so troublesome that TWA had purchased an air force cargo airplane as a flying machine shop that carried a spare engine and crew of mechanics. They would fly to a disabled airplane, like mine in Colombo, and change engines. The rescue ship was so heavy thus fitted out that our VP of International Operations, Larry Trimble, had a small jet engine mounted on top of the airplane to help the propeller engines get the load off the ground. Two French pilots were kept on standby in Paris, and when an engine failure was reported, they gathered the mechanics and took off with the spare engine. They got our call in the middle of the night, and off they went for the long grind to Colombo with my new engine. This was a marvelous crew that did superlative work.

The engines were fussy on the ground, too. As we'd wait in the long line for takeoff at Kennedy, the idling engines loaded up and ran rough. The standard procedure to clear this involved running the engines at higher power and leaning them out so they got hot and burned the oil and foreign deposits off the fouled spark plugs. This was done just before takeoff and could create an anxious, frustrating moment as we tried to get the engines running satisfactorily while the tower urgently called, "Cleared for *immediate* takeoff!"

Weather radar, its antenna behind the black nose ones sees on aircraft, also became standard equipment in the early 1950s—but not without a battle.

Airlines at this time were experimenting with radar for thunderstorm avoidance; American was active in this research, as was TWA. I flew a

WW II P-61 (Black Widow night fighter), probing thunderstorms. It was an exciting and fulfilling experience for me. I'd always had great respect for thunderstorms and, on the line, looked on them with awe as we desperately tried to stay out of them. But they were fascinating, and I wondered what they were really like. The P-61 allowed me to find out. The airplane, being a fighter, was strong, and we equipped it with instruments to measure the force of severe up and downdrafts and weather. I would fly right up to a menacing black, green, and yellow thunderstorm and, confidently in my sturdy airplane, would bore right into its center. What was in there? Rain as in deluge, turbulence that bounced you hard and tossed the airplane in all directions, and lightning so close you could smell the ozone, like a burned electric wire, when a strike occurred. I had many lightning discharges but no damage larger than a silver–dollar-size hole where it exited. In one wild thunderstorm, when the gyros spilled and I was briefly out of control, the turbulent forces bent some of the airplane's metal skin—a small amount, but enough to know that Thor was telling me something. But it wasn't frightening because of the good airplane and excess power available; it was fun.

What interested me was the fact I never flew through a thunderstorm any worse than those I'd flown through in a DC-3 on the line. Without radar, staying out of thunderstorms flying DC-3s, Stratoliners, DC-4s, and early Connies was a matter of unsupported theories, witchcraft, and luck. We missed every one we could, but periodically we flew smack-dab into the center and got some pretty awful rides. One of our airplanes came apart in a thunderstorm over the San Joaquin Valley of California, killing all aboard. Later, in our research, we put early radar equipment in a DC-3 cargo airplane and flew token pieces of cargo over routes forecast for thunderstorms—the cargo was to satisfy some members of the board of directors who thought we shouldn't be spending money in research without bringing in some revenue. What we were doing then was trying to interpret the radar images, to learn how to use it to avoid the thunderstorm cells. One day when flying Chicago to Kansas City through a mass of thunderstorms, we didn't interpret the radar image correctly and plowed right into a big thunderstorm—flew right through it for a really wild ride. The copilot, assigned to me at the last moment by flight dispatch because my regular one was off sick, was new to the airline. On the ground at Kansas City, after the flight, he asked me if we ever flew into anything like that on regular runs. I responded that periodically we made bad guesses and did. He looked perturbed, thanked me, and departed. He resigned a few days later.

Proper techniques and radar with best penetration wavelengths were finally developed and offered commercially for airplane installation to help pilots miss the violent cells of thunderstorms, but when FAA suggested rules making radar installation mandatory, the airline companies balked—a crazy paradox driven by the fact that radar cost money. They backed the research but then didn't want to be forced to ante up.

FAA's rule suggestion was that the airplane be equipped with radar if it was to be dispatched into "known thunderstorm weather." The airlines said they wouldn't dispatch their airplanes into such weather and so didn't need radar. This reasoning was specious to the nth degree. What's thunderstorm weather? One thunderstorm sitting off in Kansas a Piper Cub could fly around? A sky full of cells hidden in the extensive cloud mass of a warm front, or something in between?

Pilots knew that without regulation they'd have to continue to fly as they had been, counting on experience, witchcraft, and luck. The Air Line Pilots Association (ALPA) fought to have radar required on all aircraft, taking its battle clear to the Congress. I remember appearing on David Susskind's TV show, pleading the cause. The issue was a perfect example of the industry expounding safety while actually holding back for financial reasons. The pilots prevailed, but the FAA regulation requiring radar wasn't promulgated until July 1960, although major airlines saw the wisdom of its use and installed it in aircraft before that. The jets all came equipped with radar.[1] Cargo aircraft were not required to have radar until 1966! The pilots' battle for these regulations had begun in the early 1950s. Today all airline aircraft are equipped with radar to help pilots stay out of thunderstorms' wrath. Notice I said to *help* stay out of thunderstorms: radar doesn't do the job 100 percent; actually it simply shows where the precipitation is, and experienced pilots know that one mass of heavy rain may be smooth to fly through and another rough and wild, but radar doesn't know the difference. There are other technical limitations, such as radar's inability to penetrate heavy rain, which creates a shadow on the scope that obscures potential violence behind it. Training in radar use does not come easily nor is it all good training. The guru of weather radar and its use is Archie Trammel of Trinidad, Texas. He knows more about it than anyone alive. His teaching sessions and symposia are sought after worldwide. Archie, when talking about radar shadows, says, "Never, positively never, continue flight toward a radar shadow." He also says that, "Unlike anything else in flying, reliance on previous experience can be deadly when dealing with convective weather." Convective weather

---

1. The first domestic jet service was between New York City and Miami, Florida, by National Airlines on December 10, 1958. The first North Atlantic service was started on October 4, 1958, between London and New York by British Overseas Airways flying a de Havilland Comet, quickly followed by the New York–Paris jet service of Pan American World Airways on October 26, 1958, with Boeing 707 aircraft.

means thunderstorm weather. Radar use in weather presents a contrast to most tasks a pilot performs in the cockpit that involve absolute, exact numbers. But radar and weather are abstract, requiring knowledge, imagination, and care. So a good amount of awareness about radar and its limitations is needed by pilots. Because training costs money and airlines are in an economic squeeze, training can be cut short when, in this case, it should be thorough to the last detail—as Trammel teaches it.

This, in most part, was where we were before the introduction of jets, the advancing but nervous period between 1947 and 1958. Airplanes, except for those with the turbo-compound engines, were reliable. (Actually, the engines before the turbo-compound were very reliable. I was regularly flying Constellation 749As to Europe and the Middle East at this time. During a period of three years I returned home on schedule after every trip without any mix-ups or delays because of airplanes and their engines.) Things went downhill after that until the jet era. When we entered the jet age, with its extraordinary engine reliability, it was like dying and going to heaven.

8 | THE GOOD OLD DAYS

In the dozen years after World War II the federal government was busy with committees making studies on aviation's needs, especially facilities and management of air traffic: in 1946, the Air Coordinating Committee was formed to create national aviation policy; in June 1947, the Radio Technical Commission for Aeronautics's (RTCA) special committee, SC31, met to study and develop safe control of expanding traffic; March 1948, Senator Orin Brewster from Maine reported that the "airways system of the country was near the saturation point." In December 1955, at the Aviation Facilities Study Group, W. B. Harding, chairman, noted, "Air traffic management had reached critical proportions." There was also a constant stream of reorganization plans to decide which agency was going to manage the rules, regulations, and technical matters.

On May 19, 1957, a committee headed by Edward P. Curtiss, an executive appointed by President Eisenhower, gave its report to the president and warned of "a crisis in the making . . . because of the growing congestion of air space retarding the progress of air commerce." The report concludes that many excellent plans for improving the nation's aviation facilities had failed in the past. The report also recommends the establishment of an independent Federal Aviation Agency. The positive result from the committee was the formation of FAA, now the Federal Aviation Administration, but the hoped for air traffic control solution has never materialized. Those 11 years of concern have been followed by 37 more of the same. Technology improves, but air traffic grows at a faster pace. The result is no net gain. There's still a crisis in the making.

MUNICIPAL AIRPORT, Los Angeles, California, then called Mines Field, August 27, 1929—the same LAX used today. (*Courtesy of the FAA*)

But out there flying we saw improvements on the technical side, such as the introduction of radar into the ATC system so the ground controllers could "see" the airplanes instead of having to depend on pilots' position reports. Without radar, considering the increase in traffic, the system would have been in a shambles. But because the controller could see the airplanes on a radarscope, the airplanes could fly closer together without increasing the danger of collision, thereby making it possible to squeeze more airplanes in the same area. In 1952 the radio range with its ambiguities was replaced by the high-frequency VOR (very high frequency omnidirectional range), which was static free and accurate due to the very high frequency (VHF) used in transmission. A course is available for each degree of a circle—a full 360°—so great flexibility of courses is possible. It is displayed on an instrument called the Omnibearing Indicator (OBI).

DME, for distance-measuring equipment, came into use not long after VOR. This tells the pilot the aircraft's distance from a point where the DME is located; generally VORs and DMEs are located at the same place. The information allows the pilot to know where the airplane is and its groundspeed very accurately. Since the equipment in the airplane isn't large and can be within the financial capability of even private pilots, most airplanes are so equipped.

The drawback is that very high frequency is line of sight only, which means the signals cannot go over the horizon or through a mountain range if it sticks up in the way of your line of sight to the horizon. Of course, an airplane at altitude can receive farther—at 10,000 feet a signal can be received from 122 nautical miles away—but at 500 feet the distance is reduced to 28 miles. This line of sight restriction is remedied by having lots of transmitting and receiving stations and relays out in the country or on mountain tops in order to maintain a continuous airway and serve many airports.

In addition to navigation, VHF also came into use for the airplane's two-way radio at the end of WW II, which was a great advancement as it cut out static, skipping, and all the other nasty things pilots' radio communication had been interrupted by. VHF provides radio communication as good as any telephone's, except it's a party line with many, many customers; all the airplanes within range and the ATC controllers sometimes all seem to be talking at once.

The VOR signal did away with the beam's dit-dahs in the pilot's ears. Ears now were devoted to two-way radio communication and listening to the VOR, ILS, and DME's identification to be certain the correct one was tuned in.

Another important addition was the transponder, a receiver-transmitter that the ground radar interrogates every time the rotating antenna's beam hits the airplane. The transponder is a development from the wartime IFF, identification friend or foe, which we carried in military aircraft to help prevent allies from shooting each other down. The transponder sends a coded signal back to the ground, identifying the particular airplane and telling its altitude. The data is processed by computers, and the airplane's identification, altitude (descending or climbing), and speed are displayed on the controller's cathode ray tube, (CRT), which is like a TV screen. Other ATC housekeeping information is displayed for the controller's use. These signals are lost from time to time, and all is not always perfect, which results in more communication and delays.

The transponder gives the air traffic controller great ability to move air traffic faster. The transponder also adds to the fishbowl aspect of the pilot's life because it allows the controller to see if the airplane is at the wrong altitude for some reason. This system adds safety, but it also gives FAA an opportunity to cite pilots for violations. Violations of this type are not deliberate but the result of misunderstanding of clearances or missing ATC instructions because of other cockpit distractions.

As ATC grew, a system was set up to record all communications to and from aircraft on tape, which is very useful to find errors and file violations on the part of both pilots and controllers. It's also useful for investigation of accidents. When an incident or accident occurs, one of the first actions authorities take is to impound the tapes.

In the meantime, radar in the airplanes became universal as an aid to manage flight through thunderstorm areas. By this time, the airplanes were mostly pressurized. Before pressurization the aircraft were not allowed above 12,000 feet because the passengers would suffer from lack of oxygen, but with pressurization passengers didn't suffer from oxygen want. Flying higher

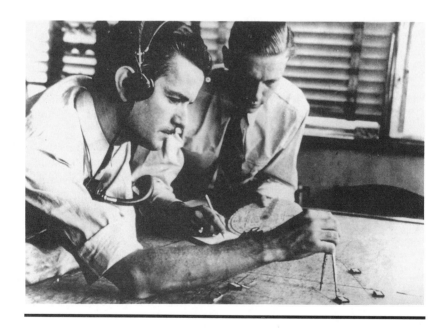

EARLY AIR TRAFFIC CONTROLLERS, before radar. Airplanes were represented on the map table by small figures called "shrimp boats." An aircraft's current position was obtained by radio from the aircraft. (*Courtesy of the FAA*)

MODERN CONTROLLER'S PANEL with radar that shows aircraft's position at all times. (*Courtesy of the FAA*)

helped pilots avoid weather and put the airplane up out of most convective turbulence, which was a great help to passengers' stomachs.

In the West, daytime rough air is simply air that rises sharply from the hot ground in chimneylike drafts that go up to about 14,000 feet, which was above the normal cruising altitude of DC-3s and other nonpressurized aircraft of the era. The airplane flying through these vertical currents heaves up and down and, because of its stability characteristics, also swings side to side, which is very uncomfortable for the occupants. I flew the San Francisco–Winslow, Arizona, portion of our transcontinental flight for a time. The flight took place in daylight and was advertised as the scenic route over the Grand Canyon. The passengers, however, saw little as they remained stretched out with eyes closed and a cold towel on their foreheads, their skin color greenish yellow as they concentrated, not always successfully, on keeping their cookies down while the DC-3 wallowed and bounced through the clear morning sky. The advent of the Boeing Stratoliner and its pressurization and, after the war, the Constellations and DC-6 aircraft cured this problem as they flew undisturbed above the turbulent layer, allowing happy passengers to gawk at the beautiful sight of the Grand Canyon and the Southwest in serene comfort.

The pressurized airplane of the 1950s mostly still flew through the stuff when bad frontal weather covered the route, calling for pilots to do battle with ice and thunderstorms. In some conditions—warm front thunderstorms, which are higher and difficult to see because they are buried and hidden in the front's cloud mass—the situation could be worse. Flying through fronts meant problems with ice. And ATC made the situation of being higher in bad weather worse by keeping you up there until lower traffic was sifted down to make room for you.

The problem of getting on top has never been completely solved, although each airplane advance increases the capability for higher flight, making it possible to fly in less bad weather. "Weather flying" en route has been reduced but not completely eliminated. The jet gets us way up there but still not on top of everything—the top often seems just a tantalizing bit above the current maximum attainable altitude. There's a story about an early space capsule with a monkey as the pilot. During an orbit the ground called the monkey and asked how things were going. "Fine," he answered, "but if I could just get another thousand feet I think I'd be on top."

The high-flying modern jet may top most of the visible weather, but the invisible jet stream often has its turbulence that is not always avoidable. It's called clear air turbulence (CAT), and while uncomfortable and annoying, it is not as dangerous as tabloid journalism would have you believe. It extends into the lower layer of the stratosphere where the temperature is warmer and jet airplane performance may suffer and not allow the aircraft to climb high enough to get above the turbulence.

The first pressurized airliners probably flew 50 percent less weather than had the DC-3, and the jets about 85 percent less weather than the DC-3s. These are only opinions based on experience, not scientific facts. But one thing is certain for all aircraft: they have to get up and get down, which means going through the lower-level weather where the old DC-3 prowled—levels where thunderstorms and ice live, which must be traversed by all. Even space launches have been delayed when low-level weather was unfavorable. Not surprisingly most accidents related to thunderstorms take place near the airport when the airplane is climbing soon after takeoff or descending to land.

Landing in low ceilings was much improved by the universal use of instrument landing systems (ILS), the horizontal and vertical beams leading right down the runway. The beam is not always perfect; it has bends and scallops that keep safe minimums 200 feet or higher. An ILS system only serves one runway, so if a landing on another runway is necessary, generally because of wind direction different from that on the ILS runway, the pilot has to make an approach using a VOR station, or nondirectional beacon. Neither offers precise vertical guidance; the airplane's altimeter provides the only vertical intelligence, but it doesn't identify where you are along the approach. You might also make an approach via ILS with higher minimums, such as 800 feet; at that altitude, if the ground becomes visible, the ILS is abandoned, and the pilot breaks off and circles to land on a different runway. This maneuver is called a circling approach and is notorious for its potential danger; once the circle is started, the pilot is back to barnstorming.

One night I made a circling approach into Boston in a 707 with an FAA inspector riding on the jump seat behind me—in heavy rain, doing the juggling act of staying far enough below the clouds so as not to be enfolded by them yet high enough to avoid hitting the ground. It was a squeeze play: making the circle as tight as possible to stay within the limits of visibility and flying turns to precise headings to be certain we'd finally get lined up with the runway. It reminded me of a landing on Johnston Island in the Pacific one night when the lights on the island had gone out and our only guidance was the headlights of a jeep parked on the runway. There I was, flying a B-17, aiming at a light in a black void with no other point of reference. I flew both approaches the same way: looking at the instruments to determine attitude, altitude, speed, and heading and taking short, periodic looks outside, when the wings were level, to see how it was coming. To do it by looking out all the time was impossible because there's no reference in the dark; the jeep lights zoom above you or below whenever the airplane is banked for turning, and sensory illusions can easily fool you so a gradual descent goes unnoticed and the airplane loses altitude to eventually smash into the sea. While Boston has more lights in the vicinity than the single jeep on Johnston Island, sensory illusions are still a serious danger. But the landing went off fine, and the FAA inspector never said anything aside from a grunt of approval. What I did was legal though primitive in both cases.

The airline pilots made strong pleas for ILS equipment on all runways, but due to cost and bureaucratic slowness it was many years before installations were added to more runways of an airport. Now, with multiple ILSs, circling approaches are rarely done at major airports. In airports serving lesser cities, however, there is often only one ILS, or none at all, so passengers will occasionally experience a circling approach. This is especially true on airports served by commuter airlines.

As the era drew to a close in 1958, we were flying airplanes like Constellations, DC-7s, and Stratocruisers on long-range flights; loaded full, the planes weighed about 150,000 pounds and carried up to 90 passengers or so. The airlines were small and stable as far as operation and schedules were concerned, which meant we flew with the same people over a long period. We knew each other's moods, characters, and peculiarities. The crews didn't split up but flew together perhaps a month or more at a time; we didn't change the cabin team at stops as is done now but stayed together, flying, for example, to Paris and back—or Paris on to Rome, Athens, Cairo, or Tel Aviv. There was more than just comraderie; the atmosphere was warm and familylike and yet thoroughly professional. From cabin attendant to captain everyone understood the operation.

One morning on a New York–Paris flight we had crossed the coast of Brittany and were only an hour from Paris, with the half-light of dawn turning into the bright light of day and the brightness burning into our sleepy, sandy eyes. Grimy and tired after the long overocean night, we flew in quiet fatigue. They were serving breakfast in the back when the cockpit door burst open, and Jackie Dakletter, hostess, said in a matter-of-fact way, "Oil's pouring over the right wing." As quickly as she'd appeared, she turned and went back to the cabin and continued serving breakfast. The flight engineer looked up from paperwork he was doing to the oil pressure gauges on engines numbers three and four. I looked back at them, too. The needle on number three was approaching zero.

"We'd better feather it," he said to me.

"Go ahead, feather number three." He looked up, then reached for the red feather button and hesitated a second, looking at me for confirmation that I agreed he had the correct engine, knowing that if he acted in too much haste the wrong one could be shut down. I nodded, he pushed the button, the engine stopped, and we flew on to Paris with no difficulty. At Paris, maintenance found a serious oil leak, but we'd caught it in time, and there was no engine damage. Jackie, in checking the wings now and then as she went up and down the cabin, had saved an engine. I took her to dinner in Paris for that one. But that was crew cooperation, coordination, CRM, or whatever you want to call it. "Hostesses," as we called stewardesses or cabin attendants, were not—are not—simply high-flying waiters and waitresses, and ours knew they had a strong safety role to play as well, so as they went about cabin duties, they also kept a sharp eye for anything that looked or acted unusual.

By this time we also had the luxury of good heating, windshield wipers, and defrosters. We felt that our pleas for better equipment, such as weather radar, had paid off, improving safety as well as creating some peace of mind. In those gentle, terrorist-free days we often invited passengers into the cockpit, and the response was always amazement at all the "things" we had to know and use. It built our pride. In that era the public and co-workers respected pilots. It encouraged our efforts toward maintaining high professional standards; we tried to look the part, with clean, pressed uniforms, jackets always buttoned, and shoes shined when within public gaze, and we tried to respond to crew members and co-workers by appreciating their problems, as well as listening to and taking seriously their ideas before acting clearly and decisively. It was a golden age whose like will never come again.

There was a disquieting feeling, however, that occasionally slipped into our thoughts, as pressures from ATC increased, along with more FAA rules and surveillance that seemed excessive. And back in our minds was the knowledge that the jets were about to come over the horizon. Would they be difficult? Would school and checkout prove beyond our ability? We'd soon know the answers.

9 | THE JET AGE BEGINS— WITH SOME RELIEF

T he jets—Boeing 707s, quickly followed by Douglas DC-8s—arrived on wings of rumor and considerable pilot concern. The concerns were not about safety but competence; the rumors said ground school would be demanding in ways we'd never seen before. The fear was enhanced when the company gave us, before the airplane arrived, a series of six books titled *Basic Electronics and Basic Electricity* to study, with examinations enclosed. The checkout promised to be very difficult, the FAA requiring perfect pilot performance—and on and on. A concerned old-timer I talked with over coffee told me he might pass up the jet and take early retirement: "The farm's paid for and I've got some savings—and I still know how to farm." We talked him out of it, and he passed through school easily and flew 8 perfect jet years before being forced to retire at the FAA-mandated age of 60.

The first pilots to fly jets were mostly senior captains in their 50s. Interestingly, with these "old-timers" doing the flying, the first 3½ years of 707 operation were free of fatal accidents. This pattern was repeated, for over 4 years, when the Boeing 747 was introduced.

After the nervous times of flying turbo-compound engines the change to jets was like a refreshing breeze on a hot summer's day. Jet engines don't have the banging back and forth of pistons, the making and breaking of ignition systems, or the problems of carburetor ice, mixture controls, and manifold pressure versus RPM. They only go around, spinning in a smooth fashion, turned by a turbine spun by exhaust coming from a burner that, in a very crude way, is like a blowtorch. The jet engine is not only much more reliable than the piston engine, and especially those turbo-compounds, but it

BOEING 707 with fan-jet engines. (*Ed Betts Collection*)

is less complicated to operate as well; there's one lever, the throttle. (Some call it the "thrust" or "power lever," but most stick with the old-fashioned word, "throttle," and that's what we'll call it.) You push or pull the throttle to increase or decrease power, and that's it; no propeller pitch controls, no mixture controls, no carburetor heat controls, no oil cooler door controls, and no cowl flap controls. Just that one lever.

Icing is handled by flipping a switch that gets heat to the cowling, and that's it. The important instrument is an exhaust gas temperature gauge, and as long as you don't allow it to exceed certain limits (and essentially that's controlled by the throttle), no harm can come to the engine. A jet engine also starts easily: you just spin it by an auxiliary means, open a valve and let the fuel into the burner can, and light it with a spark plug that is shut down after lighting off so there's no ignition; the fire supports itself. Ignition is switched on at certain times such as during takeoff, icing, turbulence, and heavy rain as a precaution, but to do it, you simply flip a switch and forget it. Starting doesn't have all the temperamental vagaries of a piston engine on a frigid day—or a moist and hot one. The jet doesn't load up and need burning off if you're holding for takeoff; you can sit on the taxiway waiting for takeoff with no problem until the fuel runs out.

Jets do, however, burn a lot of fuel. Fuel use on jets is different than on piston engine–powered airplanes; the jet engine consumes such big quantities that questions of how much remains and how far there is to go demand priority in pilots' thinking. As a task and concern it takes the place of some of the problems and complexities of the piston engine, so you don't get all the jet's gains in simplicity for nothing. The early jets were very fuel-critical; those of today are much, much better. Economics, however, have cut down fuel reserves on flights, so even though modern jets burn less fuel than the early ones, the pilot is often on the edge of the seat worrying about reserves for ATC holding or going to an alternate. This comes about because it costs money to carry extra weight—extra fuel—so the economic bottom line improves if you carry as little excess fuel as possible. Add it all up, however, and the jet engine gives a comforting feeling of reliability that never existed before. Now oceans are flown with twin-engine airplanes, on the Boeing 767 and others. That would have been impossible with piston engines; there was just not enough reliability.

Heaven-sent though it was, the jet engine does act differently than other engines in some areas, and pilots had to become accustomed to these differences and learn to fly with certain new concepts. Take the way power responds to the throttle movement, for example. A piston engine responds quickly: when you open the throttle, the engine accelerates almost as the throttle moves. This is not so with a jet. Big throttle movement doesn't get much response from the engine if it's applied when the engine is idling; rather, there's an appreciable lag as the engine spins up—until the engine comes up to about 65 percent of its power, after which the acceleration is fast and follows throttle movement closely. What does this mean to a pilot? Anticipation. You must anticipate the fact that if an engine is at idle it will take 6 to 8 seconds before power comes up. So control inputs to stop a fast descent, for example, must be thought out ahead of time. A last minute blast of the throttle will not do much if the airplane is coming down at a high rate and is near the ground with the engine at full idle (the expression for that is "spooled down" or "spun down").

Propeller airplanes have another advantage when power is applied because the propellers create a blast of air that flows over the wing and immediately adds lift. Jets, however, don't have this blast, so there's no additional lift until the jet engine is up to speed and putting out enough power to shove the airplane and its wing through the air faster for more lift. Pilots have to know about this and add the knowledge to their thinking and action.

On normal landing approach jet engines put out a high percentage of power because the airplane is "dirty," meaning it has lots of drag from things sticking out in the airstream—the lowered landing gear, for example, and big flaps hanging down. It takes a lot of power to overcome this drag, so the throttles are kept forward and the engines spun up in that 65 percent range with their response immediate, and corrective control of the flight path is relatively simple. On the other hand, the power may be cut way back, under some conditions, such as the aircraft being pushed upward in the early part of flying into a wind shear condition. The pilot pulls the power off, combating this severe upward force; in an instant, however, descending air is encountered, pushing the airplane down so harshly it almost falls out of the sky, requiring lots of power and control movement to stop the descent before hitting the ground. With throttles full back, however, the power response is slow and the situation serious. On some occasions ATC will put the pilot in a situation where a fast descent is needed with power full back. Generally this occurs at an altitude high enough for recovery to be made before it becomes serious. Additionally, of course, the pilot must remember that "pouring on the coal," or opening throttles for more power, still doesn't give a blast of air over the wings for instant lift. The entire combination of power and lift must be part of the pilot's knowledge and a factor to consider when getting into any abnormal descent situation.

Day after day, however, thousands of jet airliners take off and land free from any dire consequences because pilots are imbued with the knowledge that has truly become second nature. Procedures also help as copilots, during the approach, call out sink rates: the rate in feet per minute seen on the vertical speed instrument as an airplane is descending. An automatic device— the ground proximity warning system (GPWS)—also announces excessive sink rates on approach.

There were other differences in flying jets rather than the earlier airplanes, among them that the power of those reliable engines allowed for such increases in speed and altitude that a differently designed airplane was required. The prejet propeller airplane had thick wings, had lots of drag, and couldn't get near the speed of sound. The jet airplane, on the other hand, can approach the speed of sound easily in descent if power isn't reduced. And when you fly near the speed of sound and in the thin air of high altitude, unusual things happen, some of them a little spooky.

At high speeds, where one approaches the speed of sound, velocity, *V,* is referred to as Mach, *M,* the symbol for the speed of sound. This was named after Dr. Ernst Mach (1836–1916), an Austrian physicist and philosopher who investigated the relationship between the flow of gases and the speed of sound. Mach 1 is the actual speed of sound, about 741 MPH at sea level. (Mach speed changes with temperature—the colder, the slower.) Airplane high speeds are expressed as a percentage of that speed; M 0.82, the speed most commonly used by airliners, is 82 percent of the speed of sound. The Concord zips along at M 2, which is 200 percent of the speed of sound.

The "spooky" part of a jet's high speed comes as it approaches the speed of sound—Mach 1. Even before it is reached, shock waves develop on the wing. If the speed continues to increase, the shock wave will cause the airplane's nose to go down; a situation called "Mach tuck." To prevent this nose down action from worsening, a gadget called a "Mach trim" was put on jets; it simply provided automatic control inputs to keep the nose from dropping. In training pilots all had to go through an exercise in letting the speed build in flight with the Mach trim off to experience the feel of the nose starting down all by itself. Actually it wasn't difficult to overcome the problem with a little nose up trim, but designers and FAA felt the Mach trim gadget should be installed.

The V speeds were changed and V_{ne} became V_{mo} or M_{mo} (mo for maximum operating speed). V for airspeed is expressed in knots (nautical miles per hour); M for Mach in percentage of the speed of sound. A pilot looks at the airspeed indicator and thinks V up to about 25,000 feet. Above that altitude the pilot looks at the Mach meter and thinks Mach—M. This change is related to high speed and our old ghostly friend, the shock wave.

Because of drag and their ability to approach the speed of sound, jet airplane wings are swept back; the wing tips are behind the center part of the wing in a form approaching a V. This allows a closer approach to the speed of sound without deleterious effects.

The idea of wing sweep developed both in the United States and abroad before WW II but wasn't used extensively until the jet airplane's development. While the sweep benefits high-speed flight, it also brings with it certain undesirable instability. One aspect of this is called "Dutch roll"; it is also called "roll-yaw coupling" or, in typical British lingo, "oscillatory stability." Whatever you call it, the tail swings, or yaws, causing a wing to lower perhaps 10°. Then the yaw pauses, due to the fuselage's fin and rudder, and the wing stops going down. Yaw then starts the other way, and that wing lowers. Then the process reverses and starts all over again. It's a repetitive, drunken, rolling, swaying sort of motion, and a Boeing 707 does it in about a 7-second cycle. Dutch roll is aggravated at high altitudes and gives the swinging motion one sometimes feels in an airline airplane when standing way back in the rear toilet.

Exactly why all this occurs is complicated to explain, but it's sufficient to say that's what one gets with a highly swept wing. It isn't difficult for the pilot to correct unless it's excessive, and jet airliners are designed so that will not be the case. Nevertheless, it would be an exhausting, full-time task to keep the Dutch roll subdued, so a gadget is installed in most jets to do the work. It's called a "yaw damper" and works with a gyro and some electric-hydraulic wizardry.

Once I flew with uncontrolled Dutch roll in a slightly bizarre research airplane at Princeton University that was equipped with two sets of controls—one the normal set and the other computer controlled so the airplane flight characteristics could be changed. One of the things we did was to set the computers so the airplane had severe Dutch roll. I was cocky-confident because I could correct this in a 707, but this roll was so violent I lost control until the test safety pilot shut down the computer and took over the normal controls. This airplane was a lot of fun to fly because you could create all sorts of conditions that you would never experience in a licensed airplane, such as moving the center of gravity so far back the airplane couldn't be controlled.

I also flew a supersonic transport simulator at NASA's Ames Laboratory. This was a diabolical device with a small cab mounted on gimbals at the end of a 20- or 25-foot centrifuge arm, so the cab could be slung around and tumble any which way. I was wedged in the seat with metal plates on each side of my head to keep from snapping my neck in case the rig had problems and became violent. The research was to see how an airplane going at Mach 3—about 2000 MPH—would act if the engines on one side were suddenly shut down, simulating a failure. The idea was to learn how much correction, via computer, the control system would need for a pilot to be able to handle it. To do this, we started from an uncontrollable condition. It was quite a thrill; the instruments in my cramped, hot, dark world indicated I was screaming along, 2000 MPH, at 70,000 feet altitude; then the engines were cut on one side, and severe yaw and rolling immediately started, as in a Dutch roll but this went right on rolling despite my frantic control corrections until I was upside down and being swung around. We tried this numerous times with small corrections by computer after each go until the situation was manageable, thus learning how much control augmentation would be needed in a real airplane. An hour of these maneuvers left me with an aching head and nausea near culmination.

The yaw damper on jet airliners does a good job, but some aircraft are limited to a lower altitude if the device isn't working, because Dutch roll is worse at high altitude. As design knowledge has progressed, Dutch Roll has become less prevalent in the latest jet airliners. Yaw dampers are still fitted, but the need for them and restrictions for their use have been reduced. Pilots, however, must be aware of this instability, the devices for its correction, and the devices' limitations.

During checkout on our first jet, the Boeing 707, one of the exercises involved turning off the yaw damper and inducing yaw by firmly pushing on a rudder pedal, which dropped a wing and started the cycle. Once in the condition the pilot corrected it manually. This proved to be quite easy when you applied a simple trick of aileron use—just a little jab of control wheel motion toward the down wing as it was starting up stopped the Dutch roll.

The size and speed of jet airplanes resulted in high-control forces, meaning it would take more strength to move them than humans can provide. Direct cable connection between control surfaces—elevator, rudder, and ailerons—and piloting wouldn't be possible simply because of these forces. So the controls were given power; at first they were partially hydraulic powered, with an additional system using a balance panel, which was ingenious gadgetry using airflow to help move the control. Eventually they became all hydraulic powered, and later pneumatics were added as backup. These new control systems called for pilot knowledge as to how they worked and what to do if failures occurred; the pilot might have to adapt to anything from flying with partial control to using muscle. Some system failures might give too much power and enable the pilot to move a control so far into the airstream that structural failure was a possibility; with this type failure, pilots must fly below certain airspeeds. This is crucial: pilot, know that one well!

Additional surfaces, called "spoilers," were part of the jet's control system. Spoilers were old stuff to glider pilots because high-performance sailplanes have spoilers that reduce lift when deployed, so the glider pilot can land in a small area. The jet spoilers are panels that come up out of the wing's top side; as they stick up in the airstream, they kill part of the lift by disturbing the smooth airflow.

The original 707 had two sets of spoilers on each wing, with all four coming up after landing to kill lift. In flight, however, one set of spoilers on each wing moved in small amounts to help the ailerons bank the airplane. The 707 also had two sets of ailerons for lateral control. One set was locked and unable to move in high-speed flight after the flaps were retracted following takeoff and initial climb, but the set came back into use for more control when the flaps were lowered for slow speed flight and landing. The latest Boeing aircraft, such as the 767, basically have this same control configuration. The control system was a far cry from the Pitcairn's ailerons, elevators, and rudder. Recently I dug out the plane's first manual (a 707 manual I used while going through ground school at the Boeing factory), and I saw notes and drawings I'd made creating a diagram to show what the controls did and which control was in effect during what flight regime. This, at first, was a new and confusing ball game.

What we're pointing out, in all this, is that the basic control of my old biplane was becoming a thing of the past; certain restrictions and aids were being put in the airplane's systems to help the pilot or to keep pilots from making errors (the pusher on stall, for example). Each aid required important knowledge the pilot had to have and remember. How much pilot authority could be taken away and what psychological effect would that have on command and the pilot's feeling of full authority and autonomy of decision? This question becomes more vital as today's computerized airplanes mount the skies. But more of this later.

Jets have wings that allow flight at high speed—swept back and thin. These sorts of wings don't produce lift as the old fat ones did. At high speed such thin wings are excellent, but the speeds required for takeoff and landing would be prohibitively high if retractable flaps (high-lift devices) were not added to the wing. Before takeoff, these flaps are extended to slide out behind the wing, changing its shape and adding to wing area. Small flaps also hang down from the front of the wing to help contour it for additional lift. These let the airplane take off, and land, at an acceptable speed. After takeoff the pilot has to go through a careful drill to retract the flaps, doing so at specific speeds. If flaps are retracted, or extended, improperly, either stall or structural failure can result. For landing even more flap is extended to create drag as well as lift, which work together to reduce the landing speed.

A jet's wing, with the large speed range—from, roughly, 140 MPH to 575 MPH—creates the need for longitudinal trim in order to relieve forces on the pilot's control wheel. The method of trimming used on older airplanes required the use of a small, separate, moveable section of the elevator that the pilot moved via a control wheel mounted on the cockpit pedestal. Movement of the small surface, called a "trim tab," shifted the elevator up or down to correct out-of-trim conditions—the conditions where constant pressure would be required on the control wheel to hold steady flight.

This configuration doesn't work for a jet because too much elevator would stick up in the airstream, causing drag and reducing speed, which, in turn, makes the airplane less efficient aerodynamically and would make the airline less efficient economically. But economy wasn't the only reason that a different method of trim was needed: lots of trim is needed to handle a wide range of the center of gravity (CG) position, which is important in airline work with the ever-changing loads of passengers and freight. In addition, the big wing flaps require large trim changes when extended or retracted, and covering the large speed range mentioned would be an impossible task for a simple trim tab.

So it was decided to move the entire stabilizer (the surface to which the elevator is attached) with hydraulic power turning a screw jack. And that screw jack turned into a culprit, as explained later. But the *idea* of moving the stabilizer wasn't new, except in big airplanes—the famous Piper Cub, for example, was so equipped—and it was a good idea because the stabilizer is large, which means that small movement produces lots of trim and the elevators remain streamlined behind the stabilizer, thus creating a nice low drag profile.

In effect, the stabilizer became the dominant control, and the elevator secondary, for changing pitch. This was okay, but meant you could "run out" of elevator (not have enough for control) if the stabilizer wasn't used properly. So it's necessary for the stabilizer to be set properly before takeoff; if it is not done properly, there is a chance that there might not be enough elevator to lift the nose and fly. The stabilizer is trimmed by pushing a button on the control wheel one of two ways, one for nose up, the other for nose down. On the pedestal is a stabilizer position indicator marked in degrees. The correct setting for takeoff is computed for each flight, and the pilot sets it via the buttons; when set correctly, the indicator reads inside a green color band. One important item on the checklist, read before takeoff, is "Stabilizer trim?" with the response, "In the green" or "____ units set."

One thundery day—February 12, 1963, to be exact—a Northwest 720B (a variation of the 707) departed Miami and climbed toward cruise altitude; near 20,000 feet, for some reason probably connected with turbulence due to a thunderstorm, the airplane's nose pitched up severely. The pilot pushed forward on the elevator control, but this wasn't enough, so the stabilizer trim button was pushed for nose-down trim, and shortly the airplane's nose headed down, very quickly picking up speed that took the plane beyond V_{mo}. Now the pilot pulled back, but the elevators were ineffective, so then he pushed the control wheel button to change the stabilizer and bring the nose up, but the stabilizer didn't budge; it could not overcome the tremendous force of the high airspeed. The jack screw stalled—"jammed" would be a more descriptive word—and the airplane dove into the ground, killing crew and passengers.

This sequence of events was deduced from the airplane's flight recorder, which wasn't as good as present-day recorders. It took fewer points of data than today's, so there were some gaps in the theory of what happened. Two months later, a United Air Lines jet was climbing through 38,000 feet toward 41,000, trying to avoid thunderstorms, when the same pitch-up, dive, and jack screw stall occurred. This time, however, after a wild, screaming, out-of-control dive, the pilots were able to raise the nose and recover. That the plane could recover was a tribute to the strength of Boeing airplanes, and the excellence of Boeing engineering, because the airplane had exceeded M_{mo} by a large amount. While the jack screw was jammed, the effects of Mach and shock waves—the speed was tremendous—entered the situation, compounding the problem of getting control back. Finally, when the airplane dove lower into altitudes where the air is more dense, the Mach decreased, and sufficient air flowed over the elevators to allow them to take effect. The airplane pulled out and landed successfully. The United pilot's experience tallied almost exactly with the hypothesis on the Northwest crash. "Jet upset," as they called it, suddenly became a new aviation buzzword.

Captain Paul Soderlind was Northwest Airline's technical pilot of the time. A brilliant technician who investigated the Northwest upset with Holmesian intensity, he performed many tests, including making dives to lock up the stabilizer deliberately. He also consulted with Boeing, the FAA, and other institutions. He analyzed all the data and developed a complete picture, which resulted in a training course for Northwest pilots. It was so successful that Soderlind was called on to give the same lecture to other airlines, both domestic and international. How to prevent jet upset? First Soderlind explained the best airspeed and method to fly through turbulence; he also warned pilots not to be too quick to run the stabilizer forward when a pitch-up occurred, to stay away from high-altitude turbulence, and if in a dive, to avoid pulling back on the controls but instead to let up the pressure on the elevator, which would, in turn, relieve some of the load on the stabilizer, allowing the jack screw to move. In other words, Soderlind told pilots they would have to act against all natural instincts. The course of instruction also emphasized that when the airplane got to lower levels the chances for recovery were high; the airplane might even recover itself. Soderlind received many awards and wide acclaim for his work on jet upset.

For a few years, all pilots were given training to cope with this phenomenon, but as time passed and jet upsets weren't experienced with any frequency—although there were a few more and especially in the general aviation sector of the business—there was a tendency to slide over this training in a perfunctory way. It's unlikely that many of today's new pilots have it embedded in their minds the way we did back then. Might an airline jet upset occur again, particularly if this training and knowledge is not covered properly in new pilot training? Possibly.

The aerodynamics of the jet were different from any pilots had been accustomed to, yet little information was given about them in training, particularly in relation to high-altitude, swept-wing flight. Part of this was that only aerodynamicists and advanced test pilots were privy to the real knowledge. Most airline operational people didn't have it, and no one along the way thought to pass it on—or at least it seems that way. The new concept of the adjustable stabilizer with the great power it had and the diminution of elevator control wasn't covered in courses; the nuts and bolts of how the stabilizer moved, and not what resulted, was the focus. Perhaps the instructors didn't know themselves, but the knowledge, which was available, might have prevented the Northwest plane's dive to destruction.

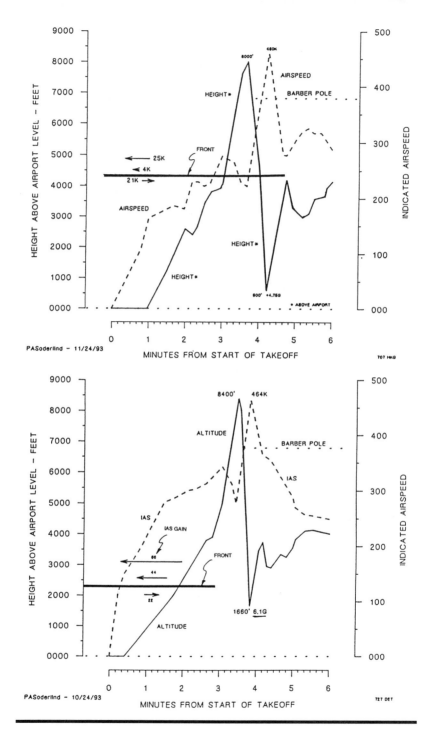

PLOTS OF FLIGHT PATHS by Captain Paul A. Soderlind of two jet upsets, one near Hong Kong and the other at Detroit, Michigan. The signature is almost exactly the same, starting with a pitch up when crossing an area of wind shear. Similarities such as this aided Soderlind in uncovering the problem and developing its solution. (Solid line represents altitude change and dashed line, airspeed.)

A jet engine, in effect, is not supercharged, so as the airplane flies higher the power available lessens, and the airplane becomes power limited—"thrust limited," it's called. Simply put, this means an airplane can get to an altitude at which the power available isn't adequate to push it along fast enough to give a large margin above stall. Other things happen, too, as the airplane approaches high speeds, such as problems with buffet. At high altitudes, there simply isn't sufficient stall margin, and stall is a real possibility if the airplane isn't managed properly. Paradoxically, up high is where the jet airplane is most efficient, where it gets more miles per gallon. So pilots want to fly as high as possible for best fuel economy—or simply more miles per gallon if they are trying to make a long flight.[1] This makes flying a tricky balancing act of being high enough for efficiency but not so high that stall and buffet is encountered—an act the pilot must fret about and make computations for.

Computers in most modern aircraft help with this, but there are still decisions based on judgment, experience, and feel. A big variable in this problem is the tropopause, the point in the atmosphere where the troposphere in which we live ends and the stratosphere above it begins. What happens at the "trop," as pilots call it, is that the temperature no longer decreases with altitude but levels off; when the airplane actually climbs into the stratosphere, it may find a higher temperature than that last experienced in the troposphere. The higher the temperature, the higher the density altitude. So if we've computed that we can safely fly, with good margins above stall, at 39,000 feet, for example, and suddenly fly through the trop into the stratosphere, the temperature rises and so does the density altitude, and we mush along closer to the stall than we want to be. The trouble is that the trop is different over different parts of the earth and varies with the weather patterns below it. It's a weather-forecasting problem, and we know about weather forecasting.

I used to fly a nonstop 747 flight from London to Los Angeles. In the early 747s, this distance was right at the airplane's maximum range, so flight planning and management was important. (How high one can fly is a matter of weight, too. This meant that right after takeoff the maximum altitude

---

1. Actually fuel is referred to in pounds. The engine uses air in pounds, so it's logical and useful in computations for the fuel to be expressed the same way. Also the weight of a gallon varies with temperature and is computed on a current basis when airplanes have fuel added. Standard weight for a gallon of jet fuel is about 6.7 pounds, but it varies as much as 0.3 of a pound plus or minus depending on temperature. A Boeing 767 at 39,000 feet will burn about 9000 pounds per hour, but that's a rough number because consumption varies with airplane weight and altitude. Pilots now think in pounds, and if you ask one how many gallons it took to fly to Paris, you'd probably get a blank stare.

might be limited to 33,000 feet. As fuel burned off, the airplane's weight was reduced, and it became possible to climb to 35,000 and even later in the flight 39,000, ending finally at 41,000 feet.) There were two problems: ATC and the temperature aloft. The weather data given included a plot of the temperatures and the trop levels from London to LA. If the forecast was accurate, you could tell about where a climb could be made. The ATC problem was different: ours wasn't the only airplane on the route; Pan Am had a London-LA flight with the same scheduled departure time as ours. The anxious pretakeoff frenzy needled the ground personnel to get us out before Pan Am got out, and the same push was probably going on at Pan Am's terminal.

If we got out first, our chances for making the altitude changes we wanted would be good. Our starting clearance was at 33,000 feet; then around northern Scotland we were light enough to climb to 35,000. We'd make a request to ATC, and if no one else was on our same track, the clearance came to climb to 35,000 feet. Toward the western part of the ocean the weight was down, so a climb to 39,000 was possible. But before requesting the change we studied the weather folder provided before takeoff to see how high the trop was and what the temperature would be above it. A trop above 39,000 feet was fine because we'd still be in the cool enough air. We didn't take it for granted, however, but reviewed how the forecast had played out so far; had weather and temperature been about what was predicted? If so, chances were that the trop forecast was accurate. If the weather had been different, then we studied the difference and attempted to see if the weather had moved along faster, or not as fast as forecast, and from such study, plus hunch based on experience, we made a decision. The reply would come from ATC: "Cleared to flight level three nine oh."

We'd push up the power and climb; 36,000 37,000 38,000, then about 38,500 feet, a slight turbulence jiggled the airplane. "Damn." We didn't have to look further: the turbulence indicated the boundary between the troposphere and the stratosphere was lower than forecast. Our eyes whipped to the outside air temperature gauge; it had been a comfortable $-55°C$; now as we entered the stratosphere, the temperature gauge registered an increase to $-50°C$, and at 39,000 it settled down at $-48°C$. Cruise power would not keep the speed up, so climb power had to be maintained, which uses more fuel and makes engines run hotter. Now came a figure-balancing act; how long at climb power and this temperature before the weight would be down so cruise power could be used again, and how much fuel would this waste— enough so we couldn't make LA? The questions rattled around. I've seen this condition so severe—although infrequently—that once it was necessary to call ATC and ask for a return to 35,000. Sometimes ATC already had given it to another flight that had been anxious for a higher altitude. Then followed lots of negotiations and squirming. It wasn't always a nice, tranquil ride.

What if Pan Am beat us out and the higher altitudes weren't available? We kept plugging, kept figuring. Before calculators and computers, we'd have a pile of paper slips on the little shelf to our left, covered with figures as we computed each groundspeed change and wind forecast that LA sent us. Over various airports in the western part of Canada, and later the United States, refiguring was done; the question was whether we should land in Calgary for fuel or press on. We reviewed fuel, groundspeed, weather. The last desirable airport to get fuel was Las Vegas, Nevada. How much fuel would we have in LA? More than just fumes? What was LA weather? We made a request to ATC on the chances for delays in landing and put it all together and decided to press on, seeing Vegas slide behind as our eyes looked ahead toward the mountains, behind which laid smoggy LA. All the chips hadn't been tossed on the table yet, however; there was still Palmdale, out in the desert, 50 miles north of LA if something desperate occurred. It may seem irrational to worry about making an extra stop to that degree, but the schedule says nonstop, you're in a competitive world, and it's your job to make it if you can safely, so the stress of the decision rides heavily on you, the pilot.

The working of altitude versus miles per pound of fuel, versus speed, and versus stall margin is a big part of jet knowledge, and despite computers, which do help, pilot judgment is an important part of it all. Temperature is also a factor because temperature changes the altitude as far as the airplane and engines are concerned. The altitude you read on the altimeter is one thing, but apply temperature to that, and the result is density altitude, and that's the real world, the criterion that performance goes by.

There's a chart showing standard temperature with altitude, and that's what engineers use to compute performance; standard temperature for sea level is 15°C, at 35,000 feet it is −54.3°C. The standard is calibrated for an average trop height; actually, it's lower over the poles and higher over the equator and variable all the time. The official standard atmosphere chart puts the trop's end and the stratosphere's start at 36,000 feet with a standard temperature of −56.5°C. It holds steady at that to 65,617 feet, and then the temperature slowly increases with altitude and at 200,000 feet it's −20.4°C. Of course, very few days are "standard." How many days where you live, if it's near sea level, is the temperature exactly 15°C (59°F), which is standard? Not many.

So when flying, the difference between standard temperature and what is registered on the thermometer is really important, and pilots must constantly think of this, have a gut feel for hot days and the resulting performance deterioration, and then use charts or computers to anticipate what the airplane will really do. This affects takeoff distance, climb, ceiling, maximum range, altimeter readings for low approach, terrain clearance, engine performance, and almost every facet of the airplane's efficiency.

I rode the cockpit, as an observer, on a Concorde test flight; the test was a flight from Toulouse, France, to a point off the coast of Iceland, where we turned around and flew back to Toulouse. The distance was about the same as Paris–New York. One part of the test called for holding over Toulouse for 30 minutes before landing, simulating an ATC delay at New York. It was a beautiful flight, except the actual temperature at altitude was almost 10° above standard, so all we did at Toulouse was make a quick circle and land. The 30-minute holding fuel had been used up as we struggled through that warmer air, albeit at about 1300 miles an hour. But even that speed was affected, and we limped along at 900 MPH for almost half the flight until the weight was down enough to get to 60,000 feet and Mach 2.

Going from Constellation-type airplanes cruising at 18,000 feet to jets at 35,000 introduced other high-altitude problems.

If pressurization was lost in a Constellation, the sudden increase in cabin altitude to 18,000 feet wasn't going to be fatal for passengers and crew (except possibly for some people on board with serious medical problems); there was a reasonable bit of time to descend to more breathable altitudes. But a jet at 39,000 feet is a different story; suddenly going from a cabin pressurized for 8000 feet to 39,000 can kill people in a minute or so. The airplanes, as any rider knows, are provided with oxygen masks that drop from overhead above the seats for passengers to clamp over their noses and use until the pilots dive to a lower altitude.

There were two developments as a result of the new altitudes and possible decompression; one was an emergency descent procedure developed for pilots. Oxygen masks for the crew are placed on a quick release strap behind the shoulder of each crew member. If the airplane loses pressure, you grab the mask and slam its harness on your head and the mask over your nose, then pull back the throttles, open the speed brakes, roll into a 45° bank, and shove the nose down, double-checking that the passengers' masks have dropped down. The procedure has been modified over time, but using the mask and getting down fast is still the key. When the 707s first arrived, part of the training was to climb to 35,000 feet and do an emergency descent in order to satisfy the FAA. Now it's done in a simulator, which saves the airline an appreciable amount of money over climbing a real jet to 35,000 feet and screaming down just to see if the pilot knows how to do it. (Actually it's an easy maneuver.)

The other nasty part of the beginning of the jet age was that one pilot had to wear an oxygen mask all the time when the airplane was flying above 25,000 feet in case a decompression occurred. This was damned uncomfortable to say the least, as a comfortable oxygen mask has never been invented. I feel sorry for the military pilots who wear them all the time. We alternated wearing the masks, captain-copilot-captain-copilot, at 30-minute intervals. The pilots yelled long and loud about this silly rule, and finally the FAA was satisfied that we could get the emergency masks put on and start descent soon enough, so the rule was changed to say that one pilot must have a mask on, using oxygen, when the airplane is above 25,000 feet only if the other pilot leaves his or her station for any reason, such as a visit to the john. Otherwise, with both pilots on duty, no one has to wear a mask unless the plane is over 41,000 feet. The latest jets, such as the Boeing 767, however, are allowed to operate above 41,000 feet, so then we're back to the situation that one pilot must wear a mask all the time when flying above 41,000 feet.

When in the territory of 40,000 feet and above, a sudden decompression can kill you in seconds—or at least cause brain damage. Not to worry, however; the record is excellent. Very few decompressions have ever occurred, and those that have gave the pilots enough time to get down to liveable altitude. An instant decompression would require a very big hole in the airplane, a catastrophic occurrence difficult to visualize unless the airplane was hit by an unfriendly rocket or such. Simply having a window blow out might play havoc with the people sitting right next to it, but the airplane's pressure would not all rush out instantly. There is enough time, with a small hole, for the passengers to don masks and for the pilots to descend. Other pressure loss could come from the system malfunctioning, but there are enough backups and warnings to catch this, and besides, this would probably be a slow depressurization.

In the days of Constellations we were still allowed to bring passengers into the cockpit, which we did fairly often, especially children. On one otherwise serene flight over the ocean, as we were cruising along at 17,000 feet, a hostess brought a cute child—perhaps three years old—up front. The outflow valve controls (the valves one could open to dump the pressure) were located, on that model Connie, on the rise of the step down into the cockpit, a place handy to the flight engineer but unhandy to anyone else. This child entered the cockpit and then, as though he knew the location perfectly, turned around, bent down, and flipped open an outflow valve! Our ears "bubbled" as the air pressure rushed out. Luckily the flight engineer had an eye on the child and got the picture instantly; pushing the child aside, he quickly moved the valve to its correct position. The cabin altitude only climbed 1000 feet during the episode and was quickly restored to the proper level. But we really watched children after that.

The jet came equipped with the flight engineer's station much as it was in the Connie—a separate seat behind the pilots', facing sideways toward an instrument panel that covered electrical, hydraulic, fuel management, air-conditioning, and pressurization systems. As in the past, the F/E was a useful part of the crew, but someone was already thinking of a way to get rid of that position. The telltale item on the new F/E station was the lack of engine controls. Connies give the F/E throttles, but the 707 F/E's station didn't have them. To move throttles, the F/E had to turn his or her seat and slide it toward the pilots' and then reach ahead, in awkward fashion, to adjust them—a real chore because during a flight it was necessary to adjust throttles many, many times. This diminution of the job's activities was a clear signal of what was coming: the end of the F/E and introduction of a two-person crew. Interestingly, the F/E's station, being behind the pilots' and lower, allowed the F/E to see forward and up at a piece of the sky cut off from the pilots' view. During approach to a busy airport flight engineers scanned that portion of sky; I've had the F/E point out many airplanes that neither the copilot nor I could see. This was a safety factor disregarded when officialdom decreed the demise of the position.

Such was the start of the jet age. The new techniques were interesting and demanding, the engine reliability soothing.

Times and eras generally don't end neatly as though cut off by a knife; the old, in various forms, hangs on while the new is introduced. This is very true in aviation, where the DC-3 of the 1930s is still occasionally found prowling the sky. The early jets, DC-9s, Boeing 707s, and even piston engine Connies and DC-7s are out there demanding old techniques and knowledge. But the basic force of progress pounds ahead, curing some problems, retaining many of the old, and creating new and complex ones.

10 | LEARNING JET FLYING
THE TRIAL-AND-ERROR WAY

With the jet airline age came new
concepts and new management techniques, both financial and
operational, along with a contest for aircraft command between
the pilot in the cockpit and the people on the ground with the
rule books and balance sheets. It also marked the start of a dramatic
and major change that has created a poorly defined area of conflict
between technology and the pilot, a strange situation in which the
pilot, while appreciating technology's benefits, recognizes that it must
be a servant, not a master, and that it is not always a reliable servant.

At the start of the jet age, with the 707 and DC-8, we were still
flying very much in propeller airplane ways, which encompassed the
character developed from open cockpit biplane to Constellations. The basics
of that pioneer age were valid and still are, but the jet airplane, with its
performance, and compromises contrived to get that performance, demanded
new disciplines.

The V speeds we spoke of earlier were being used during later Connie
days in the 1950s but weren't as crucial. Runway lengths weren't as
marginal, so pilots could still decide, in many cases, if they wanted to lift off
a bit early or hold the airplane down and gain extra speed before climbing
out. Liftoff speed was mostly the result of pilot opinion, based on
experience, without much scientific data to back it up. I remember line
checking a senior captain in a Connie, and he only used about three-quarter
power for takeoff, making the takeoff run very long, which in turn would
make obstacle clearance at the far end a serious matter if an engine failed.

I criticized his stingy use of power and tried to explain why it wasn't the
proper thing to do, but he was firmly of the opinion that he never wanted to

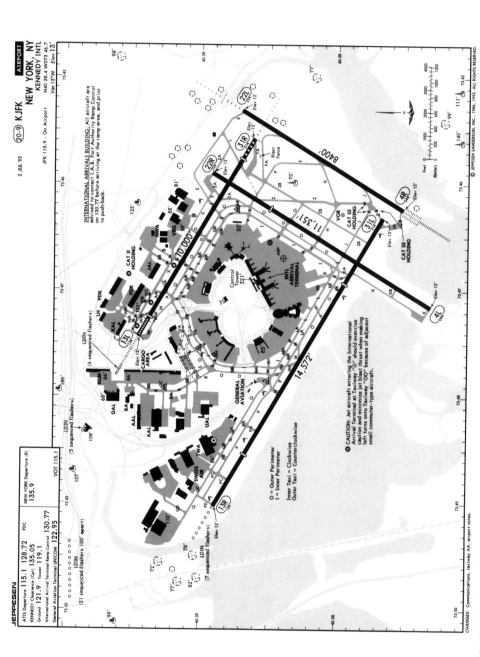

DIAGRAM of John F. Kennedy International Airport's taxiways and runways. Pilots study such diagrams, sometimes in a dark cockpit, to sort out taxiway routes as directed by the control tower. (© 1986, 1993 Jeppesen Sanderson, Inc. *Reproduced with permission of Jeppesen Sanderson, Inc. Reduced for illustrative purposes. Not to be used for navigation.*)

open the engines to takeoff power and put all that strain on them. Using reduced power, he thought, made for less chance for engine failure. He wouldn't believe that the engine had been designed, tested, built, and certified to be able to withstand the high power required for takeoff. We made a number of takeoffs on this trip, and I had him do them the proper way, but I'm sure once I was out of the cockpit he went back to those reduced power takeoffs. Interestingly, he flew to retirement with a perfect safety record. Was he lucky never to have had an engine failure, or did his conservatism protect him from any failure?

Landing presented a similar situation in that approach speeds, in propeller airplanes, were pretty much as the pilots thought they'd like them considering current conditions of wind, weather, and what their instincts told them they ought to be. With the jet, however, the V speeds for takeoff, climb, and approach to landing had to be precise and obeyed. They were taken from charts and rigid rules. They were absolutely necessary because the airport margins for safety were drastically reduced as we made jet airplanes fit propeller airplane runways. I got a terrible shock when studying our first International 707 performance data; I discovered that the required runway length, full load, was 10,500 feet! That included, of course, the V_1 stop business with an engine failure or ability to climb out and clear a 35-foot obstacle. But JFK's longest runway at the time was only 11,000 feet (it's almost 15,000 feet now), and other runways were shorter.

The difference in takeoff speeds was impressive—V_r for takeoff was 108 knots in a 749 Connie but 144 knots in the new 707, which means the pilot used a lot more pavement to take off.

The higher landing speeds meant more runway was needed to land and stop as well, so the recommended approach speeds were important, with little tolerance for deviation built in. Again, for comparison, note that the 749 Connie used an approach speed of 102 knots. The first jets upped this to 132 knots.

Since jets, which don't have propellers, aren't as efficient as propeller airplanes for reversing and stopping on the ground, a jet on a wet runway was a nervous proposition, especially on runways like JFK's 4R instrument runway of 7000 feet. This fact made one stick very closely to approach speeds. Through time, that runway has been lengthened to 8400 feet—the useable length is listed as 7393 feet—so little has been gained, and it's still an uncomfortable feeling when landing on it under slippery conditions. There is a 4L runway available now for instrument approaches, with a useable length of 10,151 feet, but illogically and I know not why, the minimums on that runway are higher than the shorter 4R. So in conditions of the lowest ceilings, the shorter 4R has to be used. Because of problems like these, the introduction of the 707 and DC-8 demanded new, inflexible discipline of pilots. The latitude allowed in the old school way of doing things was drastically reduced, and the pilot found tight constraints in all aspects of flying, which was quickly ceasing to be an art and becoming a strictly disciplined science instead. There was a feeling, flying the new jets, that margins for error were squeezed tighter, that jet flying took you closer to the limits, that you had to fly nearer the edge of the airplane's safe parameters. The high altitudes that put you closer to the stall or buffet regime were kind of spooky, and flying at 39,000 feet on a hot day created a slightly uptight atmosphere in the cockpit. Most of these demands, by now, have become routine in jet flying, but without doubt, flying jet airplanes has increased the need for closer pilot attention and more precise flying techniques. Although the jet engine has relieved the old anxiety of engine failure, new concerns have taken its place on the list of things that furrow a pilot's brow. And high altitude on a hot day is still spooky.

There is scientific exactness to the new methods, but their use also, though subtly, removes initiative from the pilot. We're not saying this is all bad, but the move to jets was a move toward doing things by rote, doing them as though directed by a mysterious "they" down there somewhere on the ground. Did this change make the judgment of pilots less individual and more dependent on others'? Certainly these methods placed new and additional responsibilities on the pilot. Did they increase the pilot's mental load or, instead, give him or her direction so that off-the-cuff judgments weren't as necessary? There's a lot to explore in answering these questions, plus the need for a close examination of how much "art" is still essential in flying.

One thing this exactness provided was something for FAA to inspect in a pedantic manner. While judgment cannot be written into rule books, things like V speeds can, so FAA air carrier inspectors watch, hawklike, on check rides to see that the pilot performs perfectly with regard to the numbers. The inspectors also do a lot of nit-picking things like writing up pilots if they start to taxi away from the gate while even one passenger, whom the pilots cannot see or be aware of, is standing in the aisle stuffing luggage in the overhead storage compartment. But FAA inspection doesn't reveal the pilot's ability to make a judgement. A pilot may do a masterful job of making an emergency landing in severe weather, but what got the pilot in that weather jam in the first place? Might it have been poor judgment? Ruling on judgment is a difficult and arguable process, so FAA has to fall back on the precise rules for censuring pilots, which almost develops into a game—a serious one, however, because there are many rules, and pilots, although thinking they are doing everything correctly, constantly wonder what rule they may have overlooked. Pilots are always on tenterhooks whenever an FAA inspector is around.

An interesting part of jet introduction was the schooling we received; mostly it was nuts-and-bolts stuff, covering hydraulic, electric, fuel, and 14 other different systems. Certain useful information was missing from the curriculum, however, such as the differences between jet and propeller airplanes and the problems we would encounter flying the line—jet upset, for instance. The gut stuff about how a jet fits and operates up there wasn't learned until actual line flying began and pilots encountered things that mother didn't tell them about. Passing a pilot friend of like seniority in a layover hotel or the operations office often produced conversations that might open, "Hey, you know what I found out? If you turn B this way, you'll get x result." Something that never came out in school. Probably you had one for him too, perhaps about flight characteristics: "Brother, if you're right at ref and cut the power and try to flare, she'll fall outa the sky like a brick!" (A landing approach.)

This kind of information exchange is important and much of the lore finally finds its way into revised manuals and then into the school for use by later pilots. It's also part of the reason for the reply I received when I asked a very senior pilot why he hadn't bid to fly the jets: "Naw, I'll wait till they've been on the line awhile—I don't believe in mixing airline flying with test flying," he said.

We also learned, by the hard knock school, the craftiness necessary to get a higher altitude while dealing with the ATC system—a bundle of tricks like getting requests in ahead of other airplanes, changing track, taking a higher altitude before you were really ready for it, and expecting to burn more fuel hanging there with less efficiency perhaps but benefiting in the total sense by getting up there. Jockeying for higher altitude was a constant game, the rules for which were not learned in school. Interestingly, hard-nosed domestic pilots accustomed to the cat-and-dog fighting for position necessary for getting into busy places like Chicago or New York seemed to carry their "street smarts" with them when they moved over to the higher-paying international jet operation, beating out the staid overocean regulars for number one to approach London or Paris. Today, of course, there have been millions of hours of jet experience, and new pilots learn much of this lore in their training, as well as when flying copilot with experienced pilots.

The F/E's job became easier as it was spared the complexities of piston engines and propellers, but good use was made of the F/E's so-called spare time. Soon the F/E was responsible for duties such as routine company communications, gathering weather reports, and periodically going back in the cabin to correct a complaint from a cabin attendant that the coffeemaker wasn't working, that the movie projector was busted, or that there was a strange smell or noise. This relieved the pilot and copilot of distraction and concern.

Pilots liked other things about having an F/E, especially during preflight aircraft inspection and their check on fuel load. Going through the checklist reinforced mutual respect and cooperation; it was mighty reassuring when, before starting up, the flight engineer entered the cockpit, doffed cap and jacket to get ready for flight, and commented on the condition of the airplane, what problems it had coming in, how they had been fixed, whether or not any problems still existed and what their effect might be on the flight. This helped you decide, after some back-and-forth dialogue, whether or not to go with the plane in that condition, or this information was put in your knowledge bank as a factor in how you would manage the flight. Then there was the final assurance of a definite reading of how much fuel was in each tank, information the F/E had from being on the ground double-checking the fueling. This discussion was not only informative but it set a tone of cooperation and mutual respect that today is called CRM but that we simply called people doing a job together. It's difficult to understand why the airline industry feels it's not cost efficient to have an F/E on the $135 million, 400+ passenger 747-400—or on all new airplanes, for that matter. Aside from cost there is an added safety factor, no matter how forcefully industry people argue against this safety premise. Computers now take the place of the F/E, and if you are confident that computers, and the pilots programming them, will never make errors, then you'll feel comfortable without the F/E.

The instruments of the jets heralded the age of computers. The flight director and autopilot of the 707 had built-in "intelligence" that did a certain amount of "thinking" as to what corrections the pilot should make to successfully fly down an ILS. This was and is a big help, as it relieves the pilot of the inexact guessing game of what the next heading change should be to stay on the ILS; the computer does all the anticipation for the pilot, and it does the same for staying on glide slope. The flight director made low-ceiling approaches a lot easier, although it did not obviate the need for high concentration during this procedure. And its introduction meant we all had to go to school and demonstrate our ability to shoot a 200-foot ceiling, albeit in the simulator.

The autopilot was a more sophisticated system and included a function called "control wheel steering," which, in its simplest form, was a way for the pilot to move the control wheel to turn the airplane but have the autopilot do the work. It was marginal in its usefulness, and I rarely used it. But all in all, the autopilot of the 707 era was a big improvement over past autopilots.

Our early 707 autopilots had a turn knob on the pedestal, so if a turn was needed, and you weren't using control wheel steering, you simply twisted the knob in the desired direction. This caused the airplane to turn, the degree depending on how much one turned the knob. Return it to center, and the turn would stop as the knob slipped into a shallow slot called a "detent." The problem was that the detent didn't always grasp the knob and center it. The knob might stay out of center by a small fraction, causing a very subtle turn with very little bank angle. One pilot, flying the North Atlantic, eastbound, made a 30° course correction and then stopped it by returning the knob to center. The airplane flew through the night, all smooth and well, except that later the pilot did a double take when he looked out the left window, up at the northern sky, and the Big Dipper and North Star weren't there! When he asked the copilot to have a look out his right side window, they found the stars had moved to the copilot's side! They had turned completely around, as a quick check of the compass revealed—the airplane had made a big, sneaky, shallow turn. The pilot got it back on proper course, and from then on always double-checked to be certain the control knob was firmly in the slot. We complained about the design, but it took a long time to get it corrected.

All in all the autopilot was an advancement, allowing for smoother flight, and in general was quite reliable. It did fail from time to time, however, so constant checking was necessary, as it still is despite a warning light and horn if the autopilot shuts off on its own. Autopilots are designed to keep airplane and autopilot synchronized in regard to trim and control wheel forces, but this feature doesn't always work perfectly. A typical result might be that while flying along smoothly the autopilot could be out of synchronization with the trim. If the pilot turned the autopilot off with such a condition—by pushing a button on the control wheel—the airplane might jerk toward its trimmed position, an action which, while not particularly dangerous, would be sufficiently noticeable to startle passengers. An instrument was supposed to show the synchronization between autopilot and an airplane control's trim, but its indications were often invalid. We quickly learned that the trick was to have a firm hold on the control wheel when pushing the button for disengagement and be ready to overpower any jerk toward nose-up or down. All this isn't a big issue but is representative of the many, many small items about which pilots have to be knowledgeable. (Passengers who have felt this jerk in-flight should not worry; all is safe.)

Since the autopilot could do a variety of things and be set in different modes, turning it on or off wasn't just a matter of pushing a button or flipping a switch; rather, there was a middle selector with six different settings depending on what you wanted to have it do. And it could do a lot: hold altitude and heading, respond to commands for up or down pitch changes, fly down the ILS for an instrument approach, follow an Omni course en route, or follow the heading a pilot would set. This is good, helpful stuff, but you still don't turn the device on and go out to lunch; you watch it and see that it's doing what it should. Today's autopilots on airplanes like the Airbus 320 and Boeing 767 are so sophisticated they make the 707 autopilot seem primitive, but you still don't let them mind the store without constant and careful surveillance.

Little things about the autopilot, unknown or unattended, could cause serious consequences. It would shut off, for example, if the pilot grasped the control wheel and gave it a small push, pull, or twist exceeding a force of six pounds—this amount varied with airlines and engineering department opinions. But any poundage involved was relatively small; if it were larger, it would be too difficult for the pilot to overpower the autopilot in an emergency. So what could happen? Middle of the night, crew sleepy in the dark cockpit. Copilot decides to answer nature's call and squirms out of his seat and goes aft. Unseen by either pilot, his knee hits the control wheel as he gets out of the seat—with a force greater than six pounds. The autopilot disconnects, and no one realizes it. In a few moments, the pilot discovers they've lost 500 feet and the heading is off by 20°. The pilot knows what happened, cusses a bit, and puts it back together.

That is a simple case, but there could be more tragic disconnects. One happened over the Florida swamps when a Lockheed 1011 was having landing gear problems. Too many people were fussing with the landing gear problem; they couldn't get a green safe light on the instrument panel, indicating the gear was extended and locked. Unbeknownst to them, a jar had disengaged the altitude mode of the autopilot, which had no warning alarm, and the airplane flew a shallow descent into the ground, resulting in a major crash with many fatalities. Of course, someone should have been "flying" the airplane, if not with hands-on control then at least by watching the three keys of altitude, attitude, and airspeed. It seems logical that one of the pilots would catch such an irregularity, but one pilot might be off-station, or both might be distracted by other things to watch or functions to perform, such as tending to paperwork, answering ATC radio calls, and more. The only warning of the autopilot's altitude going off was a click when it disengaged—a sound of low enough intensity to be easily missed. (Whenever one hears even a subtle click, it's a good idea to start looking around for its source.)

The idea of an autopilot to relieve the crew of manual labor and to do certain demanding tasks, such as making a low instrument approach, is all to the good, provided the crew has time to monitor the autopilot's performance. Unfortunately, the trend hasn't been thus; rather, the autopilot is usually used to relieve the crew of one duty in order to perform another. A method of monitoring without constant attention for irregularities in the autoflight system came with modern aircraft in the form of situation conditions announced on a CRT (cathode-ray tube), with warning lights and sounds. If the crew is busy and not observing certain aspects of autoflight, then warning lights, bells, and horns light up or sound off to get their attention. In addition a situation display announces, through lighted sections, what modes the autopilot is set to perform.

And now we must ask ourselves if flying has become easier or, in fact, more distracting and demanding. Advances have certainly added to the human's task, and the proof seems to be in the simple matter of various airlines requiring one pilot to monitor the "raw data"—the basic old style information—while the other pilot uses the fancy systems, a telling development that seems to detract from the gain of the new system. If it's necessary to monitor the old system plus the new, then an additional load on the pilots has been created; they now have two systems to manage and monitor, rather than one. An additional question is how much the crew knows about the system. Training centers on the how-to-use-it aspects, with little knowledge imparted of how the system works. Of course, the argument is advanced that the pilots don't have to know the system's inner workings, but a certain amount of knowledge of the system's innards may help solve a difficult problem that might have serious consequences. We knew more of the system's workings in the past, and this knowledge often helped. Of course, the old systems were not as complex as the new. This argument of how much pilots should know about systems goes on without promise of solution.

When the 707 came into service there were few enough jets that ATC could provide special handling if needed, and it was needed on occasion, as these first models burned a lot of fuel.

I came westbound from Paris to New York one night, flying a track very far north in order to escape head winds. I planned on getting 39,000 feet altitude, where the fuel flow would be low enough, so making New York wasn't going to be a serious problem. Over Labrador, after we'd made landfall, ATC called me and said to descend and cruise at 29,000 feet! This was a disaster. I protested but was told the military had blocked the higher levels. This happens when it is conducting exercises or making extensive refueling contacts.

We slowly descended and, once leveled off, read the fuel flows and calculated against groundspeed and distance. Things were going to be tight. It was shaping up that the judicious thing to do would be to land somewhere such as Albany, New York, which was on our path. But Albany was a marginal field for handling jets at that time. Approaching Albany, I got the New York weather, which was clear; next I told ATC my problem and asked what the chances were for a no delay clearance and special handling to avoid the normal circuitous route into JFK so we could cut down the distance.

"No traffic, you're cleared direct, present position to Kennedy. Descend your discretion."

We stayed up as long as possible and then, just south of Albany, cut the throttles and, essentially, glided all the way to JFK without touching the throttles until on final approach to the runway. We landed with just enough fuel to be safe—thanks to ATC's cooperation.

Today, of course, the airplanes are almost all jet-propelled and special handling when seriously low on fuel comes only after the pilot has declared an emergency.

The jets, because of their speed and lower operating costs, plus their large capacity, caused a dramatic increase in air travel. The airlines were soon busily expanding schedules and competing for advantageous departure times, which makes for more airport confusion as a dozen airplanes all want to taxi and take off at the same moment. But the push was, and is, on for more schedules and more business, multiplying the problems of air traffic control. The competitive and economic push is reflected in the cockpit, where sophisticated aircraft systems compound a pilot's list of things to know, watch, remember, and be wary of; the pressures ATC creates make the cockpit environment more stressful. Creating additional stress is FAA's constant rule-making to fit all problems. The rules create a false safety net, implying as they do that if a pilot goes by them all, never slips from the complex, confusing regulations and procedures, all will be safe. But this is a fallacy because humans err, and if the demands they are asked to meet are impossibly large, then accidents will happen—pilot error will occur. And it's safe to argue that these demands now exceed the reasonable, that it is unrealistic to expect perfect performance from a human all the time.

11 | PILOT AUTHORITY ERODES

When the airmail service oper-
ated in 1919, pilots were expected to fly in any weather. The
supervisors, who did not fly, demanded pilots take off in fog,
snow, sleet—any condition. The accident rate was appalling, but
it was fly or be fired.

July 22, 1919, marked the beginning of the end of such folly. In
the previous two weeks 15 airmail service airplanes had crashed, and
two pilots had lost their lives. July 22 was a morning of dense fog at
the Belmont flying field near New York City. Pilot Leon D. Smith
waited as the mail was loaded and the airplane readied, but Smith
didn't climb in and take off; the weather was too bad, and he said, when
asked why he didn't fly, "I'll be damned if I'll kill myself for a sack of two-
bit letters."

Smith's supervisor fired him and called E. Hamilton Lee to make the
flight. Ham, as he was called, also refused and was promptly fired. Then all
the other pilots refused to fly—the first pilot's strike. It was settled four days
later, on July 26. The U.S. Post Office appointed flying supervisors who
would decide if the pilot should be able to make it under current weather
conditions. Ham Lee was rehired, but Smith never was, the reason lost in
time. The settlement was half a loaf, however, as pilots were still pushed to
fly in weather and competition between them was fostered by such incentives
as extra pay for weather flying—things unheard of today.

There were difficult years ahead as pilots attempted to organize for
greater safety and for better pay and working conditions. Finally, on July 27,
1931, in a Chicago hotel room, the Air Line Pilots Association was founded,
headed by a lion-hearted pilot, David L. Behncke. He was tough, abrasive

A SWALLOW BIPLANE of the early airmail days—April 1926. The pilot is Leon Cudderback. The large wheels in back are not the airplane's but are on a dolly placed under the tail skid to aid in moving the airplane while it was on the ground. (*University of Texas History of Aviation Collection*)

to management, but politically astute, playing President Franklin Roosevelt and the Congress off against each other to ALPA's advantage. Fiorello La Guardia, then a congressman, was a great friend of Behncke's and of inestimable help in ALPA's difficult early days.

While airline management looks at ALPA as an economic adversary, ALPA is also strongly motivated by safety concerns and spends a good portion of its income from dues on such matters. As early as 1944, ALPA established an official Engineering and Air Safety Department; Ted Linnert, an aeronautical engineer, had been hired by ALPA to work on safety in 1940 and eventually became head of the department. Many pilots donate their time, promoting safety concepts and technology as well as taking part in accident investigations.

The story of ALPA is long, taking many twisting paths; it is best told by George E. Hopkins in his book, *Flying the Line*. The important point to us here is that from the time of its founding ALPA has been a strong advocate of the idea of the pilot as final authority to judge if the airplane flies or not. Every airline flight is given a clearance signed by an airline dispatcher who can say the flight will *not* fly but can never say it *will* fly unless there is complete agreement by the pilot. An absolute must is the ritual of the pilot signing the clearance, signifying that he or she accepts the flight and is satisfied that all matters of safety have been fulfilled. A typical clearance might once have read "Flight 7 A/C 351 cleared Newark/Chicago instruments 600 gallons South Bend Alternate: SCD." The important part was the letters "SCD," which stood for "Subject Captain's Discretion." SCD summed up those years of trial and tribulation that established who was boss and that made clear that the final decision was the pilot's. Actually, today, clearances seldom include the initials "SCD," but they are understood to be there as part of the regulations. I wish they were still present to remind the pilots that they are the bosses, in command of and responsible for their flights.

Being in command means making and carrying out decisions. A thunderstorm is over the airport; the pilot thinks that's a hazard and tells approach control (a part of ATC) that the airplane isn't landing but it will pull out and hold for the storm to pass—or go somewhere else. That's the pilot's good judgment at work.

In days gone by, the ground personnel would understand the pilot's action and do everything to cooperate, keeping in mind, first, the safe progress of the flight. In those days airlines were, in the main, run by pilots. While pilots weren't the most astute financial people, they did know operational problems and fully understood the actions of the pilots in the airplanes. Command wasn't influenced by people on the ground. In that era, the pilot's judgment prevailed; he or she was concerned primarily with what was best for the safe progress of that flight and was able to push aside other factors, like the federal rules, to worry about later. Is the situation different today? Of course, everyone says—and means—flight safety is first, but have operational changes put a kink in that thinking? Do other factors detract from the pure, straight-line consideration of the safest way? Has pilot judgment been diminished by other people and interests getting in the act?

The first piece chopped out of total cockpit command came with the growth of air traffic control, which happened along with traffic growth—not in one sudden time frame but gradually from the late 1950s on. Before radar, instructions were sent by radio for the pilots to hold or make an approach at a certain time, to fly at a different altitude, or to make some other adjustment necessary for traffic control. The pilots, however, didn't feel their realm was being taken over, at least partly because in the early days of ATC, the controller always told the pilots why something was being done: "Your traffic is Eastern ninety-one at seven thousand." That was why the pilot had to stay at 6000.

But when radar control entered the picture, and traffic grew, the pilots felt their command was diminished. An order such as, "turn right to two one zero" said what course to fly. A pilot, following such a command, then went off in a direction that was not in the flight plan. The pilot was not quite certain where the airplane was headed, if there was high terrain ahead and if the ATC-assigned altitude would clear it. It wasn't the pilot navigating, knowing the airplane was safely above the terrain, but someone on the ground in whose hand the pilot was supposed to place the flight's safety. People today may laugh at this charge, but the original transition was difficult for pilots.

In the beginning, old-time pilots were shaken. "No summabitch is gonna tell *me* what heading to fly," you'd hear in the 1950s—an empty exclamation as pilots resisted the idea of the word "instructions." Don't ask for taxi instructions, was the underground message going around; ask for taxi clearance or information, but not instructions because that suggested you were asking ATC how to fly the airplane, thus violating the idea of the pilot managing the airplane. During the height of this resistance, I once heard, at La Guardia airport, New York, a pilot call the tower and ask for "taxi instructions." Immediately another pilot, probably parked at a gate waiting to go, grabbed his mike and broadcast, "Release the brakes and open the throttles," letting all tuned into the tower know what he thought of the other pilot asking for instructions.

As traffic increased, communications grew, and there wasn't time to tell pilots what their traffic was except if it was useful in the process, such as, "keep traffic ahead in sight" when approaching to land. Soon operating in the ATC system began to carry the atmosphere it has today of operating in a vacuum. You generally don't know of the other airplanes out there and see only a small portion of them.

Navigation, the challenge of finding your way and finally finding the airport runway, has diminished, as has the feeling of being in total command from takeoff to landing. If you're naturally lazy, it's easy to get in the habit of sitting back and letting the ground do it.

This isn't a clever idea, though, because ATC makes mistakes. Even though given seemingly random headings to fly, the pilot should try to keep reference as to where ATC is taking the airplane (although, for technical reasons, this isn't easy to do), if for no other reason than to be certain ATC hasn't made an error and taken the pilot too low over high terrain. This happened to me when I was being "vectored," as the heading procedure is called, by Rome, Italy, control asking me to descend while flying north toward hills I knew were there. I challenged the command and got it changed. There have been similar cases in the United States; on one occasion a private aircraft was vectored smack into a California mountainside.

Similarly, strong arguments have occurred between ATC and pilots about weather. Say you're up there and straight ahead is a thunderstorm. You ask ATC to allow you to make a 30° right turn to avoid the storm. "Unable," ATC replies, and the argument begins. The ground controller has other aircraft in the area, and your turn would conflict with it.

I've had ATC, in such a case, tell me the storm wasn't bad, that "others had gone through it." And I've told it, "Friend, I'm sitting up here staring a big black storm in the eye, and I'm not going to fly through it." Sometimes it almost seems to be blackmail as ATC tells you flights ahead of you have gone through with no trouble; what ATC may not be aware of is that a thunderstorm is never static and can grow to violence in minutes.

Since ATC's radar is specialized to see moving airplanes, with its capability to see weather a second priority, you don't have confidence in ATC saying the storm isn't bad. You know better than it. ATC's objective, as written in the basic charter, is to separate and expeditiously move traffic; it isn't to steer airplanes through weather or have anything to do with the aircraft operation that doesn't directly apply to traffic movement and separation. Naturally, ATC will help when it can, and it has saved lost airplanes and airplanes in trouble, and given certain aid in relating weather, but those tasks are secondary, and should be. If they aren't, then ATC is, literally, flying the airplane. This is an important point that pilots must understand, or judgment and decision from the cockpit deteriorate.

The issues are, of course, a bit more complicated; if a pilot is in trouble, and there is no one to turn to, the pilot can call ATC and ask for help. ATC, itself, may not be able to help, and it may direct the pilot to someone who can help or direct such help to the pilot. But, and this is important, pilots should not lean on ATC, or think of it as a mother to run to anytime they are in trouble. The newspaper-type accusation that "the pilot did not contact the ground by radio," or some such phraseology, shouldn't condemn the pilot; in many cases, it should be understood that the pilot was busy flying the aircraft and didn't have time to make a radio call. Ninety-nine percent of the time, if an airplane is in trouble, a pilot should be grabbing the controls and not a microphone. You cannot fly by mike. Modern instruments and aircraft

operations refer to radio usage so much that neophyte priorities mixed up at times and think using radio comes b~~

A close friend made a date to fly from Rutland, Vermo~~ Vermont, near where I live, for lunch. This pilot had about ~~500 hours flying~~ time and was flying a small four-passenger airplane. It was a beautiful day. About 11:00 A.M. he called and canceled the date. He said he couldn't make it because the radio transmitter in his airplane wasn't working. It's only 41 miles from Rutland to Sugarbush, neither airport has a tower that requires radio, no ATC is needed, and there's a road to follow. I chided him a bit about not coming. "Oh no, I wouldn't take off without a radio," he said.

I thought back to my first seven years of flying, which included flights from coast to coast and from New York to Mexico, to Havana, Cuba, and to a lot of other places, and I didn't even *have* a radio in the airplane. Have we lost the art of teaching self-reliance? And what does this cost us in safety?

By any measure ATC tends to diminish pilot command. Of course, ATC is needed, and pilots must comply with its requirements, but we should also consider how this has affected the basic role of flying the airplane in all its phases. An experienced pilot is able to be cooperative within the system but remain the one handling all aspects of flight, normal or emergency. Have we passed this ability along to others in modern training and concepts? The evidence suggests that we may have, possibly to a serious degree.

Many airline pilots these days are ex-military, accustomed to taking orders. Does this type of pilot subconsciously think of ATC as a command from authority that must be obeyed under all conditions? I don't know, but the thought concerns me.

The heavy traffic that crams airplanes into a close elephantlike, tail-to-trunk flow is almost overpowering. There are airplanes landing ahead and others close behind as you fly down that path to a runway. You have a speed to maintain: go too slow and you'll foul up the line behind; go too fast and you'll catch up to the guy ahead. Now say that the air is electric, that there are thunderstorms in the area, and that one is building along the approach path. Are you thinking primarily of the thunderstorm or of keeping the system moving and landing? And besides, the pilot ahead of you just flew through that shower and landed without trouble. But thunderstorms can develop very fast, so the difference in time between the pilot landing ahead of you and your landing may be enough for the storm to have become more savage. Calling to say you're pulling out will cause all sorts of problems, and Lord knows where ATC will send you. Without doubt, this awareness affects your judgment.

Historically pilots refer to airline flying by talking about "flights." Each trip is a "flight"; it's written that way on schedules. Most pilots say, "The other day I was on a flight from St. Louis to KC," "My flight was delayed," or "The flight had a mechanical." Always the reference is to "flight."

Too often, these days, one hears the word "mission" rather than "flight" used, especially by the younger ex-military pilots. "Mission" connotes a task to finish even with great odds or risk—at least in military thinking. Does some of this creep in and affect an airline pilot's judgment? Does this have anything to do with approaching through a thunderstorm—a desire to complete the mission? I don't know, but I do know that if I were VP, Flight Operations, of an airline, the word "mission" would be made taboo.

ATC gives commands pilots hear every time they fly: "Climb to and maintain two five oh," "Descend immediately to one four thousand," "Turn left to three one zero," and "Maintain one eight zero knots."

There are many such orders—necessary, of course. But deep in a pilot's psyche these orders cause some degree of resentment. And if a pilot is a Milquetoast type, the orders may take precedence—however subconsciously—over judgment

It is important to know that no regular airline pushes its pilots to fly weather; in actual fact, conservatism is encouraged. At times it's the pilot pushing and trying to get in for a number of reasons, such as beating a flight by a competing airline, even though his or her company doesn't even suggest this. In fact one major airline I'm familiar with campaigned using bulletins and discussions at pilot meetings to discourage pilots from such attitudes. But the pressure of the system is strong—that tight-up pressure of airplanes behind and ahead, of things moving fast, and of the paramount problem, the flow of airliners rather than constraints of weather.

And sometimes pilots have a case of "get homeitis." They've been out on a trip for days; they're tired; someone in the family is ill; if they don't get in at the home base airport, they may miss their next trip, which could carry an economic penalty—there are many reasons. It takes cool judgment not to let get homeitis take over.

Another nudge toward the ground assuming control comes from the noise aircraft make that other people don't like. When I learned to fly at a country airport so many years ago, I heard my first noise complaint from the farmer who lived just off our takeoff path: "You make too damn much noise and it scares my chickens."

Yes, noise complaints go way back. During the propeller-piston era there were enough complaints that we tried to do something about them; we tried to avoid certain areas—to not fly over hospitals, for example. We also made power reduction as soon as the landing gear was retracted, but this wasn't a hardship because with piston engines you were already anxious to reduce from the high power of takeoff to a level called METO (Maximum Except Takeoff) because the FAA and the manufacturer would only allow takeoff power to be used for 5 minutes as a structural safety limit. But starting in the 1950s, the request was tied to noise, and for the first time the words "noise abatement" came into use.

With the introduction of the jet the problem zoomed to big proportions; the jets made much more noise. The noise brought on serious complaints, even threats, phone calls, demonstrations, pressure on members of Congress, and any other method that got the attention of government bodies and airlines. And given the jet's thundering, roaring noise on takeoff and its whine on landing, as offensive as a blackboard chalk screech, there was justification for these protests.

Neither industry nor FAA could find a technical solution in design or construction at that time, so everyone turned to focus on another area: the airplane's operation. FAA introduced regulations that required special departure and approach routes, minimum altitudes, preferential runways, and detailed takeoff and landing maneuvers for pilots to follow. Once again, as in so many aviation problems, when the answer could not be found, the problem was dumped on the pilots, demanding they follow new regulations and procedures. Again the "paper" cure became a pilot burden; the powers that be decided that a difficult problem could be solved by adding another page to the manual.

The pilots objected to the prescribed maneuvers, which were designed to turn the airplane away from the noise-sensitive area and to reduce power if over it. The maneuvers presented a head-scratching contradiction; deep in a pilot's psyche, put there in earliest training, is the idea that takeoff is made by applying power, rotating, climbing, and above all, not making turns or doing other maneuvers until all is settled down and safe altitude gained. Noise abatement procedures counter this basic, safe flying practice; now the drill was takeoff and make an immediate turn and reduce power to what became known as "quiet thrust." Pilots referred to the turn as an aerobatic maneuver. Certainly, at best, it was an unnecessary, unwelcome distraction from good flying—and at a critical time of flight.

An American Airlines 707 departed runway 31L at Kennedy on a beautiful, clear, but gusty and turbulent March day in 1962. The procedure on that runway is to make a left turn immediately after takeoff—at at least 300 feet altitude—and shortly after reduce power. This 707 did just that and flipped over to dive into Jamaica Bay, killing all aboard. The official accident report did not tie this to the noise abatement procedure (the accident was due to a rudder control malfunction, the report said), but line pilots felt that if the pilot hadn't been in the unusual attitude due to the noise abatement procedure he'd have been better able to cope with the rudder control problem. We'll never know, of course, but certainly the maneuver required was not normal or prudent flying but shamefully was—and still is—approved by FAA.

Noise monitors were put off the ends of runways in the late 1950s. They were located anywhere from one-half to 2 miles or more from the runway. They monitored and recorded noise levels. I shouldn't put this in the past tense, however, because they are still used today. If the aircraft passing the monitor produces noise levels above the prescribed level for that monitor location, a report is filed, and the pilot finds a note in his or her mailbox a few days later requesting an explanation.

In my years of flying the line, I had more than one such note in my box, and my response was always the same: a note to the chief pilot saying that I had followed all procedures necessary to the safety of the flight. That always seemed to put an end to it. But if an airline produces too many excessive readings over the monitors, the airport authority may put restrictions on that airline. This is especially true in London, and we had to work very hard to keep noise levels down in taking off from there; if we hadn't, TWA would have not been allowed to take off after a certain hour at night—11:00 P.M., as I recall. As we had a flight to Frankfurt, Germany, about that time, keeping quiet was important to our economics. Pilots developed tricks to help keep the noise recording down, and one such was to push the nose down, from climb attitude, to a near-level attitude when passing the monitor so the tail pipe (exhaust pipe) wasn't aiming down toward the ground where the monitor was; in level flight, the noise blasted toward the horizon, so there was less noise on the ground. It was a safe maneuver and not drastic, just a little push on the wheel worked out by the pilots on their own to cheat the monitor.

The turns required took on an almost desperate, must do atmosphere. One night I was being given a line check on a JFK to Paris flight in a 747. We were taking off on runway 4L at JFK, which required a right turn at 400 feet altitude. This night was a nasty one with rain, low ceiling, and gusty, turbulent winds. I lifted off and quickly went in the clouds; my concentration was primarily on properly flying the aircraft under these conditions. Suddenly I heard the loud voice of the check pilot—our chief pilot: "Turn! Turn!"

His mind was on that noise monitor below. I flew straight ahead until a few hundred feet more altitude was gained and then turned. He lit into me, saying, "Goddamit, you'll get a high reading, you should have turned at 400 feet."

"I should fly the airplane the way I think is safe and not to satisfy some goddamn noise shack."

We started an argument that seemed to go on halfway to Paris. But such was, and is, the airline's emphasis, with little consideration for wind and weather.

The system of preferential runway use to satisfy noise problems also compromises safety. Certain runways send the takeoff and landing flight paths over the least noise-sensitive areas, so they are used whenever possible—naturally only when it's proper and safe, especially with regard to wind. But the definition of proper and safe is constantly stretched, and there are times when the preferential runway is still being used after the wind has changed or weather conditions under good flying practice would require the use of a different runway.

One night coming from Milan, Italy, to JFK, I arrived over JFK to find poor weather and a delay because airplanes were missing their approaches to runway 4R. It was obvious that the preferential runway was being used even though a tail wind was causing excessive descent rates, resulting in the missed approaches. I called approach control and said I wanted to use runway 22L, which I knew would have a head wind, normal descent rates, and a better chance for a successful approach. But 4R was preferred because its approach path comes in over water, not people.

ATC was taken back by my request; the controller told me that I would have a long delay while ATC worked me in between flights landing the other way—probably 45 minutes or more. It was a form of blackmail to get me to stay with his runway. As it happened, I was on a cargo flight, so there were no passengers to inconvenience, and I had plenty of fuel.

"Roger," I replied, "I'll hold for runway two two left."

Actually I only held for 15 minutes and made a normal approach under a rainy ceiling without trouble. My descent rate down the ILS was slower than normal, indicating the people approaching from the other direction must have had a difficult time scrambling to keep on the glide path, fighting excessive descent rates.

Even today—March 1993—pilots carry in their brain bag a page on La Guardia (and such pages exist for other airports, also) that says, in big letters at the top, "NOISE," and right beneath:

CAUTION
CLOSE ADHERENCE TO
STANDARD NOISE
ABATEMENT PROCEDURES
IS IMPERATIVE

The sheet then tells where the noise monitors are located and that they can be avoided by a heading change. The big stick statement is "following noise abatement procedures will prevent additional noise violations and fines."

There are also noise curfews, which require that operation be stopped after a certain hour. The concept sounds innocuous, but it has subtle effects on safety. One summer I flew a flight pattern from New York to Paris and after a brief stop continued to Rome. The flight was scheduled to land in Paris at 10:00 P.M. and be out by 11:00 P.M., after which a curfew stopped Orly Field operation for the night. So my eye was on the clock between New York and Paris to get in there and get out before the curfew. A foggy night in New York and long delays waiting to take off could make the Paris ETA an anxious number, and while we didn't do unsafe things to make it, we did pour on the coal and cut any possible corners. Although the curfew wasn't directly a safety matter, it piled on another factor to all the others we pilots already had to think about.

The original jets were noisy and gushed out black smoke—they were, as we called them, straight-pipe jets. In the early 1960s, the high bypass engine, in which a fan spinning around sends part of the airstream back through ducts in the cowling and out without going through the engine and burning, was introduced. This fan moves air much as a propeller does. The multi-blade fan is contained inside the cowling and doesn't stick out like a propeller. The "turbofan," as the fan jets are generally called, produces a quieter engine and a more efficient one especially at lower altitudes. So two gains: less noise for the public and less fuel consumption at lower altitudes for the pilot, which meant the need to battle for higher altitudes was lessened. All airline jet engines now have turbofans. The downside is the noise turbofans produce in the landing phase, when the whirling fan blades create a sirenlike noise, very annoying to anyone under it, as the airplane slides down the landing path. But all in all, turbofans are a big improvement in the noise department. Noise abatement procedures, however, are still in effect.

Adding to the pilot's exasperation in the noise abatement department is the construction of buildings on takeoff or approach paths of airports. Then, after construction, the people in the new structures—built after the airport was—raise particular hell about airplane noise, adding bitterness to the pilots' annoyance with the "dangerous" noise abatement procedures they must follow. Cities and their planning commissions seem impotent in their ability to restrict such construction. I landed time after time on runway 22R at JFK and watched a school being built just off the approach end. After the school was completed and occupied, complaints started as parents screamed of the potential danger jets created for their children. Why didn't someone take this into consideration before the school was built? Similarly, at JFK, takeoff on runway 31L requires a quick left turn because of a housing development built directly in line with the runway—and I watched the houses go up, noting the construction progress on each takeoff. Recently a parking garage was constructed off the end of San Diego, California, airport—runway 27—that is so close to the glide slope pilots are warned of it and the glide path guide lights are set for an approach path steeper than normal. And pilots of all airline aircraft are warned of the close proximity of this building and the dangers of getting the least bit low on approach for fear of hitting it.

ATC and noise abatement are both areas where the ground, to some degree, moves into the cockpit. Most distressing to pilots is the fact that the authoritative people on the ground are not always flying people. True, some are "pilots," but what kind of pilots? Private, commercial, airline, military? The task of each is different; as an airline pilot I wouldn't presume to tell military pilots how to do their jobs or what their airplanes should be like. Why should they tell me how to fly?

A ground person, even though he or she can fly, isn't qualified to call the regulatory or communication shots on an airline pilot unless that person knows what flying the line is really like through the year and its seasons. A ground person should know the pressures of responsibility, what it feels like to be dog tired and make an approach through low ceilings and rain at 4:00 A.M., to worry about an aircraft problem, weather, fuel reserves, alternate airports, and in the days after deregulation, whether or not the company might be broke tomorrow. When you're an airline pilot, you're in a goldfish bowl with everything you say and do recorded, with each airplane maneuver etched in the black box. Close tolerances are required, the haunting possibility of an unrealized error by you in the ATC system becoming a violation filed against you by FAA. And always there's the long list of persnickety FAA regulations—many written because there's no other solution than to dump them on the pilot (that "added page in the manual" again).

There are many "experts" who really feel they know better than the pilot. In each cockpit, behind the captain, is an extra seat—the "jump seat" in the industry's parlance—where special people are allowed to ride. These special people are FAA inspectors, psychologists making studies, engineers, human factors experts, NASA research people, and occasionally the press—a plethora of types. They watch each move of the crew, make little marks on their pads and notes in their notebooks, and feel certain they know what goes on and can report, enforce, build, and legislate as a result. The facts are, of course, that while these specialists observe what's in view they don't know that multitude of thoughts racing through the pilot's mind, and unless they do, their conclusions and results are flawed.

I don't mean to say only airline pilots can create the rules or design the airplanes and the system. There are people out there who have wide experience: some manufacturers' test pilots, retired airline pilots with FAA, research people who listen to pilots, and others. But too often the final stamp of action—what's regulated, devised, put into effect—is done despite their views. Test pilots aren't always listened to in high places nor are FAA lower-echelon types. Critical issues frequently get action by the "higher ups" and "experts" who jam something through to cover the problem, unrealistic though it may be.

A dangerous fissure exists between the hard, real world of flying and the one perceived by regulators and industry leaders, a world developed from incomplete knowledge and lack of real world awareness. This fissure, either unrecognized or ignored, increases the possibility of pilot error as economic pressures, under the guise of "progress," erode pilot command and judgment.

AIR TRAFFIC CONTROL: THE BIG SQUEEZE

We have referred frequently to air traffic control because it's a star player in the potential for accidents.

The simple fact is that there are more airplanes using the airports of major cities than there is room for. The basic problem is a dearth of airports. The popular wisdom is that additional controllers and new computer systems are needed. And they are: they will help smooth out the operation, make it somewhat safer, and perhaps move more airplanes. But more controllers and computer systems are not enough to cure the problem unless the real need, the one that *must* be satisfied, is met: more airport capacity and runways. And no matter how you attack the situation, that's the major constraint.

New airports don't spring up overnight. First of all, they are about as popular as nuclear waste dumps; people don't want the noise, hazard, congestion, and smell. Furthermore, since a new airport is largely paid for by the city it serves, a bond issue is usually involved, and bond issues are generally unpopular. But let's say all those problems are satisfied—generally by moving the airport a long way out of town, as is the case for Dulles in Washington, D.C., and Mirabel for Montreal, Canada. It still takes years before an airport is completed and in service. Ten years is a good average figure. The only new airport presently scheduled in the United States is in Denver, Colorado. It was first discussed in the 1980s, was scheduled to open in March 1994 and be completed in 1995 at a cost of $2.3 billion. The federal government will kick in about $501 million toward that. Munich, Germany, opened one in late 1992, and it took over 20 years to build.

Airport inadequacy is evidenced by the constant effort to improve what we've already got. Pilots comment that they virtually never fly in and out of a completed airport; there's always construction of some sort going on. In my 37 years of airline flying, this has certainly been the case.

In 1989 U.S. airlines carried 430 million passengers; by the year 2000 the total is expected to be 1 billion, which will more than double the number of flights flown in 1980. To build enough airports to handle the traffic will be impossible, so delays and crowded skies will not go away.

In its annual report for 1993 the International Air Transport Association (IATA) stated that airways and airport congestion is "the greatest long-term threat to industry viability." The report went on to say that a lack of adequate air traffic control and airport infrastructure may "limit the size and scope of the future" (*Aviation Week and Space Technology,* November 1, 1993).

This situation is worse in Europe, and serious studies call for a total reorganization of Europe's air traffic system. There are 42 air traffic control centers in Europe, more than twice as many as in the continental United States, which covers an area twice the size of Europe. They need a central authority to integrate it all, which means a lot of countries getting together and agreeing on a system and organization. Things like that aren't done overnight; just look how long it's taken to get the EEC organized. Europe's airport situation is as bad or worse than ours, so don't be impatient during delays when arriving in London, Rome, Paris, and other popular European spots.

Weather can still shut down flying; there's no such thing as all-weather flying. Airport inadequacy makes this problem worse because if weather shuts down one airport all those airplanes headed toward it have to go elsewhere, and most head for the same alternate, which creates a big mess there. JFK fogged in one evening in 1973 as I was approaching from Paris. I did a quick turn and got to Boston before most of the mob, but even so, we sat on a taxiway, with no gates available, for 1 hour and 30 minutes. Over 40 unwanted and unscheduled airplanes piled into Boston, most of them 747s. During two days in June 1990 there were 4000 delays nationwide, with 37 percent of them occurring in the New York area because of thunderstorms.

Adding runways allowing two aircraft to approach and land at the same time on existing airports—a system called "simultaneous approaches"—will help. Originally the runways had to be a mile apart, in case one of the airplanes wandered from course, to satisfy safety; now the distance has been reduced to half that. As traffic flow increases, more demands are placed on the human to maintain safety—the controller, who has to watch the radarscope and be ready to act if an airplane veers off course, and the pilot, who carries the extra mental load of knowing there's another airplane in the clouds right or left, leaving no room for error.

When runways are only 2500 feet apart, the airplanes are not sliding

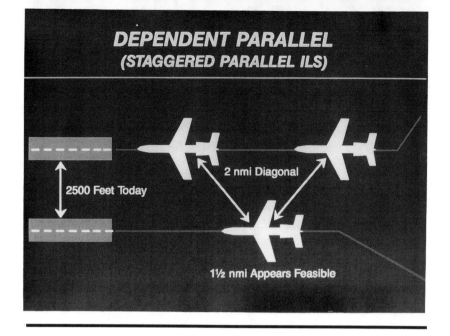

Inside the figure:

DEPENDENT PARALLEL
(STAGGERED PARALLEL ILS)

2 nmi Diagonal

2500 Feet Today

1½ nmi Appears Feasible

A DIAGRAM showing parallel runway operation and separation distances. (*Courtesy of the FAA*)

down the ILS side by side; rather, they are cleared alternately to the runways, like alternate feed from a four-lane to a two-lane highway. The alternate feed is done by a controller using the old eyeball method of watching a radarscope. Although they are under development, computers, as yet, aren't smart enough to handle this one; it's an art with heavy controller responsibility and pilot awareness. It's important to remember, also, that unlike cars in alternate feed off a highway airplanes cannot put on brakes and wait—everything is moving fast and without any ability to stop while the sticky situation is sorted out. But even with the alternate feed the airplanes are only 1.5 nautical miles apart.

Other tricks are used to get more use from existing runways: when winds are light enough, pilots may be told to take off on a runway that crosses another on which airplanes may be landing. Typically, a pilot is cleared to land but commanded to stop short of the crossing runway because an airplane may be taking off across the landing aircraft's nose. Under some conditions takeoffs are made partway down a runway, which reduces the safety factor that comes of using a full runway. Even ground vehicles like trucks may be using the other part of the runway, which cuts down or removes extra runway normally available for emergency stopping or as a buffer in case of brake or reverser problems. Using only part of the runway for takeoff or landing was allowed only when the runways were dry (for good braking), but FAA now allows this with wet runways provided braking is reported as good—and we know the uncertainty of that. Airplanes on approach to a runway have been separated by 3 miles, but the zeal for cramming more airplanes on a runway in the shortest time has reduced this to 2.5 miles. One can almost feel the pressure to move it all faster, to close the gaps between airplanes, to make more use of the runway. How much do these pressures reduce safety? How little room remains to cover human error? As a wise man said, "Things break, and people make mistakes." Have we provided a sufficient buffer to allow for this truism?

A recent proposal to squeeze in more airplanes came from the prestigious *ICAO* (International Civil Aviation Organization) *Bulletin,* September 1989 (ICAO is the aviation part of the UN). The article describes methods for staggering approaches to runways that slant inward to finally meet or cross. The article's title: "New Display Aid for Controllers Could Improve Airport Traffic Capacity." It also refers to necessary procedures and safety rules to be adopted—rules added for protection against new hazards created by the procedures.

The improvement is described for Logan Airport, Boston, Massachusetts. It states that on a clear day staggered arrivals are made with visual protection to runways 22L and 27—runways that converge at an angle of 50°. Such a procedure, under instrument conditions, could increase the Boston traffic flow from 34 aircraft per hour to 48—an advance for airport capacity. Price? A degradation in safety because pilots cannot see the other aircraft in bad weather. Then it's up to a controller staring at a radarscope.

All through the Federal Aviation Regulations (FARs) the pilot is left with the final say to accept or refuse such abnormal capers. This out gives the FAA the ability to sit in its ivory tower and say, "The pilot used poor judgment; he should have refused the intersection operation under the prevailing conditions." The FAA's rules do not consider the pressure the pilot is under to avoid disrupting the system flow. Imagine that you are a captain approaching to land at a busy airport with airplanes close ahead and behind. The emphasis is to keep 'em moving; the airplane that just landed is being urged to get off the runway so you can land, and then the pressure will be on you to land and clear the runway as soon as possible.

Your landing clearance includes "hold short of runway three one," which means stop before you get to where runway 31 crosses. You don't like it; while the operation is possible, you'd feel more comfortable not worrying about the adroit technique needed to land short and stop. But with the pressures, the tension, the babble, and not knowing if you'll simply be cleared to use the full runway, are you going to be a maverick and refuse, with Lord-knows-what implications, or do you go along with the system? These are the pressures on the follow orders type pilot; but this kind of clearance also works on the bravado-style pilot, inviting decision partially based on emotion: "Yeah, man, I can make it anytime." So macho or

Milquetoast, you continue landing—but with an added mental pressure.

When pilots learn to fly, the sanctity of the runway is drummed into them. "Use all of it!" is an early admonition; "When you land or take off, it's your runway!" You get possessive about a runway, but the authorities—FAA, airports, companies—chip away at your sense of having a free, protected zone in which to work, a zone where you can concentrate on properly maneuvering the airplane to touch on an exact spot or take off knowing there are only the normal, listed obstructions ahead and that all the pavement is yours to use if need be. But with the pressure to use only part of a runway comes a separate issue to think about, something that requires sharing the technique of good control manipulation with factors not related; in effect, the mind is required to focus on two alien actions in the "risk-laden" attempt to move more traffic into airports originally designed for less traffic. Do such things add or detract from the chance for human error? You decide.

The repeated reference in the FARs to the pilot's authority to refuse or take alternate action may require the pilot's declaring an emergency—that he or she is low on fuel in a terminal area and is asking for landing priority, for example.

The precise system of phraseology is frequently violated. Avianca, for instance, on January 25, 1990, approaching JFK in bad weather and low on fuel, asked for "fuel priority." The South American pilot had been told that that's the way to do it when you're low on fuel and need fast clearance to land. But the ATC rule book's fine print says fuel priority means the airplane is low on fuel and *may* need special handling on arrival. It isn't automatically given, however. For that, read further from the FARs: "If the remaining usable fuel supply suggests the need for traffic priority to ensure a safe landing you should declare an emergency."

The Avianca pilot didn't understand this nit-picking verbiage and so didn't declare an emergency. The final cause of this accident hasn't been sorted out, but the airplane crashed, and people were killed, and no matter how the report comes out, semantics played a part.

Pilots don't like to declare emergencies because most times it's necessary to answer for them. Now, this shouldn't be worrisome, but it is because FAA not only scrutinizes the emergency and reason for it but seems to inspect all aspects of the flight for possible rule infractions—on which the FAA is quick to pursue action. And any pilot will tell you that because of the mass of rules and their complex and obtuse format, probably *no* flight is flown without breaking *some* regulation.

Pilot reticence in reporting safety incidents goes way back. I remember a particular situation that made all pilots of the era clam up completely about anything to anyone. An Eastern DC-3 was approaching Washington, D.C., shortly after WW II when suddenly a military B-25 flew across its path, almost hitting the DC-3. The DC-3 pilot reported the near collision. Investigation found that the B-25 carried a pilot practicing instrument flying under the hood with a "safety" pilot along, and they were doing this smack through Washington's National Airport's traffic pattern—clearly a dumb act because, realistically, the pilot practicing under a hood obstructs part of the safety pilot's vision. It's hard to believe the outcome: the innocent Eastern pilot who was nearly rammed by an invading airplane was cited for violating the air regulations that say you are not to fly closer than 500 feet to another aircraft! I never knew what happened to the military pilots, but airline pilots were up in arms at the bureaucratic, legalistic approach to the problem. The word went out: "Never tell the Civil Aeronautics Authority (as FAA was then called) a damned thing!"

So exchange of information about potential accident problems ceased. Through the years, FAA attempted to assure pilots of its friendly attitude and willingness to be considerate about reported hazards, even to the extent of promising nonpunitive action for reported near collisions. But most pilots never believed FAA's attempts to be known as the Friendly Aviation Administration, and most still don't.

Thinking FAA and industry people felt a valuable source of information to help reduce accidents was being wasted. They turned to a neutral body, one that was nonregulatory in nature for help; the choice was the National Aeronautics and Space Administration (NASA). The program was set up so pilots, controllers, cabin attendants, or any crew or ATC member—even mechanics—could report hazardous incidents of all operational types and be assured they'd not be identified or subject to disciplinary action. The program, called NASA's Aviation Safety Reporting System (ASRS), was set up in 1976, and within a short time 100 to 150 reports were coming in each week.

The immunity became an important part of the program. Names of people reporting were so well guarded that NASA's department for this had a locked door feeling reminiscent of the CIA. A person reporting fills out a form that includes his or her address and phone number, but this portion of the report is returned to the sender and the phone number only used if the investigator reading the report would like more information. All on a friendly, nonpunitive basis. The system took hold, pilots and others developed confidence in its promise, and by October 1987 NASA had received 79,826 incidents with a potential for becoming accidents! During the month of January 1991, 2541 reports were received: 1855 from airline pilots,

611 from general aviation pilots, 71 from controllers, and 4 from mechanics, cabin attendants, and the military.

The system protects a pilot from being cited for a violation if a report is made within 10 days of the occurrence, and this is a big reason for its success. Of course, there is a method to prevent people reporting from taking advantage of the system if their act was deliberate or criminal, but such incidents have been few, and the overall success of the program has not been affected.

The NASA Aviation Safety Reporting System is one of the best things to enhance safety that has ever been invented. It does many good things, and one of them is to revive "hangar flying"; a term synonymous with "bull session." In the old days, pilots sat around and swapped tales and experiences, openly and honestly. On a warm summer afternoon, as a brand-new 16-year-old pilot, I often sat on the grass under an old cherry tree that gave shade from the bright sun, chewing a blade of grass and listening carefully to older pilots as they swapped yarns. I picked up and tucked away all kinds of bits and pieces of information. One day, for instance, Warren Noble, one of our instructors, told about getting in a tailspin that he had trouble getting out of and the trick he used to do it. The airplane whipped at one point in each turn, and Warren said he tried goosing the engine at the whip, and sure enough he got control and recovered. I didn't realize I'd be in the same scary situation a week later flying a Kinner Fleet, which had significant notoriety for its unfortunate spin characteristics. I did two turns in this open biplane and then went through the motions for recovery, without luck. The airplane kept right on going around but did start that whipping motion. I tried Warren's trick and got out (albeit not until I'd spun from 4000 feet down to 900!). And if I hadn't heard Warren tell his experience, I probably wouldn't have lived to tell the tale.

Hangar flying experience covered a wide range, and stories were told in an unassuming way, often as admission of doing something dumb or being lucky. The frank tone in the telling influenced character building—character that made safety the paramount issue and not ego. There were basic truths that are good pilot's gospel: avoid the terrain, don't stunt down low, have an out—*always* have an out, make sure the airplane is working right and has fuel, look in all directions, think and check before any move, respect weather, and many more. These things crawled into your psyche to stay there forever, needing only the slightest updating if you had advanced to flying a 747 New York to Paris.

With the hubbub of modern times, busy commercial flying, iron fences around airports, and people who want to do their flying and get on with their lives, these hangar sessions have faded. Oh, hangar flying can still be found in sleepy airports of rural America and among pilots getting together at air shows, although air show talk is usually more of exploits and gee whiz stuff. All in all, however, hangar flying, experiences told and good confession, has all but disappeared from flying and the benefits almost extinguished. Fortunately, the Aviation Safety Reporting System has become a modern replacement for hangar flying, especially the confessional aspect.

Early in the program, it was determined that if benefit was to be received from the reported incidents, a method of broadcast was needed. Retired airline pilots, who called themselves the Old Eagles, came on board. Rex Hardy was chief Eagle. A monthly safety bulletin entitled *Callback* was created. Hardy and other Eagles created the ideal relaxed format that allowed people to protect their identities while telling in detail the incidents right up front for all to read. This blue sheet can be had by anyone through the Office of the NASA Aviation Reporting System, Box 189, Moffet Field, CA 94035. Its subscribers now number close to 70,000, and it's free.

Among *Callback*'s diverse beneficial aspects are three referred to as "Immunity," "Philanthropy," and "therapy." Pilots are assured immunity, so they're willing to report; there's philanthropy in the willingness to share experiences for others' benefit; and the exercise is therapeutic in the old sense of confession being good for the soul.

NASA also distributes immediate danger points to the proper industry people via alert bulletins. These problems are of an immediate, band-aid nature. Following, for example, is a laundry list for one month:

- Reliability problems with an East Coast VOR.
- Altimeter missetting in low-pressure conditions.
- A faulty motor pump assembly in a light plane.
- Visual approach procedures at a West Coast airport.
- Inexperienced cabin crew members scheduled on the same flight.

The alert bulletins have resulted in resurfacing a runway that was worn and slick and revisions of charts, runway markings, and navigation aid abnormalities. The bulletins have brought attention to call signs that could be ambiguous and called attention to poor automatic terminal information service (ATIS), a canned airport information broadcast.

This is all good stuff, worth the effort, and undoubtedly has done good, but ASRS hasn't been enough to awaken the industry to the large, basic changes that are needed. And the reports have shown over and over again that certain basic problems are still up there, uncorrected except for picky but ineffective regulations.

There are many types of reported incidents: pilots being at the wrong altitude, pilots making incursions into runways, pilots missing radio calls because a poorly designed volume control is swept off by a sleeve passing it, pilots not having airspeed indicators because of a poor preflight check, pilots almost landing with the gear retracted but who are saved by the tower, pilots missing checklist items, and many others. But the most glaring thing ASRS records show is the constant potential danger of the radio communications system. This is spotlighted by the fact that 70 percent of the reports received are about communications between controllers and pilots that result in situations with potential for disaster.

The entire safety of the air traffic control system hangs on communications—one person speaking to another by radio—where a penchant for error is notorious. In flight instructions and clearances there is no room for error. The controller tells the pilot what altitude to maintain, what airspeed, what places the pilot's cleared to, what heading to point the airplane, what altitude to descend or climb to. The controller's job is to keep departing, arriving, and cruising airplanes from colliding. But a typical error occurs when airplane B is cleared to 11,000 feet and airplane A to 10,000, and B misinterprets and thinks its clearance was to 10,000 feet and goes there, but A is already there. So there's a chance for collision, and only luck and a big sky prevents it. Insiders shake their heads and mutter, "Some day there's going to be a lu lu." A missed altitude is just one aspect of miscommunication. Other typical errors include place cleared misunderstood as another place or a pilot following instructions actually meant for another.

A controller gives instructions to a pilot, and the pilot then repeats the instructions verbatim so the controller can double-check that the instructions were received accurately. But the controller is often so busy that he or she has gone on to talk to another airplane and never hears the read-back, which may have been wrong. To take another typical situation, the full call sign of a flight is to be used, always—"TWA eight oh two," for example—but in haste, TWA or the controller cuts corners and replies, "Roger eight oh two," leaving out the "TWA." There may be another airline's flight eight oh two up there, and confusion results. I remember a summer of flying into Paris on flight 870 when Air Canada also had a flight 870 arriving from Montreal at the same time. We had to be very careful, and Paris at 7:00 A.M. is never as busy as Chicago at 5:00 P.M.

People under pressure frequently start talking before pushing the mike button or release it before their message is finished. Pilots are distracted by other problems—after all, the airplane has to be flown and navigated, and engines and systems have to be monitored—and sometimes these distractions result in the controller or pilot only half-hearing what was said. A common conversation between captain and first officer: "Did he clear us to one one thousand?" "Yes, I'm pretty sure he did." Yes, the pilot could make a call back to double-check, but the controller is busy now, working five airplanes further along, or even may have told the pilot to change frequency to another controller. This isn't atypical; there are lots of frequency changes. The actual count on a typical flight, Los Angeles to Salt Lake, 1 hour and 18 minutes total time, was 15 frequency changes and 55 communications, 20 within the first 25 minutes after takeoff from Los Angeles. So after a fruitless attempt to confirm, the crew gives up in favor of agreement that the clearance was to one one thousand (11,000).

A controller says reduce to 250. The controller should add knots to the request to signify it's a speed command but, in the desperate hurry up atmosphere, leaves it off. The pilot thinks the clearance was to flight-level 250—altitude 25,000 feet—and descends or climbs to it, and maybe there's another airplane there.

The proper radio phraseology and techniques, spelled out in 11 pages of air traffic control rules, are there to make certain communication is properly understood. But the pressure of an inadequate system trying to absorb ever-more airplanes during busy times at busy airports forces people into rushing, pushing, taking shortcuts.

Airplanes on the ground are affected by the same communication problems; couple this with airports notorious for their confusing taxiways, poor markings, and inadequate signals, and you have big problems. A madhouse at work is any large airport at its peak hour, when literally dozens of airplanes are all trying to get clearance from the tower for taxi and take-off. You sit in the airplane, finger on the button, waiting for the airplane currently talking to end the talk; it does, so you immediately push the button and blurt, "Kennedy ground (ground control) from TWA 800." You release the mike button, and instead of hearing Kennedy answer you, you hear the tail end of another call being made at the same time, which tells you that your call was done along with others, resulting in gibberish for the tower.

The tower: "One at a time, I can only handle one at a time."

The clearance finally comes in fire hose fashion: "TWA 800 cleared to runway three one left, proceed delta to the outer, foxtrot and zulu—hold short of three one left."

You'd better know your airport; some are so confusing that you don't learn all those taxiways by heart but have a map in your lap to help direct you through the maze. Now imagine doing this maneuvering at night, in snow or fog or poor visibility, in a kaleidoscope of lights, with ground vehicles zooming out from under you near the terminal, on poorly marked taxiways with crazy angle turns you can easily miss in reduced visibility. Think of all that, and you'll know why we've had airplanes run into each other, with one just plain being in the wrong place. I've seen runway 22R at

JFK with a 30-minute delay because a foreign airline pilot missed a taxiway and turned into the active runway instead. Luckily, no one was taking off, but it took ages to redirect him back into the line taxiing to the runway.

The United States has been painfully slow in getting good taxi and runway markings. Europe has been way ahead; clear back to Connie days, London had a light system that put a line of green lights along your path to the runway. You simply put the nosewheel on the green lights and follow them. London has a red and green stoplight system that will prevent you from getting on an active runway—unless you have your eyes closed. The United States, today, is experimenting with such systems but is slow, slow, slow to act. There were 252 runway incursions for the 12-month period ending July 1990; that's 37 percent more than the previous period, by FAA's data. What's an incursion? An airplane getting on a runway it shouldn't be on, one another airplane might be landing on or roaring down to takeoff.

To be spoken of later, but highlighted here, is the fact pilots are required to complete a taxi checklist to prepare the airplane for takeoff—while they are taxiing through the maze and reading and responding to other crew members to be certain things like takeoff flaps are down and while their ears are cluttered by voice-overs between other aircraft and tower and maybe something else that's directed at them. Talk about juggling.

ASRS receives more than 1,000 communication error reports monthly! Why? In the most simple sense, it's a breakdown in discipline and procedure. Why is that? Simple again: because the system is being asked to do too much, and the pressure on all parties makes for fast talk, poor listening, shortcuts, and misinterpretation.

Sounds pretty desperate—and it is. The cure? Maybe a data link printout with hard copy sent to the cockpit. This promises to be good stuff, and to a limited degree it is coming into use, but if not done properly, it will multiply distractions and add work. Will the copilot have the taxi checklist in one hand and an airways clearance hard copy in the other? What errors may data link have? Each advance always seems to bring new problems that have to be worked out. And how long before all airplanes have it? A long time, from the point of urgency; small airplanes may never have it. In the meantime what? Someone has to recognize that the system is saturated and *do* something about that. ASRS isn't in a position to do the curing, but it shouts out the problem, which is a good reason for ASRS's existence.

Of course, the sky isn't always that crazy, but any major terminal has its busy hours each day. The en route airways get that way as they feed in and out of the Chicago area, New York, Los Angeles, Dallas, Miami, and other hubs.

There's a national airspace plan—FAA designed—to improve all this: to provide better equipment, computers and programs, more controllers. The plan was created a decade ago; at the moment, in spring 1993, it's already seven years behind schedule, and one portion, the advanced automation system (AAS), will not be completed before April 1995 at a cost overrun of about $3 billion.

A partial safeguard is coming into being via a gadget whose installation is mandated in all airline airplanes by the end of 1993. It's called traffic alert and collision avoidance system, or TCAS, and it is an instrument added to the panel that sends out one of two messages to the crew. First there's traffic advisory, which sounds a loud "traffic, traffic" alarm to tell the crew there's another aircraft whose proximity, closing rate, and altitude threatens a collision if both airplanes keep going as they are. The second message is a resolution advisory (RA), which instructs the crew to climb, descend—and at what rate—or stay put. All this comes with lighted symbols and arrows, on the instrument, showing which way to go.

The TCAS is a gain, although some experts say there are flaws in the system. One is the fact TCAS works by talking to another airplane's radar code transponder. Not all airplanes have this, so TCAS misses those without it. Of course, in a heavy airline environment, there will be few airplanes without transponders—and none by law in terminal areas. On the other hand only the fanciest corporate aircraft will have TCAS equipment because it costs about $100,000 per airplane. There's also some concern that TCAS will tell an aircraft to climb or descend without prior knowledge of ATC, which, if carried too far, might interfere with ATC's traffic separation function. TCAS isn't supposed to command a big enough change to cause interference with ATC. Time will tell. To date there have been two incidents with TCAS-equipped aircraft that were close enough to cause serious concern and investigation. I've never flown with TCAS, but my son, an airline captain, has, and his reports so far are good, and he's enthusiastic.

One proposal that underlines the desire to jam more airplanes on a runway is the suggestion I heard during a recent symposium that TCAS could be used for traffic separation on approach to landing: a pilot would be able to squeeze up closer to the plane ahead using TCAS for maintaining a couple of miles separation. Always the effort to put more pounds in the one-pound bag. Safe, they think, because TCAS will provide the buffer. But what about demands on the pilots—an added instrument, an added technique, an added worry at a crucial time—just to increase traffic flow? How much can we add to the pilot's task and still expect that human will never err? One pilot I talked to about this was enthusiastic: "Then, at least, I'll know how close I am to the guy ahead." But the pressure is always there. I quote from a note on an actual airline clearance to a pilot flying a Boeing 767 into Atlanta, Georgia: "LDG 26R CLEAR RWY ASAP DUE TO CLOSE INTRAIL LDG TRAFFIC." Which means get off the runway as soon as possible because there's another airplane coming right on your tail. This isn't an exception; it's the rule!

But even supposing that much is accomplished with computers and systems in the early 2000s, there still will be the problem of airports and runways to land on. Curing those problems will take dramatic action and leadership, two commodities which so far haven't shown their face, especially since the problems involve money and the Congress.

In the busiest times, ATC can occupy a pilot's mind to the extent that priorities are subliminally shuffled. ATC can slide into first place, where pilot judgment is influenced more by it than by weather and safety. Make no mistake: this is seriously suspect, with great potential for danger.

13 | THE FAA: A PARADOX

With the arrival of the jet age, our attitudes and operational methods gradually changed and the barnstorming ways fell away, although early 707 days had a delightful mix of both as the regulations hadn't yet caught up with the airplane. That era was, for me, the most enjoyable of my career, especially as I was flying international routes. The regulations said that when making an instrument approach we could not descend below the minimums, "as reported by a U.S. weather office," but of course, there were no U.S. weather offices overseas—they were operated by the country we were landing in—so we could go to whatever minimums we wanted. We made our own appraisals of weather conditions and decided whether or not it was safe. We didn't have any accidents, either. This was in the late 1950s.

It was a learning time, really an exploratory time, when we'd experiment with different techniques for flying the airplanes in all their regimes, especially descents, which, in jets, presented interesting problems: If you're at 39,000 feet and going to land at an airport ahead, just when do you start the descent? What speed is best to maintain? What were the tricks of slowing a jet from 450 knots to 200, and how long did it take? In flying Connies, proper descent was second nature, but in the swift, high-flying jet, it was all new and as we learned later, a proper descent with well-managed speed could save fuel and money. This was easy to experiment with because there were few jets, traffic wasn't a problem, and much of the time ATC would promptly allow you the altitude desired; you could start descent when you wanted and cut corners on the complicated routings.

We were serious about proper procedures and held to them when developed and set down. First officer duties included careful call outs of *V* airspeeds on takeoff: "vee one, vee r" and all such critical numbers. Procedures soon required call outs of sink rates near the ground, height above minimum altitude on instrument approaches, distance off the localizer or glide slope, and airspeed that slowed toward the danger point.

As procedures and methods developed, FAA jumped right in to make them law, so ignoring procedures would put you at risk of being cited for possible violation. FAA, a federal government body that's under the Department of Transportation, has lawmaking and enforcement as part of its charter and stands ready to make a rule for any abnormality that occurs. The 3-inch-thick operations manual that describes the airplane's specifications, systems descriptions, and operational procedures is approved by FAA, and therefore all limitations in it are, effectively, law and must be adhered to. It's as though all that stuff in your automobile owner's guide was law, and a cop could fine you for not precisely performing according to what's in there.

Further, the law requires adherence to all of ATC's commands and clearances, so if you don't comply—and perfectly—FAA's gotcha. There's an alert gadget in ATC's system that rings a bell and notes any airplane altitude deviations of more than 300 feet, and then the pilot has to answer for it. This also applies to the ATC controllers; if the deviation was their mistake, they have to answer for it. Of course you cannot fault these procedures because leveling off or maintaining the proper altitude is serious stuff, and people should realize its importance. All we're pointing out is that the regulations, created by the bushel to accommodate the complex system, are an added mental load on pilots and controllers.

There are regulated routes governing the arrival at and departure from every airport in the country with an instrument approach, and the routes and rules differ from place to place. Pilots carry books with approach plates for specific airports. These started as simple maps printed on 8½ by 11 paper, identifying the radio beam orientation and spelling out procedures for letting down through the murk, the minimums to go to, and how to pull out if the ground fails to come into view. Also noted were the altitudes of any serious obstructions close by. Today the approach plate, now 8½ by 5½, printed on both sides of tissue thin paper, is still a "map," but it comes with copious notes explaining an airport's facilities, procedures, and irregularities. For example: "CAUTION: Numerous unlighted obstacles penetrate approach light plane 43' maximum, 1546 feet from runway." This at La Guardia.

Another page shows an approach that requires the pilot to engage in the gymnastics of looking for guidance inside at instruments as well as outside at the terrain and roads. The notes for expressway approach (visual) runway 31—still La Guardia—read:

This approach may be utilized when ceiling is 3000' and visibility 5 miles or better. When cleared for an Expressway Approach to Runway 31 (while on the La Guardia VOR/DME 221 radial), cross Dials Intersection or D5.0 LGA at 2500' or above. Turn right at Dials, heading 085 and descend to Runway 31 via the Long Island Expressway and Flushing Meadow Park.

The foregoing is a contradictory mix of following radio navigation aids by instrument and eyeballing an automobile highway visually, the first demanding eyes inside and the latter eyes outside. Tennis buffs watching the U.S. Open on a brisk day with a northwest wind will know when this procedure is being used by the noisy airplanes flying overhead.

There are approach plates for each runway and procedures for area departures and arrivals; the book has 13 two-sided pages for La Guardia alone. In many respects, approach plates themselves have become legal documents; they tell what weather minimums are useable for takeoff and landing. Variables enter the rules if parts of the instrument landing system's radio transmitter or guidance lights become temporarily unserviceable. For example, ILS runway 4R at JFK has eight different minimums for transport airplanes depending on the condition of the system. These are set up in matrix form. Notes are stuck here and there on the approach plates. For example a note on La Guardia's plate for ILS to runway 4: "CAUTION: Numerous unlighted obstacles penetrate approach light plane within 3000' of rwy threshold." "So what do I do about it?" a pilot might ask, but the notes provide no answer; what the notes do is shift the burden from the FAA, La Guardia, and the chart maker in case anything happens (well, they warned the pilot). Many regulations have this effect; they free certain authorities and interested parties, such as manufacturers, from responsibility should an accident occur.

Approach charts are confusing, and vaguely written legalities may result in a pilot being cited for a violation for all sorts of things, from weather minimums to a runway being illegal to use because a cross wind is 1 knot or 2 above the limits. All airlines have special instructors who are experts in the rules, and pilots go through courses taught by such instructors every time they are scheduled for training. Difficult as the rules are, pilots must understand the legalese.

There's a fat part of the loose-leaf book called "Ops Specs" ("Operating Specifications") that spell out how the airplane and airline can operate. These specifications are very extensive and complicated, requiring a legal mind to interpret. When I was still flying the line, our "book" had an "Ops Specs" section and then right after it another section called "Ops Specs Interpretation." In other words, the "Ops Specs" were so intricate that the company decided to give us a guide to understand what the "Ops Specs" really meant.

So you looked up something in the "Ops Specs," read it, half-understood what it said, and then flipped to the "Ops Specs Interpretation" to read the same section translated into understandable language.

From all this emphasis on regulations comes a standard pilot quip about many things: "I know it's safe, but is it legal?"

This imbroglio extends into all parts of an airline operation. Take the airplane itself. Suppose you're ready to go, but a generator is not working. You call the mechanic by telephone between cockpit and ground while the airplane is on the ground and tell him it needs fixing. The phone is generally stored in the nosewheel well during flight.

So you say, "Number one generator is out. Can you fix it?"

"Don't need to. MEL says you can go with it that way," is the reply. MEL is an acronym for minimum equipment list—a list compiled for each type of airplane by the manufacturer and airline and approved by FAA specifying which mechanical items can be unserviceable and still leave the airplane safe and legal for flight.

The MEL has an interesting history. It was first created to help if an airplane was stuck with a mechanical problem at some small airport without parts or mechanic. Originally, the airplane would sit there until a mechanic and parts were flown in. If the malfunctioning part was not critical and the weather was good and night flying not a factor, it might be perfectly safe to fly on to an airport—a station—where there were facilities for repair, but you couldn't. So the MEL was created with the idea of allowing an airplane to get to the next airport where repairs were available. Not a bad idea, but it didn't take long for it to be abused; some MEL items were not in fact fixed at the next station but carried for days. In other words, MEL has been used to "keep 'em flying" even though something needed fixing. Periodically pilots complain about this to their chief pilot and, in a few cases where the complaint to the chief pilot does not improve things, to FAA directly. FAA then nudges the airline, and outstanding MEL items are taken care of with promises to do better in the future. Unfortunately, for less responsible airlines, such corrections generally are only temporary.

In addition, there isn't always a clear understanding of the MEL's legalese, and mechanic and pilot may get into quite an argument as to whether or not the airplane can fly with the bad item, the pilot saying it cannot and the mechanic saying it can. And, of course, the pilot has the final word and can say, "I'll not go until it's fixed." This doesn't make pilots popular, especially if their insistence creates a long delay.

A 747 was—and I suppose still is—able to depart on an overseas flight with a generator out. The airplane has four, driven by the engines, and they can produce enough electricity to light a small town, so there is plenty to spare. The pilot, however, is thinking about heading to Europe, where the weather is poor and the flight is scheduled for night arrival. What if another generator fails en route? The two remaining will handle the essentials, but a certain amount of caution is required; items like coffeemakers and food-warming ovens will have to be turned off. Yes, you can take off with only three generators working, but you don't feel completely comfortable about it.

Airline operators like MELs, as do mechanics, but pilots are more suspicious; they know MEL can cast a shadow. A misunderstanding about MEL and fuel gauges was one of the causes for an airliner on a scheduled flight en route to Vancouver, British Columbia, to run out of fuel and make a complete power off emergency landing—which was done successfully by the pilots doing a superb job.

The approach plate book and "Ops Specs" aren't all pilots have to be wary of. There are the Federal Aviation Regulations (FARs) with their parts and subparts. FAR 1 covers definitions, with 15 pages of fine print, 2 of which consist entirely of abbreviations and symbols. An amusing one, Part 1.3, "Rules of Construction," says such things as

(a) In Subchapters A through K of this chapter, unless the context requires otherwise:
(1) Words importing the singular include the plural;
(2) Words importing the plural include the singular; and
(3) Words importing the masculine gender include the feminine.

The FARs are written with lawyer approval, and they look it. They certainly weren't written for pilots to understand easily. Many of the FARs were created as the result of problems, accidents, and incidents, many of them simply to cover a situation in order to say FAA has responded to the problem. The number of rules doesn't decrease, and the book gets fatter with time. Efforts have been made to reduce and simplify, but take it from someone who has read them since inception: you'd never know anything had been accomplished.

An excellent example of rule-writing speciousness pertains to regulations for taking off with frost, ice, or snow sticking on the airplane. Even particles the size of fine sandpaper can dramatically reduce the lifting capability of an airplane. To attempt a takeoff with the airplane's wing so contaminated is an invitation to disaster. Experienced pilots know this and so do airline operations people. To safeguard the airplane under foul weather conditions such as wet snow or freezing rain, the airplanes are deiced by spraying the wings and important areas with a mixture of glycol and water. This removes any frozen particles. Then the airplane is sprayed with a mixture for anti-icing; this is combined, at times, with the deicing process. The anti-icing mixture, a freezing point depressant (FPD)—again glycol—is supposed to keep the precipitation from freezing long enough for the airplane to taxi out and take off. Big question: how long is the protection effective? Until recently such information was not available or given to pilots. No nastier decision rests on a pilot's shoulders than this icing problem, and I've experienced the nervousness of it many times. You taxi out with wet snow falling; the airplane has been given an anti-ice treatment with glycol. There's a long line of aircraft waiting to depart, you're number 10 in the line, and your takeoff time is probably 20 to 30 minutes away. How long will that glycol keep the wings clean? You have no positive numbers to go by; you squirm, wondering if ice is forming out there, You really sweat as you watch time click by and the line slowly move up as airplanes ahead take off. From the cockpit you cannot see the wings or the tail or the critical areas like the wing-fuselage juncture. If you go back in the cabin to look out a window at the wing, leaning over passengers who look at you bug-eyed as you squeeze across them and shine a flashlight out toward the wing, you find that the light bounces back, like headlights in fog, revealing only a blur. On some airplanes, such as the 707, a cockpit side window can be opened, and you can reach out in the cold night to feel the side of the fuselage, rubbing your hand over it and trying to determine if there's ice forming. The result is never conclusive, and the quandary remains. The 747 doesn't have a cockpit window that can be opened, so even that sketchy method is out. On the taxi strip, with airplanes ahead and behind, their engines running, swirling winds, poor footing, and no steps or ladder, there's no way to have a crew member get out and inspect wings or the top of the stabilizer 30 feet or so above the ground.

The rule states, "No person may take off an aircraft when frost, ice or snow is adhering to the wings, control surfaces, or propeller of the aircraft." But how is the pilot to see if the wing is clear once out on the runway?

Nor was there information for pilots regarding fluid-holding times, as the time of protection after anti-icing is applied is called. There was very little guidance from FAA to ensure that the de- and anti-icing procedures used were performed properly. During this period there were new fluids, developed in Europe, that were ignored in the United States.

In 1982 FAA published an advisory circular on the subject—a learned, well-done document but of a length and character appropriate for technical people, not pilots. The question of holding times is discussed at length, with a number of graphs showing how long mixtures are good for, but on each graph one finds the wording: "_____ DO NOT USE THIS CHART FOR ESTIMATING TIME AVAILABLE FROM DE-ICING TO TAKE OFF."

The circular includes no precise information for pilots to use to determine how long the deicing would hold. So pilots were still in the dark.

The document also carries the usual, unrealistic statement: "Just prior to taking the active runway for takeoff or just prior to initiating takeoff roll, a visual pre-takeoff inspection should be made." Any pilot would tell you that the author never sat in that long line of rumbling airplanes on a cold, snow-swirling night at a busy airport. It's an example of rules that are impractical, and the creator of the rule either knows this or is ignorant of the real world. It doesn't seem honest for government to write rules impossible to comply with.

The distribution of this circular to pilots was essentially nil although the FAA administrator of the time assured me, in a letter, that FAA would see to it that it would be required reading for pilots. I've asked pilots from three different major airlines and none have ever seen it.

It's only logical to assume that if pilots have any doubts, they should not take off but return for additional deicing. The real world isn't that simple. The perturbing thought of getting out of line, losing your place for takeoff, returning for deicing, which takes half an hour at best, and more likely an hour, and then taxiing out again to start all over at the end of the line with a long wait affects your judgment, so does worsening weather at either your departure or destination point. And the situation is always made more difficult by the lack of precise knowledge of how the fluid is holding.

That's how the situation was in 1982 when Air Florida crashed at Washington, D.C., the result of ice in the engine instrument system and ice on the wings. The National Transportation Safety Board (NTSB), which investigated the accident, charged that the FAA should, among other things, require that airlines: "Immediately review the predeparture deicing procedures used by all air carrier operators engaged in cold weather operations and the information provided to flight crews to emphasize the inability of deicing fluid to protect against deicing resulting from precipitation following deicing. (Class 1, Urgent Action)."

All in all, NTSB gave FAA 10 recommendations it called "urgent" or "priority" as a result of the accident. Like FAA, however, NTSB made one recommendation that was the unrealistic coverall, "Immediately require flightcrews to visually inspect wing surfaces before takeoff if snow or freezing precipitation is in process." Of course there were no suggestions on "How ya gonna do that?" FAA responded to NTSB, saying air carriers had been notified of the NTSB's recommendations. FAA also put out various warnings and guidelines, but the substance was weak and, as always, covered by "Flight Crews must use the 'clear aircraft' concept specified in current rules." Of course the final say so should be the pilot's, but FAA and NTSB failed to acknowledge the difficulty flight crews face in trying to accomplish such an inspection. And they turned their backs on the pressures flight crews experience, as well as avoided the question of fluid-holding times, except for a weak statement that said, "Under some atmospheric conditions ice may form in a much shorter period." NTSB had said caution is needed if 20 minutes have elapsed since the last deicing. FAA pointed out that 20 minutes is "not considered in the best interests of flight safety." That was the only mention of holding time. All this went on in August of 1982.

While doing some work in 1982 during the investigation of the Air Florida crash, I discovered that the Europeans had been using fluids developed in the wake of research, much of it in Sweden and the former Soviet Union; these fluids have longer holding times than the glycol used in the United States. Most European carriers used them when needed and had been doing so for at least two years—since 1980! The United States did not adopt these fluids, although people in the FAA knew about them. FAA, as can best be established, felt they wanted to test the fluids and research their effectiveness. The "not invented in the United States" syndrome was at work since the fluids had been thoroughly tested in Sweden and the Soviet Union and adopted by all European countries. But in the United States it has only been since 1989 that some carriers started using the longer-holding fluid called "type II." (It is a glycol fluid with corrosion inhibitors and a proprietary thickner.) Dow Chemical Company began its production in 1988 under the name Flightguard 2000. In the 1989–90 period the airlines used approximately 9.6 million gallons of glycol for deicing, and less than 0.5 million gallons of the type II fluid.

Little more was done during the ensuing years by FAA. The Europeans were active, and a special working group was set up by the Nordic countries of Sweden, Norway, Iceland, Finland, and Denmark to work on the problems of deicing and anti-icing of aircraft. Their work was reported at the European Civil Aviation Conference (ECAC) at Strasbourg in June 1982. The FAA decided not to send a representative, saying it appeared that a deicing discussion would not be a major part of the meeting. This seems a very apathetic way of dealing with things, to say the least—FAA had representatives in Paris who could have gone with little expenditure of time or money. One would have thought FAA would be eager to learn anything possible following the Air Florida crash.

FAA and the industry did little to solve the problems until the crash of USAir flight 405, a Fokker, at La Guardia, March 1992—the result of an icing problem—10 years after Air Florida. Then type II fluids got press attention, and an FAA official said, "USAir 405 may turn out to be a watershed accident." He was 10 years late. Air Florida was really the watershed accident.

After the public awareness of the La Guardia accident, FAA began to move. In May 1992 it called a conference of all interested parties including those from Europe. The conference was called a big success. Then FAA developed and printed an advisory circular with much data and recommendations, and FAA changed the FARs to fit. The good part: good information and, at last, some tables to show holding times in various conditions and with the two different fluids. The tables are called "guidelines" but carry the warning, "These guidelines should only be used by air carriers as a part of, or in conjunction with, an approved ground deicing/anti-icing program." Whatever that means. The pilot was not forgotten and a section in the circular is called "Practices for Pilots to Ensure a Clean Aircraft." There are 16 items for pilots to know, many of them simply impractical to respond to in the daily operation of an airline. For example: "Ensure that deicing and anti-icing are performed at the latest possible time before taxi to the takeoff position." With delays, passengers showing up late, the many kinds of confusion possible at departure, how are pilots able to know what time they'll depart?

An additional item shows the still-unknown time that the fluids hold off freezing and the way the responsibility is passed along to the pilot: "Be aware that the time of effectiveness of FPD deicing or anti-icing treatment can only be estimated because of the many variables that influence this time (holdover time)."

The last item says, "Do not take off if possible evidence of a clean aircraft cannot be ascertained." This is a good admonition, but if followed, the rate of aircraft returning for additional deicing/anti-icing, and consequent delays, will noticeably increase. There should be no complaints because it's a safe procedure.

The circular is a good one, full of valuable information, but the gray areas still are there. The final judgment is the pilot's, and it's a difficult one because of the pilot's inability to really inspect the airplane properly just before takeoff.

How could we do better? A means of deicing just before takeoff near the end of the runway. At present FAA and the industry are studying this, and some airlines are setting up areas, close to the runway, to do deicing as close to takeoff as possible, but let's go back to Europe again. In Paris, at Charles de Gaulle airport, a huge structure like a carwash is available for an airplane to pass through just before takeoff, getting deiced in the process. This was installed in de Gaulle in *1977!* Since then a second structure has been installed for the narrow-body jets. The time for a jumbo jet to get deiced is 8 minutes; 5 minutes for the narrow body against about 30 minutes in the United States. The system at de Gaulle is also environmentally sensitive because the fluid drains through grating after spraying the aircraft, is filtered and reused. There are other structures like these at various European airports, Munich, Germany being the latest.

Station De Dégivrage, or station for deicing aircraft, at Charles de Gaulle airport in Paris, France. Aircraft pass through just before takeoff and are deiced. This station was installed in December 1977. There are none in the United States. (*Photo by Alex DeGrimm*)

Where has the United States been during all these years, when Europe was miles ahead? In the 10 years since the Air Florida crash, there has been a noticeable lack of action in getting things accomplished—such as installation of the de Gaulle "wash" system, or an inspection by a person from the outside, just before takeoff, who can tell if the airplane is clean, or devices on the airplane, allegedly under research and development, that can tell the pilot in the cockpit that there is or isn't ice on the wings. FAA has been slow in pushing this research.

It is a sad story, and the time that passed, the 10 years, is appalling. Certainly FAA must come in for a big share of the blame. The winter of

1992–93 showed much positive activity and attention to the de/anti-icing problem, much of it the result of FAA's advisory circular and rule changes, and FAA is to be complimented, but most all of it could just as well have been done 10 years previously. Where was FAA?

Did the unrealistic FAA rule "No person may take off an aircraft when frost, snow, or ice is adhering." produce an attitude of complacency in FAA? Did FAA feel, "Well, by God, it's the pilot's problem," and let that take the place of action? How much did this have to do with the dark and shameful decade 1982–92?

FAA is chartered to control the regulation of air commerce, as well as its development and safety and efficiency, to consolidate research and development of navigation facilities, and to promote the development and operation of air traffic control. Under this umbrella of fancy words comes the stack of regulations, licensing of airmen, airplanes, and procedures—a mass of things. But many of these regulations, made to cover a problem, not cure it, are a clear demonstration of FAA's failure to lead and coax the industry.

An interesting aspect of FAA's regulations is their effect on pilot training. When a person studies to pass the FAA's written examination for a license, he or she simply learns the answers to the multiple choice questions that make up the exam. You don't actually have to know the subject, just which answer to check. Lists of these examination questions are published by FAA, albeit without the answers. However, other publications publish both the questions and answers. Various schools advertise cram courses of only a few days' length to allow you to pass the tests successfully.

The question being asked by many in the industry is "Does this exam method create a rote pilot who knows the answers but lacks the true knowledge?" FAA acts as though judgment can be created by regulation, which is an extremely doubtful proposition. Certainly the multiple-choice questions for FAA don't test judgment. Instead, the mass of rules and the multiple-choice answers to exams have created an industry of aviation schools focused on passing tests. There are exceptions, of course, but the dominant force is the quickie, let's-get-by way, and industry emphasis, to various degrees, is to train to pass exams, not to learn the subject.

What proper training should do is make certain the student knows the reasoning behind the answer, not simply the answer. In many countries—Sweden, for example—tests for pilots require essays that show if the student knows the subject. Our system doesn't do that, probably because we have many more applicants for licenses than any other country and the work of reading and appraising essay exams would be too big to handle, but this reason tends to become an alibi rather than a cure for a poor system. It's generally accepted that if the percentage of people passing a multiple-choice examination is under 75 percent the exam is effective, but FAA's rate of successful exam results, is about 96 percent—showing the exams to be weak.

FAA's task is too big to respond effectively to all of aviation's diverse needs. Its research is ponderous, results slow; action on programs, procurement, and installation are stretched out over years. For example, in 1991, a serious accident occurred at Los Angeles when a landing aircraft collided with another on the runway the tower operator didn't see. In September 1960 the first airport surface detection equipment (ASDE) was commissioned by FAA and scheduled for installation at 10 major airports. ASDE is a radar to show the tower operator where all aircraft on the ground are located. There are about 254 airline airports of consequence where you'd expect ASDE to be installed, but 31 years after the first scheduled installation only 13 airports are so equipped. (Los Angeles happens to be one of them, but the day of the accident the equipment wasn't working.) An improved version of ASDE was installed at 33 airports between 1991 and 1993. The schedule called for replacing the original 13 as part of the total 33.

It is apparent that there is no government organization or process that holds FAA accountable; no one asked why ASDE had not been developed and installed or had the authority to see that it got done; there is no one responsible for seeing that the airways modernization program moves ahead and doesn't fall 10 years behind, as it has. No one had the authority to keep pretakeoff deicing from becoming such a fiasco.

There's a dangerous zone between the National Transportation Safety Board, which investigates accidents and determines cause, and FAA. NTSB makes many safety recommendations, generally to FAA. These aren't always acted upon; although NTSB says 80 percent of its recommendations are acted on, it doesn't say whether or not the action taken is satisfactory. There's reasonable doubt in this area as many recommendations are excused away in letters to NTSB from FAA. There is a need for an organization truly responsible for aviation matters, one which would see to it that aviation and its safety goals move forward in a timely fashion.

The administrator of the FAA is appointed by the president of the United States; the position has no tenure, and the turnover is fast—the average length of an FAA administrator's service has been 2.8 years since FAA's inception, which is a pretty short time to get one's teeth in the job, much less effect real change. The FAA administrator's qualifications are not spelled out as a requirement. FAA relates predominantly to civil aviation, yet most administrators have come from military backgrounds—retired generals and admirals with little or no civil aviation experience. Although some, like Admiral Don Engen, understand the civil part quite well, it's doubtful they can have the deep feel for it that someone who's battled through civil aviation's ups and downs would have. Najeeb Halaby was perhaps the most-balanced civil-military person to fill the job. He was appointed by President John Kennedy and continued under President Lyndon Johnson, but the political atmosphere changed, and Halaby's hands became tied in a political morass so untenable that he finally resigned. Perhaps it will be different this time around as President Clinton has appointed David R. Hinson as FAA administrator. Hinson has all the qualifications, including experience as an airline pilot, airline executive, general aviation pilot and in the miliary; we'll see if this well-qualified man can make some of the changes urgently needed or if the entrenched federal and FAA bureaucracy will curb his efforts.

The FAA is part of the Department of Transportation, and at times, the secretary of transportation overrules—"interferes" might be a better word—with the judgment of the FAA administrator, which is an unhealthy situation. As the situation is at present, FAA is like Big Brother watching over the pilot and the controller, as well as others, adding stress to their jobs. Although FAA says it isn't a cop, that it's friendly, most on-line airplane people are skeptical and treat it like a growling dog whose owner says he doesn't bite.

Still, paradoxically, there's a bright side to FAA, areas where it does a magnificent job. All the navigation aids—omni stations, DMEs, lights, and communication hookups—work in excellent fashion, as do, for the most part, ATC's radars and computers, even though many are old and out-of-date. When you're sitting in the cockpit, you know that out there somewhere is a silent, unseen, very able cadre of people who go about their business and keep things running—like the gardens in Paris, which are always beautiful even though you rarely see anyone working on them. FAA also has many people working nationwide in district offices called FSDOs (Flight Standards District Office), giving license tests, making inspections, and providing the myriad of answers and actions the FAA rules and structure require. These are dedicated people, from pilot to clerk, but they don't make policy, create reforms, or change FAA. They do their jobs, generally in a thorough, cooperative manner away from the morass of Washington, D.C. They are not the problem of FAA.

Despite all the criticism and fears for potential disaster the air traffic control part of FAA does an excellent job. Yes, there are major yowls and complaints about delays, but ATC's first task is to keep airplanes from running into each other and that it does marvelously despite old equipment, a shortage of people, and constant pressure to move traffic faster and tighter. These pressures reduce the margin for error and if continued may mar ATC's good record. The controllers, with these constraints, perform admirably.

By the time the 747 came into view our black bags and the manuals and rules they carried had become considerably heavier. In past times we'd only see FAA inspectors occasionally, but now they seemed to be peering over our shoulders much of the time. The regulations, ATC, and added pilot responsibilities had grown to a menacing size.

14 | BOEING'S 747 AND NEW CONCEPTS

The arrival of the 747 in 1970 caused excitement and change, although not as drastic a change as going from propeller airplanes to the original jets. The issue with the 747 wasn't that it was a jet—by now we knew about jet flying—but its size. The announced dimensions of the 747 were impressive: 710,000 pounds gross weight—roughly 400,000 pounds heavier than a 707—with a wingspan of 195 feet—65 more than a 707. Most awesome was the cockpit's height above the ground: three stories high, a two-story jump from the 707.

Among pilots rumors flew about such things as the difficulty of trying to judge a landing when perched 30 feet off the ground and whether or not, if a low-level go around was required, a 570,000-pound mass (the landing weight) could accelerate fast enough to abort the landing and climb away without hitting the ground.

During the development stage, Boeing built a simulated cockpit mounted on a truck with allowances made for all the 747 dimensions, including the landing gear geometry, to find what problems might exist when taxiing. It was dubbed "Waddell's Wagon," after Jack Waddell, the test pilot who would make the first 747 flight. Assisting him were Boeing test pilots Brien Wygle and Jess Wallick. Jack "drove" this rig around Boeing Field, Seattle, trying various maneuvers and learning the problems of handling the big airplane on the ground. When news of this experiment got out, pilots worried even more about the mysteries of flying this monster.

Of course, all the rumors of difficulty were unfounded. A pilot could certainly judge landing from a height of 30 feet, although many would use the radio altimeter that shows altitude right down to the ground. And going

THE LATEST BOEING 747-400. (*Courtesy of the Boeing Company*)

around on a 747 was just like doing it with any other airplane; you could decide to abort a landing 3 feet off the ground and climb smartly right from there. Taxiing would prove more difficult, at least for me, because I couldn't tell where those wheels were, way down and in back. Then, too, from the high cockpit, a taxiway looked mighty narrow. I cleansed my mind about this by driving an auto behind a 747 as it wound through the taxiways on TWA's practice airport at Salina, Kansas. From there I could see there was lots of room for a 747 to maneuver on a taxiway. Boeing made part of the landing gear capable of swiveling, like the rear wheels on a long hook and ladder fire engine, which made it possible to do tight turns. Once accustomed to the 747, I could wind through the maze of twisting turns at JFK with more dexterity than I could with a 707.

When training started, we quickly found that, big or small, airplanes are airplanes, and doing the usual transition flying was easy—steep turns, stalls, simulated engine failures, landing, takeoff, V_1 engine cuts, the lot. Basically the 747 flew like any other airplane, from Piper Cub on up.

Pilots adjust pretty easily to differences in airplanes if they look them over carefully and go over the process slowly. Their judgment doesn't get stuck on one size airplane; it's flexible. While flying 747s, I was also actively flying gliders on my days off. I'd land a 747 from Paris one day, with my eyeballs 30 feet off the ground, and be in Vermont the next day landing a tight-fitting fiberglass sailplane, with my eyeballs only 36 inches above the ground. Making the necessary adjustment was very natural, and I'm certainly no exception; all pilots with reasonable experience can do it.

But if the flying was relatively easy, the ground school was more effort. Much of the instruction reminded us that the 747 was a Boeing and a direct descendent of the 707s. There were even a few leftover traits that go back as far as the B-17, like a crossbar, located just below the instrument panel to rest your feet on. I had put my feet there for many hours during WW II on a B-17, and here it was on the 747—made me feel right at home. The ground school instructors frequently said, as they lectured, "same as," meaning the system being explained was the same as a 707's. The main differences were improvements such as pneumatic power added to move some of the flaps and back up the hydraulic system.

The class attention getters were the navigation and automatic flight systems. Navigation on the 747 was by a totally new principal called "inertial navigation," which eschewed the magnetic compass altogether.

In DC-3 days, navigation was done by compass, map, and flying the beam. Flying over oceans, we used celestial, taking sights on celestial bodies to determine position. The course was always followed by compass. At jet speeds, celestial navigation began to show its tedious side, which was better geared to ships of 15 knots than to 500 MPH airplanes.

The airplane navigation problem has always been groundspeed and drift. In airplanes you cannot see or feel drift, and for a long time there was no instrument to show it; you learned where you were after the fact. You'd find your position over the ground or water: ah, 10 miles right of course, which means 13° drift, and the spot is 100 miles from the last fix; you've been doing 180 knots. Then you would use that information to guess what new heading to fly and estimate arrival time. Then off you'd go, following the new heading until the next fix, be it looking at the ground and matching it with a map or a star fix. Navigation, essentially, was historical; you'd take old data, make a new start, and try to funnel down toward the destination.

Midway through the 707 era Doppler came along. The Doppler system consisted of an electronic device that sent a signal to the ground or water—whatever was below. The signal then bounced back at a slightly different frequency because of Doppler effect, the same principle that makes a train whistle change pitch as it goes toward or away from you, named for the German, Christian Doppler, who discovered the phenomenon in 1842. With fancy computer work a standard-sized instrument on the airplane's panel displayed drift and groundspeed constantly! Very neat, although the system had its problems: if the water below was glassy smooth, the Doppler signal wouldn't bounce back, so no information was available until the sea became at least a little choppy. Not a big problem but a problem nevertheless.

Of course, the drift information had to be applied to the compass for a correct heading to fly. A compass reading is not precise because it's affected by various things—not only magnetic items in the airplane but variations in the earth's magnetic field, which are capricious and don't follow the charted values in standard use. The Davis Straits, located between Greenland and Canada are notorious for this, and the possibility of course deviations in that area kept you on the alert.

But Doppler was a big improvement over the old navigation methods. An unfortunate aspect of its introduction was the demise of the professional navigator as the airlines gleefully rubbed their hands together over the possibility of dumping a crew member and all attendant expenses. Of course, this was not done without a fierce battle between a company and the navigator's union. The company won, but the navigators got a monetary settlement and passes on the airline for life.

Now navigation was handed over to the pilots. It wasn't as simple as just following the Doppler instrument needle; we also had to take fixes to be certain all those compass variables hadn't thrown us way off course. For this we didn't use celestial but a radio system called Loran (for long-range navigation), which was based on a hyperbolic medium-frequency radio transmission from known points. To use it, you huddled over a cathode-ray tube and watched dancing spiked green lines. The trick was to match two stations by superimposing one wiggling green line over another in a three-stage operation. From this puzzlelike game you got a number. The overocean chart had long swooping numbered lines in pretty colors. You found the one with your number, and that gave you a line on which, somewhere along it, you were located. To find out where, you tuned in another set of Loran stations and repeated the process; where the two lines crossed was your position. The vagaries of this exercise were many; reception was affected by distance, time of day, sunspots, and two different radio waves—ground waves and sky waves—that you had to sort out. You had to develop a certain craftiness. You could call taking a Loran fix an art. Today Loran has been all cleaned up and works almost by magic, with no need to play games with spiked green dancing lines; instead, you simply read the numbers displayed in digital form, with the art part being done by computer.

I was saddened to see the end of celestial because it had been a skill learned that linked me to navigators of the past, and I felt the lore of that kinship. I'd learned the stars and related to them in a personal way, as friends. Suddenly the knowledge was useless, except when I was outside on a clear night and could look up to see these faithful old friends above me. Some stars bring memories, like bright Sirius and a night in my B-17 heading for Midway Island from Adak in the Aleutians. For complex wartime reasons, I had no navigator and so did the navigation myself. The weather was terrible as we flew in clouds with no fixes, but suddenly a shaggy hole opened and almost mystically Sirius's brightness sparkled through. I took a quick sight for a much-needed and useful line of position, and then the hole closed, and we were back on instruments. Thank you Sirius.

During 707 times, we also lost the radio operator. The long-distance radio transmission was changed to Single Side Band, which gave much better reception. SELCAL (for Selective Calling) was installed about the same time. Its use meant we didn't have to constantly have headsets clamped to our ears or be beaten by the chatter and ear-bashing static of long-range radio, just in case there was a message for us. SELCAL assigns each airplane a distinctive code for the ground to use when calling. A call to you, from the ground, activates a loud chime and flashes a yellow light in the cockpit; then you answer the phone, so to speak. With improved reception and SELCAL, the powers that be decided pilots could handle communications themselves. And so went the radio operator—more money saved—leaving two pilots and the flight engineer, who, incidentally, took over much of the SELCAL answering duty.

The most impressive and eye-opening system on the 747 was the INS (for Inertial Navigation System). This system caused head-shaking wonder; no more compass—INS doesn't need it. From the legend of lodestone use by the Chinese, to the Age of Discovery, and right up to 707s, all navigation had followed a compass of some sort. Now it was gone! A small standby magnetic compass was half-hidden up above the windshield, but it was there largely to pacify old-time pilots who couldn't quite develop 100 percent faith in the idea of going across an ocean without a compass! After all, you don't abandon 900 years of use just like that! The little magnetic compass also gave some sort of secure feeling in case the INS failed, but there were three INS systems, and the chance of all three failing at once ran up into the million to one shot sphere.

INS brought with it the long-dreamed-of ability to know groundspeed and drift at the moment, all the time. How? To go into the deep theory, which relates to the earth's center and enough math to fill a couple of blackboards, is, frankly, more than I can handle; suffice to say the intelligence of the original INS was a combination of very precise gyroscopes and accelerometers. The gyros kept the accelerometers level, and they measured any force moving the airplane; that information, via computer, is changed to groundspeed, drift, and heading.

Dr. Charles S. Draper, of MIT's Lincoln Lab, was the dominant INS inventive force in the United States, and the first aircraft to fly a successful INS cross-country was a Draper-supervised, specially fitted B-29 that flew coast-to-coast nonstop in the last days of WW II. Computers were at an early stage then, still run with vacuum tubes; the whole computer unit weighed 3000 pounds and filled the B-29's bomb bay. A special air-conditioning system was installed to keep those tubes cool. INS advanced with the computer, and the military latched on to it for submarines, aircraft, and missiles—all very secret. Finally, in the late 1960s, INS was removed from the secret list and approved for general use. The 747 was the first commercial aircraft designed with INS as a standard system.

Today's INS is called IRS (for Inertial Reference System—nothing to do with taxes), and the intelligence of the system comes from a 6-inch triangle with laser beams tearing around inside. It all fits in a container not much bigger than a shoe box and weighs about 25 pounds.

Before a flight takes off, during the prestart checklist, the crew types into the Control Display Unit (CDU) the exact longitude and latitude of where the airplane is parked. It takes about 10 minutes for the IRS to digest all this and align itself, and during that time the airplane cannot be moved. Once taxiing starts, the IRS, knowing speed and drift, keeps the position updated and reads out, in the cockpit, the latitude and longitude of the aircraft second by second.

The crew's important task, during preflight and while the IRS is aligning, is to type into the Flight Management System the route to be flown, via various places called "way points"—Gander, Newfoundland, 50° north latitude/ 50° west longitude, and each 10° across the ocean. Flipping a switch connects the autopilot to the IRS; the crew then sits back while the airplane automatically proceeds along a perfect course line. Accurate? In 3600 miles New York to Paris, the error might be 2 or 3 miles. As we fly, the FMS displays groundspeed and drift, moment-to-moment position, and gets a constant fix—the ultimate navigation solution!

IRS intelligence is all contained within the airplane. You need no radio from outside, nothing. It gives the pilot a wonderful feeling of independence; it allows you to thumb your nose at the ground below.

At first pilots were taken back a bit: "No fixes? How do you know where you are?" It was difficult to let go of old concepts and put all navigation eggs in that one INS basket with never a fix to prove it was doing its thing properly. Some even predicted there would be airplanes lost as the system failed. In about 3000 hours of 747 INS operation, I once had one of the three systems develop a 35–nautical mile error—the biggest in-flight irregularity I ever had. Worldwide, the IRS reliability record has been phenomenal.

Nothing is perfect, however; there must be a hitch somewhere. Unfortunately, there is: the possibility of human error when typing in the coordinate for alignment or the way points for en route. Typing numbers on a keyboard can easily result in transposition; 4554, for example, can be entered as 5445 or some other combination of the numbers in the wrong order. There is chance for error in the initial entry for system alignment, and if that's in error, everything that follows will be too. Paris, France: 48°41' north latitude/2°23' east longitude. Note *east* longitude. Most U.S. pilots were accustomed to west longitude—even London is west if only by a little bit. It is easy to put Paris in as west longitude if you're rushing and not concentrating. Another kind of error: I once typed in a way point as 48°00'N/7°00'W, and the first and second officers checked it as okay. When the autopilot picked up the signal to head on that course, we seemed to make a larger turn than I thought necessary; I checked the CDU for the way point—yes, it was proper. The F/O and S/O checked it again; okay. But things felt wrong, so we went over the numbers again, very carefully, and there it was: I'd typed in not 48°00'N/7°00'W, but 47°00'N/8°00'W. A simple transposition of the numbers, and we were headed 60 nautical miles too far south. Our first quick check of the numbers had seen all the correct numbers—4s, 8s, and 7s—but they weren't in the correct order. The whole incident had only taken five minutes, but it made a serious impression, and I developed procedures to minimize such errors in the future.

The key to IRS operation is the use of procedures that make certain the inputs are correct. If the crew stays alert and uses the procedures, the numbers of IRS human errors should be very small.

The IRS of today has done much in design to prevent errors; for instance, the computer stores the lat/lon of all airports and gates, so the pilot simply types KATL B-7, which is a gate at Atlanta, Georgia, for example, and the computer automatically places the position in the IRS. Of course, the wrong gate or airport could be typed in error, but it seems less likely than the numbers of lat/lon.

If a conscientious pilot wants to check that the entries have been correctly accomplished, it's necessary to get out a book or map to look up the coordinates of that airport and gate for confirmation that it's right. Some do this; many do not. Should they? Computer people will say no; there are so many computers in the modern airplane that one simply cannot check everything they're doing. How good or bad this is and what safeguards are or are not needed becomes an important provocative and ultimately unanswered question, but willy-nilly, pilots are being forced to have lots of faith in computers. An important aside, in this case, is the pressure and rush that's often present as pilots get ready to start up and taxi out, that doesn't give enough time to dig into a book to read out lat/lons and to check them.

Great as IRS is, a better system is lurking right around the corner; Global Positioning System, or GPS, which has been adopted for the future air navigation system by International Civil Aviation Organization. A flock of satellites squawk from the sky and send signals the airplane can receive, and through computers and other electronic massaging, display the airplane's exact position in the cockpit—within a few feet, not a few miles. There are 20 satellites up there now, with more scheduled to go up until there are 24 parked above the earth. New airplanes being delivered have provisions for GPS antennas, and many general aviation aircraft have systems installed and in use, although these are not as precisely accurate as the eventual system will be when airlines start using it. The delay is a military-civil mix-up that has to do with security. The possibilities of the system are astonishing; eventually we will do away with all ground navigation aids—Omni, DME, and some day, even ILS; experimental blind approaches and landings using GPS have already been accomplished. GPS will also replace, or become an adjunct to, the present altimeter, which measures pressure. GPS can place you within a few meters not only laterally but vertically as well, which translates into altitude above the earth. The uses for it will not be confined to airplanes; boats, trucks, and even your automobile will have a GPS. There are some available now, small enough to fit in your shirt pocket, for instant position information. GPS is indeed a marvel, but I'll still miss that independent feeling IRS gives. I suppose, however, that with each day it is more difficult to be independent in this world.

But let's get back to the 747. The complexity of the big aircraft's systems removed it far indeed from the simple airplane of old. Four independent hydraulic systems powered by engine-driven pumps, augmented by pneumatic pumps run by air bleed off the engines, move many things, including controls, retraction and extension of the landing gear, and wheel brakes. The complexity is created, in part, by safety concerns, so there will be redundancy, a backup that ensures that another can take over if one system fails. In other words, on the 747, and all airline aircraft, all systems don't have to work for the airplane to fly safely. Yes, with the loss of each system you may lose part of a control, or electric supply, but the airplane will fly, in limping fashion, even with only one hydraulic system. That's one reason the 747's safety record is so good.

The electrical system with its four generators—and 635 circuit breakers—runs many things; instruments, IRS, and even the machine that makes coffee and the ovens to heat food. The system doesn't miss a beat if one generator fails; with two out some functions are lost; with only one remaining much has gone, but we're still flyable. An added ace in the hole is a small onboard jet engine way back in the tail called the Auxiliary Power Unit (APU); it runs a generator, plus other things, to aid the system. The

APU is also used on the ground when all engines are stopped to keep lights on and air-conditioning operating and, when the time comes, to start the big engines. At first we were not permitted to run the APU in flight, but now advanced design allows it.

Of course, the system comes with warning lights to show when something goes wrong so the problem can be diagnosed and proper procedures followed. Most system warnings were back there with the flight engineer or second officer. The S/O also managed the pressurization system, air-conditioning, heating, and the fuel system. The latter is made up of seven tanks with pumps, pressure and quantity gauges, and switches that direct valves to open or shut. This allows the use of fuel from different tanks; the sequence of which tank to use first is a function of the airplane's weight. Of course, if an engine fails, the fuel for it will be directed elsewhere; if a pump fails, there are a bunch of possibilities to take over its work. But each component has that redundant backup character, so no one thing can knock the plane out of the sky. The S/O has to keep an eye on these things and do the fancy work when needed.

Up front on the pilots' instrument panel, overhead and on the pedestal between the pilots, are a plethora of warning lights and sounds to tell if something isn't working properly—the Instrument Warning System (IWS) with five different lights to come on and say if something's askew. The lights mean one thing if flashing, another if steady. The instruments themselves have warning flags—little signs that pop up or change in a window—to announce something has failed; all in all, there were 22 flags in the instruments. There were also warning lights on the autopilot and INS. And to make certain you get the news, there were also warning sounds—bells, chirps, and Klaxons, both steady and intermittent. I say were because I'm talking of the first 747. The 747 is different today, but the warning systems are certainly no less complex, and lots of the early 747s still prowl the world airways.

The warning lights and flag signals aren't simple to interpret because different combinations indicate that different things are wrong. You have to see the lights and flags, then analyze the situation and take corrective action. Not surprisingly, the airplane manual had upwards of 16 pages of drawings and explanations to cover this.

Sample situation for analysis on pilot's ground school exam: "Red flashing warning light, yellow altimeter light, autopilot red light, flight director flag in the attitude indicator, flag in the altimeter, Mach meter and True Air Speed indicators out." What happened?

Hummm, some brain storming and the answer: "CADC (Central Air Data Computer) failure. What do we do? Static selector to alternate, "A" autopilot off, "B" autopilot to command. Note: autolanding cannot be accomplished in this configuration."

Remember, there are 16 pages of combinations in the manual. The flags and lights come on, automatically, when something goes wrong—a sudden surprise to the crew. And sometimes this happens during a tight moment; on final approach only three minutes to the runway, on instruments with the ceiling reported at 100 feet, your concentration deep and focused on the approach—then this disturbing occurrence that requires fast
analysis and action.

This is just a sample of the parts and pieces of the airplane; there's more, and a good pilot must be a good diagnostician, looking for clues, working with the F/O and S/O for advice and help. You always have to be alert for irregularities—the funny smell that could mean a hot electrical wire, bleed air from an engine, or something burning in the cargo hold. A strange noise, an instrument even slightly off the normal position, all go into your awareness for possible trouble.

I often felt a certain wonder, as I pulled into position for takeoff, the checklist complete and airplane ready, that everything was working; all the motors, pumps, instruments, relays, generators and a host of things hidden away, scattered with order throughout the innards of that big airplane. The whole preflight ritual had some aura of a space shot countdown, but the procedures do work—a credit to our research community, engineers, test pilots, and manufacturers.

With experience you make a philosophical adaptation to overcome anxiety about the multitude of things whirling, clicking, sucking, blowing, flowing, and Lord-knows-what in that monstrous machine strung out behind you. You separate it into individual systems, each specifically designed, tested, and manufactured to work. No reason why it shouldn't. Each has been tested for reliability and operating life and comes with a program of replacement and overhaul that swings into action before a part's probable failure time. Critical proof in the pudding: accidents due to mechanical failure are but a small fraction of the whole. The odds are better than anything you can think of—even staying in bed.

The early period of flying a new airplane is the time to shake out and deal with problems that all new things have. And so it was with the 747. I held the enviable position of being number one on the seniority list at the time, so my checkout was early, and I got in on the action.

While landing the airplane was easy, we had to recognize and remember that the wheels on the 747 were way behind and hung down much lower than on other airplanes. This was especially critical when landing with the nose haughtily pointing up at the sky. On a normal glide path, if the cockpit was 40 feet above the ground, the rear wheels would only be a scant 2½ feet above it! So skinning over the end of the runway for a short landing might result in the wheels hitting the ground before the airplane got to the runway. Fortunately, the radio altimeter showed actual altitude above the ground, and I quickly latched onto the concept of never allowing the cockpit to cross the runway's approach end without 100 feet showing on the altimeter.

A major difficulty we soon learned about the 747's engines had to do with starting them, which was tricky. You placed the start switch to on, eyes glued to the N_2 RPM indicator; at 20 percent, you raised the start lever and then watched exhaust gas temperature (EGT) like a hawk. It was normal for the EGT to rise as the engine lit off, but it had to rise at a proper rate. If it started up quickly, then chances were it was a bad start, with the possibility of doing $250,000 worth of damage to the engine. So you learned to spot a quick rise and slammed the start lever off and stopped all fuel flowing to the engine. After it cooled down, you'd try again. It was tricky business. Engines had been damaged by bad starts. The procedure became a routine matter but was always cautiously performed—like walking on slippery ice. Once started, the engines were reliable and ran faithfully hour after hour.

The engine was also sensitive to compressor stall: a condition when there isn't enough airflow through the engine, and to put it crudely, it backfires. This sensitivity was a bother especially after touching down on landing when the pilot wanted to use reverse thrust to slow the airplane. Our orders were to come out of reverse when the airplane speed decreased to under 100 knots. Not using reverse thrust under 100 knots meant the wheel brakes had to be used more, with resultant excessive wear.

The engines used water injection on takeoff—water was forced into the engine by high-pressure pumps. The water lowered the exhaust temperature and gave a 3 percent increase in thrust. The water flow lasted about 2½ minutes. It was an added bother because you wanted to be aware of when the water was exhausted and be ready to change the airplane's attitude after the power reduction. But actually it was a fairly trouble-free system.

On takeoff with the 747 we were using reduced thrust, less than full takeoff power. The objective was/is to reduce maintenance costs on engines—it's solely a matter of economics. There were restrictions as to its use; the runway had to be dry, all engine gauges and wheel braking antiskid working, for example. A lot of us didn't like the idea; reducing thrust lengthens the takeoff run and lessens initial climb out. Reduced thrust use also increases the hazard of a rejected takeoff because it moves V_1 closer to the end of the runway, leaving the pilot less room to stop. If the pilot decides to keep going rather than stop, she or he must not forget there is more power available and to pour on the extra throttle, which is another factor to pile on the many that pilots must not forget for use in making their decisions. Economics again compromising safety. Of course the captain could refuse to use the reduced thrust, but refuse regularly and the chief pilot would ask why.

There was opposition to reducing thrust on takeoff. Full power, which was what the engine was designed for, got you off the ground and up to where power could be reduced to climb values quicker; you also got up and away from noise-sensitive areas sooner, and it can be argued that using full thrust, considering the quicker climb, saves some fuel. But the combination of money saved in lessened maintenance and certain manufacturer guarantees if reduced thrust is used have made it de rigueur in the industry—all airlines and aircraft now use reduced thrust. Now it has been given euphemistic names: "flex thrust" or "alt thrust" for flexible and alternate or, sometimes, derate; in the Boeing 767 there are two derate types. In number 1 derate the thrust is 8 percent less while in derate number 2 the thrust is 17 percent less. Computing reduced thrust was also a chore. I use "was," because doing this is past tense for me, but the basic things are the same today, except thrust reduction is computed by a computer, and all the pilot has to do is push a button to get it.

The most interesting aspect of using reduced thrust has to do with human factors, and that translates to the pilot forgetting, in an emergency, that reduced thrust is being used and there's extra power available by just pushing up the throttles. The first 747 accident was a takeoff at Nairobi, Kenya, when the leading edge flaps were not extended. It was called a crew error, but the airplane had been modified to get more pressure for starting the notoriously tricky engines of the early 747s; this added to crew work load, requiring switches to be moved and introducing an extra hazard if they were missed. The airplane struggled to get in the air, became airborne, but couldn't climb out of ground effect. It slammed back to earth, killing 55 of its 140 passengers and 4 crew members of 17. No one reacted to the fact that reduced thrust was being used and there was more power available; a shove on the throttles by the pilot might have made the difference and kept the plane flying. Pilots forgetting extra thrust is available to use has been a factor in other accidents; one of them was the Air Florida crash at Washington, D.C., another, a Boeing 727 that tried to take off without flaps at Dallas.

Accident investigators and finger pointers are quick to say the pilot was in error for not using the extra power. And this brings up a point closely related to human factor errors: is it reasonable to build a trap in the system and then pile blame on the pilots when the trap springs? The industry is full of unreasonable loads placed on a human; no one ever adds them up and says, "How much load can we expect a human to carry and still perform 100 percent?"

Imagine you're a pilot tearing down the runway. V_r is reached, and the wheel is pulled back, but the airplane doesn't want to fly! What's wrong? You check instruments, try to deduce the problem from the feel of controls and appraise your position along the runway. A crew member calls out something you try to understand, absorb, and analyze, mixing it in with your own thoughts. The end of the runway is coming up. The situation is a wildly confusing time of only seconds. Under the circumstances it seems only logical to pour on the rest of the power, but there's no thought about power because it's been computed before takeoff. In the pilot's mind power has been taken care of, locked in the subconscious as a fait accompli. "Hell, we haven't got full power!" is not likely to leap into consciousness when the pilot's mind is busy trying to analyze what's wrong. Can logic always explain human thought processes in a desperate situation that suddenly develops?

A major advance in the 747 was its ability to land automatically. This gave us lower weather minimums and made bad weather approaches easier—just the ticket for places prone to fog and low ceiling, like Paris in winter.

An addition was a new type of flight director with much information on it plus an eyelike ball in the center that swung into position once you'd gotten on the ILS. We called it the "bouncing ball," and its reliability was shaky—the first 747 had some interesting hiccups in both autopilot and instrument systems.

Within the autopilot system were automatic throttles to keep the speed just where needed; unfortunately the autothrottles never worked well and tended to "hunt" as we called it. If power was required, the autothrottle firmly put it on, but always too much so the airplane headed for too high a speed. At that point the autothrottle would cut back, but too far. The throttles were always hunting for the right adjustment, but never finding it. We learned how and when to engage autothrottles for better results; this turned out to be simple, a matter of making certain you had stabilized the airplane's speed with manual throttle manipulation before flipping on the switch. Then the throttles didn't have to hunt out the speed; you'd done it for them. After that, only small variations were required, and they did those pretty well.

But there were other problems. Visualize an approach to Orly Field, Paris, runway 22L. The autopilot captures the ILS about 7 miles out and starts tracking course and descent; speed is right on, so you flip on autothrottles and let them take over. As glide slope is intercepted, the bouncing ball on the flight director swings into view, saying we're right on course; lights on an annunciator panel go from amber to green, saying the autopilot is locked on localizer and glide slope (actually there were two autopilots—redundancy again). No visibility, but hidden in the murk ahead is the runway—ceiling about 200 feet, visibility a quarter of a mile. You're relaxed, noting that the airplane is right on course, sliding down the glide slope perfectly. An automatic landing is the way to go as the gyros, servos, and computers do the manual labor, giving you a feeling of command with time to double-check everything constantly. The outer marker squawks in your ears, and a blue light pulsates in the bouncing ball. Twelve hundred feet above the ground, 4 miles out; fine. Suddenly, the peace is shattered by a wailing horn and a bright flashing red light; something has screwed up in the autoflight system, but you're too close in for analysis and corrective action—hell, you're only 500 feet above the ground, still blind. You press the button on the control wheel and disconnect everything, glue your eyes to the glide slope and localizer, horizon, airspeed, and altimeter, and hand fly it.

If you followed the rules, you'd pour on the coal, climb out, and go to the alternate or, if there was a lot of reserve fuel, wait up there for weather improvement while working with the autoflight system to see if you could sort out the problem. But the air is silky smooth; there's no wind; you're perfectly on course, speed stabilized. It's illegal but safe in this condition in your judgment. You tell the crew you're going for it.

The F/O sings out, "lights," meaning he sees the approach lights but not the runway, so you don't look up. "Runway in sight!" is the next call. Then you look up and in the mist see pavement, lights, and markings. You've got it made, and within seconds you cut the throttles and roll along the runway. A DC-3 approach in the world's most modern airplane. We did more than one like that in early 747 days; actually very few were illegal because the ceilings and visibilities were generally above the height that required autoland or a working flight director, which generally failed when the autoland did. Nevertheless, our old raw data techniques were well honed because there were lots of ceilings 300 to 600 feet that were legal for hand flying when the fancy stuff failed.

What was the trouble? Spurious signals dancing about in the system—early computer glitches. But gradually engineers corrected the problems, and the irregularities were reduced to almost zero—note the "almost" because even today on the most modern airplanes an occasional failure occurs. That's why pilots cannot simply sit back and let "George," as autopilots are nicknamed, do it without constantly watching what George is up to. Did we ever get in trouble making the illegal approach? No. After all, who was to know?

Within a year improvements made autolandings routine. Even the balky engines stopped being prima donnas as modifications were made and procedures sharpened. Initially a somewhat difficult child, the 747 became a reliable workhorse. And each new model since has been even better.

Of course, FAA got in on the act—and with both feet because it was nervous about this big first-of-its-kind airplane. Being senior and first to check out may have had its glamorous moments, but it also meant I was constantly under the FAA's gun. Checkout was a long oral exam administered by an FAA inspector asking questions on the airplane and its systems, limitations, and operations, and then there was a 2½ hour flight check, including normal takeoffs and landings with all engines, abnormal with engines cut, plus many tricky maneuvers and instrument approaches.

When actual line trips commenced, there was an FAA inspector riding jump seat, breathing down my neck for almost every trip the first month. When the FAA finally decided we could handle things and ceased riding along, I almost missed the inspector. Okay, that's a slight exaggeration. On the last trip the inspector told me things had gone well but then strongly admonished me: "Remember, never leave that cockpit except to answer nature's call—and then get back quick!"

With the 747 there was the sudden growth of the cabin crew to 12 "hostesses," as we called them, plus a service manager. The senior hostesses looked at the 747 and said, "Not for me; too many people." With a few exceptions they stayed away from it. The result was a cabin full of the most junior hostesses—just hired, nervous, not sure of themselves, and in a few cases, making their first trip ever.

While it was pleasant to have a covey of sweet young attractive attendants on board, the responsibility to make certain they were doing their jobs weighed a little heavily. Preflight briefings were part of the solution; we'd gather in a room, talk over emergency procedures, and let them know we were there to help, that if they had problems they should come up top and let us know. This was important for passenger service but even more for their part in safety. It's little recognized that cabin attendants are an important part of safety. They keep alert for sick passengers, or an oven that smokes, and take a glance out at the wings now and then to see if all is normal. They see to lots of routine safety precautions, but their big job comes with a serious accident. The general impression is that all on board die in airplane crashes, but it's not so; most accidents have survivors, and a big part of that is because the cabin team has done its job and pushed, pulled, coaxed, guided, and even threatened people out of a burning airplane. Over the years cabin attendants have done many fine and heroic things to save passengers. So in our briefing we both reviewed emergency procedures and made an effort to help them relax. I also got on the airplane early, before the passengers, and walked through the cabin to have a word with each cabin attendant, stating that it was going to be a nice trip and reaffirming the cockpit crew's readiness to help if needed.

We spent the first few months with these new cabin attendants, and they were great—quickly learning the job and becoming relaxed, efficient, and pleasant. After a few months the more senior women learned the 747 wasn't an ogre and started bidding on the airplane when vacancies opened, but I'll always remember how well the young women—and most cabin attendants in that early time were female—rose to the occasion and made flights pleasant. This story is told simply to point out that along with the many operational requirements of the cockpit, the cabin attendants, back in the passenger cabin, are an added responsibility.

The 747, in many ways, is more an institution than an airplane. You walk up the jet way, go through the door, and enter the big cabin; rows of seats seem to go on forever as you look down the cabin. There are a number of galley areas—seven on early 747s—with their ovens, storage bins, microwave units, coffeemakers, and other items that you'd see in a small, tight kitchen. You stop at the forward galley, before going to the cockpit, where a couple of attendants are busying themselves checking equipment and galley stores as the coffeemaker fills a fresh pot. After a few pleasantries, you make a request for a hotdog, for the cockpit, if it isn't too much trouble. The reason for the request: it is now 7:30 P.M., we've been busy with flight planning and getting from hangar to airplane and missed dinner, and we won't get in the air for almost an hour, after which the flight attendants will launch into their beverage and meal service. This will be a wildly busy time, with little available for the cockpit, although they try to at least get us a cup of coffee. The cockpit crew will also be busy, first with checklists and getting settled and finally started, taxiing out, taking off, and then going through the complicated departure procedures and climbing to cruising altitude. So a hotdog before starting will stave off pangs of hunger until there's time to serve the cockpit a meal—about 10:00 P.M. The flight attendant is agreeable and cooperative because the micro does the job in minutes.

From the front galley it's a climb up a circular stairway to the lounge and then forward into the cockpit. Then for the first time, it's all real. You settle in the seat, store the black bag in a place close by on the floor left of you so access to manuals and charts is easy, dig out of the bag your own headset, plug it into the radio system, and put it on over your head with the little earphone in your left ear only, the right remaining open so you can communicate, by talking, with the F/O. Now, settled, you look at the instrument panel, cluttered with familiar things that relate to all airplanes: it's then that you realize this, after all, is just an airplane. The F/O and S/O settle in, you get the checklist read, and you're ready, feeling just as you did waiting for the loading to be completed and the door closed in a DC-3.

But the importance and size create a sense of responsibility that settles you into a thoughtful and deliberate pace that will not be rushed. You follow procedures, start the engines on signal, and after fighting through JFK's tower radio bedlam for a taxi clearance, pull away from the gate. You taxi carefully, with an occasional glance at the INS speed, which acts like a speedometer on the ground. This is important because it's difficult to judge speed when sitting so high; the taxiway seems narrow, and with the wing spread wide and behind, you cannot see its tips, so you depend, once away from the station signal man, on a yellow line down the middle of the taxiway. Keep the nosewheel on that, and your wings will clear anything to the sides, although it takes a little faith to believe that.

Finally, you are pointed down the takeoff runway. The tower has said, "Cleared for takeoff," and the S/O has called out, "Checklist complete." You've made that quick, 5-second, check of killer items, a check you have personally developed through the years, a check that's above and beyond procedures. Then you look ahead and carefully open the throttles, not too fast so all that machinery has a chance to gain rotation speed or too slow that you waste runway distance. The airplane moves, gathers speed; the F/O calls, "Vee R, rotate!" and you pull back on the wheel, look at the ADI, and go for a 15° nose-up attitude. The airplane breaks away from the ground, and right then, this big complex airplane is no longer a 747 but just another airplane because it feels, flies, and responds like any other.

However, despite the feeling that it's just another airplane, the 747 breeds reverence for precise operation, for following procedures and not diverging from the norm. The 747 is dignified and entitled to the veneration one gives a grande dame. Perhaps because of this aura, well understood by the older pilots flying it, the 747 had a perfect safety record for the first four years and 10 months of operation. The attempted takeoff with the leading edge flaps not extended, at Nairobi, Kenya, previously mentioned, finally put the first blemish on the record.

15 | WEATHER DICTATES— SOMETIMES RUTHLESSLY

To remind us that we're not omnipotent, Mother Nature humbles us with weather that is destructive and unmanageable. She doesn't overlook airplanes in this, and the common term "all-weather airplane" is hogwash.

Airplanes cannot fly in tornadoes, land in thunderstorms or hurricanes, take off with deep snow or slush on runways, or land in zero-zero (zero ceiling, zero visibility) old style London pea soup fog. About 35 U.S. airports are equipped with special instrument landing systems that allow landings in weather with only 600-foot visibility, provided the airplane is set up for it with extra autopilots and a pilot that is specifically qualified, but none allow for complete blind landing, except a few in Europe. Thirty-five is a long way from the total number of airports used by airlines, but those covered are the major ones. Some, like Tucson, Arizona, where fog is rare, don't need such systems, of course.

There are other items that shut down flying, but the weather that causes problems is the stuff pilots attack with a lack of weather insight because

- They haven't been adequately informed of weather and its severity. Also, the modern technology of weather dissemination via computer printout tends to homogenize weather information so that the serious appears no more important than the trivial.
- The movement of traffic and ATC's demands have made weather, subconsciously, a secondary consideration in some pilots' thinking.
- Pilot training and retraining, from first solo to airline cockpit, hasn't done a good enough job of teaching the mysteries, uncertainty, and relevance of weather awareness.

Any combination of these factors—or all three of them at once—can come into play, but let's talk about them in sequence and start with dissemination.

The science of weather forecasting has improved over the years, but the output to the user hasn't. One reason is that the computer has taken over much of the task while the crafty forecaster's hard-won local knowledge has been put on the shelf along with old hats that are seldom used. But that's another story for another time. The process of getting weather information to pilots has deteriorated despite the fact there are masses of data gathered and many prognostications made. The gut data (How's the weather right now? How's it going to be? What's it been?) doesn't go from meteorologist to pilot but rather is disseminated in the form of printed copy, frequently dim and hard to read, spewed out of a computer. The major airlines have meteorological departments that work closely with flight dispatchers, and a pilot can contact the dispatcher via radio and talk over a tight situation, but the press of communication and time spent managing the flight in a crowded sky inhibit frequent use of the service, especially close to destination situations and in the final approach to landing. Dispatchers tend to tell pilots what to do—which way to go to avoid thunderstorms, for example—without always giving a clear picture of the storm's rate of movement and severity. While the best route information may be valuable, pilots should also know what they are up against so they can make a judgment from the cockpit if things don't turn out as expected.

In certain ways DC-3 times were the golden age of weather flying. The airlines didn't depend on the U.S. Weather Bureau but had their own meteorologists at each dispatch center, which generally coincided with pilot domiciles, where your trips started.

Almost the first thing a pilot did walking into the airport office was to look at the weather map and talk it over with the meteorologist. The pilot and meteorologist closely inspected the map, with the meteorologist pointing out weather patterns with sweeps of a hand, explaining the big picture—what the weather was along the pilot's route and what it was going to do. Most important was the very personal and honest relationship; the meteorologist would tell the pilot how good the forecast was, what its chances were of working or not, and what to look for and expect if it didn't. Today the information is a cold printout with a no-nonsense, no-maybe aura of "that's the way it is or will be."

Weather has a very capricious nature, and no matter how scientific forecasting may seem, weather periodically will go off like an errant child and do something different than predicted. Anybody knows this from comparing the newspaper's forecast for clear skies with the rain out at the ball game. What a meteorologist can sense are the chances for the prognostication to work out or not. For instance, when a nice big high-pressure area sits over New York, it's easy to forecast good weather and be sure it'll turn out that way. But things aren't always so clear-cut: on a sultry day you may be expecting a cold front that's forecast to push down from the north and come through New York, bringing fresh air and clearing skies, but the front stalls in the New York City area. The fresh, clear air never arrives; instead a low-pressure system forms on the front and crawls through New York, bringing rain, fog, and miserable weather to the area. And predicting when the mess will move off is very difficult despite computers and "modern" methods.

Say we're leaning over the weather map at Kansas City, chewing it over with a meteorologist. Since we're flying the New York trip, he or she points out the front: "That ought to be through New York by the time you get there, with good ceiling and visibility. But the high behind it isn't vigorous, and there's a chance the front could stall—and if it does, your best bet is Pittsburgh."

So you plan on the outside possibility, making certain there's enough fuel on board to get back to Pittsburgh if that front stalls, the low develops, and New York goes below landing weather minimums. On the flight over, you gather weather reports each hour and watch carefully for signs of that front stalling—ah, Allentown, Poughkeepsie, and a couple of other places haven't cleared out as forecast, and their winds haven't gone around to the northwest. Is that baby beginning to slow down? It's no big deal either way, simply an inconvenience; it's not a surprise because the honest appraisal by the meteorologist prepared your thinking and allowed you to plan for any problem.

Today, for the most part, the forecasts come via impersonal computer, seldom telling what the degree of confidence in the forecast is and what to expect if it doesn't work. Forecasts are written in coded gobbledygook created not to make life easy for the pilot but for the computer and transmission. Example:

PIT FT AMD 2 111108 1057Z C6 OVC 3S- 3215G21 OCNL C8 OVC
4L-F CHC C3 OVC 3L-F 14Z C11 OVC 6F 3113G23 OCNL C5 OVC
5R-S 17Z C20 OVC 3214G23 OCNI. 6SW- 00Z C25 BKN 3108
CHC 5SW- 02Z MVFR CIG.

Which means: ceiling will be 600 feet overcast with 3 miles visibility in light snow with a northwest wind of 15 with gusts to 21 knots, and the ceiling will occasionally be 800 feet overcast with 4 miles visibility in light drizzle and fog, and after 2:00 P.M. Greenwich time (now universal time coordinated, UTC) the ceiling will be 1100 feet overcast with 6 miles visibility in fog with wind northwest 13 with gusts to 23, and occasionally the ceiling will be 500 feet overcast with 5 miles visibility in light rain and snow, and after 5:00 P.M. Greenwich (Z) the ceiling will be 2000 feet overcast with wind northwest 14 with gusts to 23 and visibility over 6 miles with occasional light snow showers, and after midnight the ceiling will be 2500 feet with broken clouds wind northwest 8 with chance of 5 miles visibility in light snow showers, and after 2:00 A.M. Z time Marginal Visual Flight Rule conditions because of ceiling below VFR minimums. No mention of degree of confidence or anything except a cold appraisal, an aura of that's the way it will be!

In the early days, the pressure of ATC wasn't primary; weather was, and the flight dispatcher watched each report carefully and got the word to you immediately if the weather was developing into a serious problem. The urgency of weather reports at terminals isn't recognized today; what's missing are the methods and specially assigned personnel to gather the latest weather and get it to pilots fast on a serious, dedicated, priority basis. In Europe they do a much better job of this.

A classic illustration of the results was the accident in Dallas of a Delta Lockheed 1011, Flight 191, on August 2, 1985, at 1805:52 (that's 52 seconds after 6:05 P.M.). The National Transportation Safety Board (NTSB), which investigates accidents, blamed the pilot for flying into a thunderstorm on the landing approach. The report's findings are suspect when the question is raised as to whether or not the pilot realized there was a storm of sufficient intensity on the landing path to call for abandoning his approach; certainly the pilot would not have continued the approach if he knew the storm ahead was savage enough to be dangerous. Therefore, it's reasonable to assume that he underestimated the storm's intensity because of the lack of information on the storm's rapid growth and fierce nature.

This is another case of ATC being the dominant priority. Visualize the scene: the pilot is approaching the airport in a long line of traffic; airplanes have been landing; there's a Learjet less than 3 miles ahead of Flight 191 that has flown through a shower located along the approach path. The Learjet pilot doesn't report any problem in the shower. The airplane approaching the airport only a couple of minutes ahead of the Learjet is an American Airlines flight whose pilot reports flying through heavy rain, but no turbulence or wind shear on the approach. The only communication from the ground to Flight 191 about the shower is a controller's statement 9 minutes before the accident that there was "a little rain shower north of the airport."

It's obvious that the rain shower just north of the field wasn't being considered by the ground or flights landing as severe. With the frequency of thunderstorms in the Dallas–Fort Worth area in summer, pilots nip through a lot of showery conditions with thunderstorms close by; if they didn't, operations there would frequently be delayed or interrupted. The frequency of summer thunderstorms is a fact of life, but something is needed to help the pilot sift the acceptable storm from the bad. Pilots must be warned of dangerous situations with moment-by-moment reports of conditions by a trained and properly equipped observer located right in the control tower and dedicated to this task.

Three airplanes went through the shower area, which was located within 4 miles of the airport, during a total time interval of 2 minutes and 33 seconds, the Learjet 94 seconds behind American 351 and Delta Flight 191 only 59 seconds behind the Learjet—but neither American nor the Learjet reported any problems. Clearly, Flight 191's pilot had not been given any information from the ground or other flights that indicated the shower was unflyable. And the tranquil passage through the shower by the other flights, so close ahead, was a key factor in 191's pilot underestimating the weather condition.

Actual reporting of the weather from the ground during the accident period was disorganized, sloppy, and reminiscent of a Marx Brothers' comedy routine—except it wasn't funny. And the dangers of the inexpressive bureaucratic way of observing and reporting weather were never more clearly demonstrated.

The primary radar for watching Dallas area weather was located 72 miles from the airport runway. The radar specialist observing the radar was not a meteorologist and was not required to notify the airport when a thunderstorm was located near the Dallas–Fort Worth airport (DFW). The radar operator was out to dinner from 17:35 until 18:00, with no relief to take his place while he ate. However, there was a television monitor in the lunchroom, which he observed but evidently without noting anything worth reporting. Back from dinner at 18:00, he studied the radar and then at 18:04 told the Forth Worth Forecast Center of a thunderstorm cell in the airport area. A report to the airport was secondary, as the radar operator's primary reporting responsibility was to the Fort Worth Forecast Center, not the airport.

His report of the cell to the Forecast Center was 1 minute before 191's accident, but it requires 6 to 10 minutes for the computer system to get the word over to the airport after the Forecast Center receives it and decides the information pertinent enough to let the airport in on it. Thus the information was of no use to Flight 191.

The radar operator reported the storm's top at 40,000 feet; he had not found any severe weather in it and reported the cell as not equal to or greater than VIP level 4. This report is amazing because anyone familiar with weather knows a storm 40,000 feet high is an inherently violent and dangerous storm.

VIP level? VIP stands for Video Integrator Processor, a device that permits National Weather Service (NWS) observers to determine objectively the intensities of radar weather echoes. And here we run into the problem of something that was meant to do one thing being applied to another and thereby lousing it all up.

Here's the listing of VIP levels and what they mean:

Level 1 WEAK and Level 2 MODERATE. Light to moderate turbulence is possible with lightning.

Level 3 STRONG. Severe turbulence likely; lightning.

Level 4 VERY STRONG. Severe turbulence likely; lightning.

Level 5 INTENSE. Severe turbulence; lightning; organized wind gusts. Hail likely.

Level 6 EXTREME. Severe turbulence; large hail; lightning; extensive wind gusts.

Now this is an important point frequently overlooked: the VIP level tells what the radar is seeing right that moment, but it doesn't tell if it's getting better or worse. Thunderstorms, unfortunately, grow very quickly, and a VIP level 1 can become a level 5 within minutes. What the pilot wants to know is what the storm is going to be like when he or she encounters it. The VIP level concept, however, has become a criterion for how tough a storm will be when the pilot gets in it, and it's a fallacious criterion for that purpose. In addition, misconceptions have developed regarding which VIP levels are flyable. Take the following true instance: a flight took off from Orlando, Florida, and there were thunderstorms on the flight path used by ATC for departing flights. Thirty degrees to the right there was a storm-free area. ATC gave the pilot a heading to fly that would have aimed the airplane right into the thunderstorm.

"There's a thunderstorm on that heading—I want 30° right to get around it," said the pilot.

But that would have confused ATC's flow control, so the controller argued with the pilot, saying, "Oh, that's only a VIP 3—others have flown through it with no problem."

This was a case of ATC flying the airplane, saying a VIP 3 (STRONG. Severe turbulence; possible lightning) was okay to fly through. Nor did ATC realize a VIP 3 can become a VIP 5 by the time the airplane got there. The pilot in this case refused the ATC heading and finally got one around the weather.

Pilots may think the VIP level is static when actually VIP should never be used for flying purposes unless an indication of its growth potential goes with it, such as "VIP 3—expect growth to VIP 4," or whatever. Then we bring together the two pieces of necessary information—what VIP is right now and what it will develop into—for useful flight management. But that isn't done currently.[1]

In the case of Flight 191, studies made later of radarscope photographs showed the cell involved to be a VIP 1 at 17:52, VIP 3, 8 minutes later, and VIP 4, 4 minutes later at 18:04.

To drag this along a little further, it seems the forecaster in charge heard the radar operator, on a speaker phone, describe the cell as a VIP 4. The forecaster then looked at a monitor available in the Forecast Center and estimated the cell to be a VIP 3 to VIP 4 *but did not believe it was a storm of sufficient intensity to warrant issuing an aviation warning*" (italics mine). This quoted from the NTSB report. So who is deciding what's dangerous or not—a weatherman using a misguided reference or an experienced pilot?

There were two other weather sources that might have helped the pilot; the CWSU and the airport weather observer: CWSU stands for Center Weather Service Unit, the Center referring to Air Traffic Control's center. Basically, this is a weather office in the ATC department, staffed part-time and mostly for the benefit of ATC flow control for routing flights during inclement weather.

Information gets to the tower for transmission to pilots on a very low-key basis. At the time of the accident a meteorologist was on duty at the CWSU, but he went to supper between 17:25 and 18:10. Before going to supper, he checked the radar and saw no weather echoes—no thunderstorms—within 10 nautical miles of the airport. This rather substantiates the general feeling there wasn't anything of a serious nature brewing.

The third weather source is the person who makes periodic observations of the airport weather. The reports are disseminated to various airlines, the forecast office, and others. The observer's office is on the second floor of a hangar. Since only 50 percent of the sky can be seen from the office, it's necessary for the observer to go down stairs and out on the ramp to look things over. At 17:44 the observer did this, returned to the office, read

---

1. Pilots do not deliberately fly through thunderstorms and do all in their power to stay out of them by using radar, observation, and deviation. All texts, instructors, experienced pilots, and mentors say stay out of thunderstorms, they're too dangerous and have, on occasion, torn airplanes apart. Radar isn't perfect, nor is observation, so now and then an airplane will inadvertently wind up in a thunderstorm, but never on purpose.

weather instruments, and prepared a report for 17:51 that said: "Ceiling 6000 feet broken, 21,000 feet broken, visibility 10 miles and wind 070° at 8 knots," which generally indicates excellent, no-problem weather, except for a comment on the report's tail end: "Cumulonimbus north-northeast, towering cumulus northeast-south-west-north." A "cumulonimbus" is defined as a cumulus built up to very high levels with rainfall from it, and most aviation people think of it as a thunderstorm, which it generally is.

This weather report was put on the DFW ATIS (Automatic Terminal Information Service), which is a canned radio broadcast pilots are required to listen to approaching an airport. We should explain ATIS, which was introduced many years ago after pilots complained they didn't know the weather or runways in use until they were in radio contact with the tower or approach control near the airport. They wanted the information in advance in order to dig out the proper runway charts, review the information, and make preparations for approach and landing. So ATIS was set up as a repetitive broadcast on a separate frequency. It turned out to be an advantage for ATC also because it relieved it of the extra task of telling each flight the runway in use and the weather.

ATIS broadcasts are periodically recut, and a new tape runs as weather or runway changes. A pilot listens to ATIS, hears the weather and runway, and at the end of the message, hears a code word such as Romeo. When first contacting the tower the pilot says, " I have Romeo," which tells the tower that the necessary airport information has been received. If the pilot fails to do this, ATC will tell him or her to go back and get the ATIS and then call back. With a two-pilot crew flying, reading checklists, changing approach routes, descending, and doing other chores, listening to ATIS is added work. And unfortunately, some ATIS is recorded in speech fast enough to make a tobacco auctioneer jealous and frequently in the accent of the region, which a pilot from another part of the country may have trouble understanding. ATIS can also be a dumping ground for warnings and notices that add to its length. Pilots frequently have to listen to the broadcast two, three, or more times before fully comprehending its message, and their attentive listening may be interrupted by more important flying duties that necessitate their coming back to ATIS again after the chores have been completed. If ATIS is done properly and has been recorded slowly enough, accent free, and without being overloaded with extra information, it's an excellent aid, but this isn't always the way it's done.

In the case of Flight 191 ATIS broadcast the 17:51 weather report but failed to include the cumulonimbus information—the key item that would make a pilot sit up and take notice! In other words, the ATIS report also tended to downplay the possible severe weather development.

The lack of sharp, up-to-the-minute weather information and a system for getting it to the pilot immediately is appalling. The complicated lines of communication of the bureaucratic system seem to have completely ignored the need of the pilot to know what the weather is right now.

The example I've used not only shows the unfairness of dumping the total error on the pilot but also, and importantly, demonstrates the aviation trend to complicate rather than simplify, to bow to the communication system's needs rather than the recipients', to ignore the fact the pilot should be informed immediately of changing weather without the circuitous bureaucratic routing. At airports like DFW, which are subject to violent thunderstorm activity, why isn't it possible to have a weather radar and Storm Scope—another type of thunderstorm detector—in the tower, with a trained operator whose task is to spot thunderstorm location and development and transmit it to aircraft almost as a running commentary when conditions warrant? The short answer is that this is possible, but such a concept of simple, quick, and effective information to pilots would likely be shrugged off or laughed at because systems often are designed by people who may not be pragmatic or knowledgeable. FAA and NWS meteorologists, computer specialists, systems engineers, legal experts, and pilot bureaucrats sit in meetings, swap memos, and after much procrastinating create these confusing, interwoven schemes, ignoring simplicity, urgency, and pilot requirements.

Northwest Airline's Captain Paul Soderlind and meteorologist Dan Sowa developed a system for Northwest called TP (for Turbulence Plot), an immediate communications system that makes it possible for all Northwest airplane pilots to hear directly from their weather office warnings about specific turbulence areas, thunderstorms, wind shear, and any weather hazardous to the operation. It is a fast, direct system that responds to and understands pilots' needs. And the record proves it. Southern Airlines crashed in a thunderstorm that Northwest's TP message warned its flights about; there were tops to 50,000 feet—a 40-mile detour would have avoided the area. Through many years Northwest has had the best turbulence avoidance record in the business, with the fewest passengers injured in turbulence incidents.

Why isn't TP used nationwide? Other airlines looked it over, but none copied it—probably because of pride and the NIH (Not Invented Here) factor. Soderlind tried to get FAA to introduce such a system and got as far as FAA giving it a try after Administrator Langhorne Bond pressured the underlings despite their dislike of the idea. Still, it wasn't theirs, and it rocked the boat. They were determined to kill it, and they did.

I followed the trial effort. It seemed to be purposely hidden away, sent out to the field in a low-key, bottom drawer way. I asked about it in two different Flight Service Stations, and the people there scratched their heads, saying, "Yeah, I heard something about that." A search in the files brought up a letter that was vague and unimpressive. When the trial period ended, the bureaucrats said the system wasn't any good because no one used it. Of course no one used it. They didn't even know about its existence!

Everyone, by now, has heard of the dreaded wind shear. As the details of what happened emerged, the Dallas Flight 191 accident was chalked up to wind shear although the pilot was still blamed for getting into it.

"Wind shear" came into the popular parlance when an Eastern Air Lines 727 crashed at JFK in June 1975. The term "wind shear" was picked up by the press as a dramatic, mysterious, and new phenomenon, easy to explain in both words and artwork. The aviation industry, which tends to be influenced by the drama and urgency created by the press, leaped on wind shear as an important head shaker, and it also made an easy statement for nonflying industry "experts" to pronounce wisely.

What is wind shear? Something that's been around and recognized since the time of the Wright brothers. The simple case: a normal landing approach; the airplane descends, and at 1000 feet has a head wind of 20 knots, while the ground wind is only 7 knots. So there's a 13-knot loss of airflow over the airplane in the descent; the pilot hardly notices it but makes simple corrections for the airspeed loss and makes a normal landing.

If this wind difference, however, is big in number—say above 30 knots—and happens suddenly, then it takes more than a subtle juggling of controls to correct for it and maintain controlled flight. Such violent and sudden wind changes occur in and near thunderstorms. Thunderstorms have violent vertical currents; outside the thunderstorm, as an airplane would approach it, air is rushing into the storm, creating a strong updraft, but then, as you approach the storm's center, rain falls in a massive deluge, dragging cold air with it and creating a mighty downdraft. The meeting edge of these opposite-flowing drafts is an area of shear—the much-discussed wind shear. The edge of this is sharp, so the change from up to down is sudden. It doesn't take much imagination to visualize the violent change in forces acting on an airplane that encounters this shear—and the frantic and at times impossible task thrown at the pilot. But pilots have known this for a long time; airlines have, too. The July 1947 issue of the *Journal of Aeronautical Meteorology* contains an article telling of downdrafts caused by the sudden rush of air when cold rain falls in a thunderstorm. In 1958 Joe A. Brown, meteorologist of TWA, put out a bulletin warning of wind shear; he published another bulletin for TWA pilots in 1961 on the same subject. Incidentally, TWA has never had a wind shear accident or incident as of this writing. Northwest TP messages were warning their pilots of wind shear in 1968, and Northwest never had a wind shear incident, either.

Where was everybody else? I'll not dwell on it here, but it's fair to hypothesize that increased traffic in our inadequate facilities caused the high-pressure action in air traffic control that eventually shoved weather judgment into a secondary role—that plus the sluggish methods of disseminating weather information to pilots. These factors were paramount in putting us on the sinister course being flown today.

About the time of the Eastern accident in 1976, a University of Chicago professor, T. Theodore Fujita, dissected a thunderstorm's structure of up- and downdrafts and gave them the catchy names of "downbursts" or "microbursts" depending on their size. He described vortices associated with them. He analyzed the shear condition that faced Flight 191—wind change in speed acting on the airplane—of 89 knots and said the microburst 191 encountered was about 2 miles in diameter.

Fujita's work describes the type of thunderstorm apt to produce such sudden violence, the size of bursts, the difficulty of forecasting them, and other aspects. Fujita also used the word "gustfront" for that sudden wild rush of cool air any child watching a thunderstorm approaching remembers as thrilling and frightening, causing trees to crash and debris to fly as people run for cover. If the child grows up to be a pilot, the memory of that rush of air imparts the idea that a thunderstorm is a thing to keep an airplane away from.

While I don't mean to detract from Fujita's work, I don't think he really told experienced pilots anything new; he simply put a name to a phenomenon and quantified the numbers associated with it. The terms "microburst," "downburst," and "gustfront" were useful for the press, something it could use that sounded dramatic. Fujita's analysis also gave numbers that airplane operational people could look at and use to recognize what an airplane was up against. But basically the old-time pilots simply knew that thunderstorms produced strong, squirrelly winds and turbulence that a sensible person stayed away from. So why the sudden frenzy about wind shear?

Two things brought shear to prominence. One was the jet airplane, which has certain differences from the propeller piston airplane; as explained elsewhere, the engine is slow to accelerate from idle, and there's no burst of airflow across the wing, adding instant lift, as a propeller produces.

The second point is a bit more nebulous but real nevertheless. Let's go back to air traffic control and the steady flow of traffic into an airport. In the early days, in DC-3 times, traffic was not as dense, and the numbers of airplanes rushing toward an airport were far less. The airplanes weren't as subtle; they were noisy inside; they leaked in rain and bounced more because of their lighter wing loading. Therefore, pilots felt closer to the elements; weather was near and they didn't overlook its important role. The quiet, removed, shirt sleeve environment of the jet that creates a feeling of distance from what's outside didn't yet exist. Pilots kept track of weather and viewed it as an immediate adversary. If a thunderstorm was near the airport, the pilot flew elsewhere, or went off to safe territory and awaited its passing. This was easy to do, as ATC was less harried and more able to cooperate.

When a jet approaches the airport these days, the need for a fast response to changing commands of altitude and heading has pilots' minds locked on the job of flying and landing. The thunderstorm may seem close by, but one after another—as during Flight 191's approach—airplanes fly near or through it; no one yells, "Uncle." There's a subtle kind of peer pressure, also, that tends to urge a pilot to follow the airplane ahead. The weather is unconsciously set aside and relegated to a secondary position, and the lack of weather reports that reflect urgency worsens this problem. Then suddenly—as microbursts can occur in a moment when a storm dumps its rain—a flight runs into the shifting, turbulent winds. First, a strong head wind increases speed and lifts the airplane. In response, the pilot pulls back on power, lowers the nose. But just as quickly, the wind changes to a tail wind, and the airplane's speed suddenly drops toward stall. The airplane loses altitude. The pilot pours on power and raises the nose, but the engine response is slow and altitude loss continues until, horribly, there is contact with the ground.

These phenomena occur mostly in thunderstorms, although "experts" say they can also happen in dry conditions in mountainous regions with certain meteorological instability. This wasn't new stuff either as old-timers could tell you. I remember well flying DC-2 aircraft on flights to Las Vegas, Boulder City, and such places, where we stayed alert for dust devils—swirling dust kicked up in miniature tornadolike fashion—that signaled us to abandon a landing. Occasionally we could see rain dropping from tall, slim, high clouds, the rain evaporating before reaching the ground (the phenomenon is called "virga"), alerting us to the possibility of winds that might make a landing approach difficult.

Mountains, too, cause wind shear. Air spillage off a nearby hill dumping strong winds or a vertical, complex vortex twisting off the end of a mountain near an airport can do you a nasty bit. Old-timers and experienced pilots know these things; they may not use fancy names, but in any such conditions they know enough to be extra wary. Why isn't this knowledge passed along? Do we lose it in rote teaching and multiple-choice examinations? Do we want to progress so fast that it's impossible to absorb knowledge painfully learned through experience and time?

The record, as we were saying, is much in favor of thunderstorms as the cause of wind shear accidents; a compilation of 28 shear accidents and incidents shows that 25 of them were during thunderstorm conditions. One of the other 3 (an incident with no injuries) was in a strong mountain lee wave during a snowstorm that should have been forecast, another during fog and drizzle at La Guardia, New York, when the wind changed from a 42-knot tail wind at 1500 feet to a 5-knot head wind on the ground—not an unusual condition with a low sitting off Long Island and a warm front creeping northward. The third was during a frontal passage landing in fog and rain. It's interesting to note these 25 accidents took place over an 18-year period, which means passengers needn't worry that a shear encounter lurks on every flight. Twenty-eight incidents during the millions of flights in the 18-year period isn't that bad a record if you're just thinking statistics.

How have we coped with low-level, microburst-type wind shear? The first way was to "teach" pilots how to fly through it. This was a big effort with instructions by airlines, monitored closely, of course, by FAA. Simply put, the technique in question centers on how to handle the tail wind portion when the airplane has lost airspeed and is sinking: open the throttles wide and raise the nose for maximum climb. Of course, this can put the airplane close to stall, so the instructions, which varied, said either to "pull back right up to stick shaker," the warning signal that stall is about to happen, or "pull back to just before stick shaker"—with no explanation on how to do that. This would be like trying to avoid walking into a wall in a dark room without using your hand to feel for it; some said you could go a smidgen beyond stick shaker because there's a slight buffer of speed between it and actual stall—that, of course, was another walk in the dark.

Pilots were told to watch the groundspeed versus airspeed, but this could only work if the airplane was INS equipped—perhaps GPS (the satellite navigation system) might do this, but few airplanes are so equipped today. Instruments to help fly through shear have been developed and are installed in many aircraft but not all by a goodly amount.

These efforts to teach or show pilots how to fly the phenomenon are all good stuff, but does such teaching signal pilots that shear can be flown? Does it cause pilots to consider shear more benign than it is or to feel less wary when thunderstorms lurk in the airport area? The facts are, of course, that some shear simply cannot be flown successfully, no matter what the procedure, and it's not always possible to tell which are the tough ones. The problem is aggravated by the nasty way these overpowering conditions have of appearing in a matter of moments or even seconds. Flight 191 is an example: as pointed out, the Learjet ahead found manageable rain and turbulence, but 59 seconds later, when 191 got there, the shaft of descending air had developed into a fierce and desperate condition. What we're saying is that shear flying techniques and instruments adapted to help fly through shear may result in pilots having less respect than necessary for the condition.

There have also been efforts made to discover and warn approaching aircraft of shear conditions. One form of this is called Low-Level Wind

Shear Alert System (LLWSA), which consists of many wind sensors placed in scattered locations on the airport; 110 airports in the country are presently equipped. If a wind difference above a certain value exists between sensors, then an alarm activates in the tower so the tower can warn incoming pilots. The system is not very effective, however. In the case of Flight 191, the LLWSA didn't speak up until *after* the crash and until the thunderstorm had dumped rain on the airport. Flight 191's problem occurred *outside* the airport's boundaries, where wind sensors didn't exist. And aside from the problem of location, the wind sensor technique doesn't pinpoint downdrafts.

As a result of intensive research, a better system called TDWR, for Terminal Doppler Weather Radar, has been developed. In TDWR, doppler-type radar locates and measures rain rates, wind gusts, and shear conditions; the system shows great promise and in tests at Denver has spotted wind shear well. FAA has programmed the equipment for use on airports across the land. The schedule of installation is for three per month, beginning March of 1993, until 47 airports are fitted by 1994. Of course, that doesn't cover all the airports used commercially, but it covers those most shear prone and most used.

An important, nagging problem with TDWR is how the information and warning is sent to the pilot. At present, plans call for telling the tower first and then having tower personnel relay the information to the pilot. Considering how fast shear conditions can form, the fumbling way things are overlooked, and the slowness of relay, the plan makes one fear that much of the brilliant technology may be wasted.

This problem has not gone without notice, and FAA has a program in the works to send information directly to the airplane via data link—meaning it will go directly from the TDWR to the airplane and be printed out in verbal description for the pilot to read. Later systems will data link a graphic form that would be, of course, easier for a busy pilot to interpret. The idea sounds good, but it's still in development, with test-printed data link expected to be in service by 1995 and the graphic form in the late 1990s. This is still a long way off, and thunderstorms will not wait for technical development.

What to do in the meantime? Is it oversimplification to use the idea we suggested of constant monitoring and running commentary telling the precise location of thunderstorms, their movement and severity, for all approaching aircraft to hear from the tower? Airlines could set standards that spell out how far a storm has to be from an airport before a flight can land. We know over 90 percent of shear cases are thunderstorm related, so if we can avoid getting too close to a thunderstorm, the chance of shear encounters has been almost eliminated. This system might cause more diversions, which would bother ATC, but it's an inexpensive way to be safe. Such equipment is available and could be purchased and set up easily and relatively inexpensively. But this simple, old-fashioned, Midwest commonsense idea doesn't work in FAA's complicated bureaucracy. Its absence is testimony to FAA's failings in leadership and ignorance of the good old U.S. principle of doing something *now*.

To FAA's credit, the problem of getting any hazardous weather information to pilots—Doppler radar is separate from this—is being tackled. The program, Integrated Terminal Weather System (or ITWS), is to quickly inform pilots of hazardous weather via data link to the cockpit. Typically the program is slow to mature, with a demonstration scheduled for 1993 and the system in service by 1996, and I suppose at that time the Doppler radar shear warning will be part of it. But why hasn't a simpler system been used in the meantime?

Someone is sure to ask, "Why can't the pilot use the airplane's radar for this?" The answer is simply that once an airplane is close to the airport things are too busy for crew members to stick their heads down in a radarscope and study it. Reading weather on a scope isn't a simple yes or no thing; it's necessary to concentrate and study without outside interference or distraction. Attractive though the idea may be, it isn't realistic.

Periodic accidents frequently evoke a certain element of hysteria, as press and industry emphasize the current popular accident cause; as examples, wind shear and jet upset have both had their moments of fame. The overemphasis on a single problem creates a hazard within the industry, with operations people and some pilots who may jump to conclusions influenced by the cause currently in vogue, too often resulting in their missing what's really going on. Take the accident of Northwest Airlines at Detroit, August 16, 1987, when a DC-9 tried to take off without the necessary wing flaps—the pilots failed to extend them, according to the NTSB report. The airplane became airborne after a long run and the stall warning activated; normally the warning would call for lowering the nose, but the pilot, instead, held a strong nose-up attitude, suggesting the use of wind shear–combatting technique. The NTSB report says if the nose had been lowered the aircraft could have climbed out and missed the pole it struck, causing the crash. Before the accident there were thunderstorms in the area; the latest ATIS broadcast noted, "windshear advisories are in effect." Did the pilot of the unfortunate aircraft think he was having a wind shear problem? Was he conditioned to think this by the prevailing rage about wind shear, wind shear warnings, and a weather report of cumulonimbus clouds in the vicinity? Did he immediately go to wind shear–flying techniques that had been emphasized in school, training literature, and press, almost as a conditioned reflex? The NTSB gave this hypothesis a quick brush-by in its report, but it looms large and real to one who's worked in this business a long time.

So we see that weather gathering and forecasting is as good as the state of the art allows, which, while not perfect, is very good. The problem is our failure to use and disseminate this valuable information to best advantage.

Evidence is strong that pilots are generally taught weather theory once and that it's then forgotten. It would seem appropriate, during recurrent training, to review some of this basic theory along with weather's effects on aircraft and operation.

Once I walked into a weather office with a young first officer of the "modern" school. As we entered, he quipped, "What are we going in here for—we're gonna go anyway."

That wasn't quite correct, but almost. My answer, however, was, "Maybe we are going anyway, but I want to know what's out there, how far off the forecast might be, and how we handle it."

16 | COMPUTERS FLY THE NEW AIRPLANES— OR DO THEY?

And then there were none—not Indians in this case but flight engineers. Airlines and manufacturers plus a receptive third member of the buddy club, the FAA, contrived to eliminate the position of the flight engineer, saying it was no longer needed. The manufacturers, especially Boeing, had been working to eliminate the flight engineer; doing this made the airplane more economical, hence more attractive to buyers—the airlines, who loved the idea. A special board of prestigious experts was formed to advise the government. They held hearings and called witnesses—of which I was one—but the atmosphere, as I settled in the chair at the hearing table, let me know this would be a wasted morning. The air reeked of prejudice. The board said flight engineers weren't needed in new aircraft, so FAA quickly approved a two-member crew—pilot and copilot—leaving no engineer in these aircraft.

The engineer was replaced by computers and systems designed to be automatic; pilots balked at this, but their battle was short-lived and they lost. All modern airplanes (Boeing 757 and 767, even the mighty 747-400; McDonnell-Douglas MD-11; Airbus 320, 321, 330, 340; and others) have only a two-pilot crew, no flight engineer. The two 747s delivered for use by the president of the United States as Air Force 1, however, still have a flight engineer's station and engineer.

Of course, dropping the flight engineer wasn't the reason computers moved into airplanes; the computer age had arrived, and the new, advanced airplane was a perfect place to use the technology. But it didn't take long for the manufacturers to recognize that a great side benefit would be their ability to replace the flight engineer with computers. This also opened the way for

COCKPIT of a two-pilot, no flight engineer Boeing 747-400. All modern cockpits use cathode ray tubes for most of the information to pilots. Note the Control Display Unit with many buttons that programs the Flight Management System. These are common to most modern airline and corporate aircraft regardless of manufacturer. (*Courtesy of the Boeing Company*)

new design concepts in the airplane. Doing away with the flight engineer meant removing the F/E station from the airplane and redesigning the systems to respond to computer commands rather than to a person who moved switches, valves, circuit breakers, and other manually operated things. The fuel system on Boeing's 767 and 757 aircraft, for example, is more direct and simple than on the older 707 designs. It lends itself to automatic operation.

The cockpit changed, becoming more high tech in appearance. Round-faced old instruments, called "steam gauges" in pilot slang, were replaced by cathode-ray tubes—CRTs—like a TV; colors are used not to make them pretty but for codes and status indications. The CRTs are glass-faced tubes, so the modern airplane cockpit quickly became known as the "glass cockpit," and even some call the airplanes "glass airplanes." Along with this came Control Display Units (CDUs) with 69 keys and a display ready to show pages of data. The CDU programs what's called the Flight Management System (FMS), a system and unit the pilots use for many things.

There are three major aspects of flying pilots must manage. One is mechanical management of the airplane, with systems such as fuel, electric, hydraulic, and so on, previously managed by the flight engineer but now done largely by computer. However, pilots still have to be alert to warning signals when all isn't well in a system and able to take over some of the computer's work manually. The second pilot task is flying the airplane; flying it in the literal sense of taking off, cruising and landing, and managing the navigation both horizontally and vertically. The third task is responding to and performing ATC's commands.

Has the advanced technology glass cockpit airplane—often called AVTECH—made the pilot's job less work? It certainly doesn't seem so, but let's explore the question.

Back again to the early days, in respect to the chore of flying the airplane. Once there was fundamentally one way to fly an airplane, with basic controls, but the modern airplane can be flown by three different means. One is the old basic stick, wheel, and rudder; flying blind, following an ILS to make an instrument approach, involved watching the directional gyro, artificial horizon, vertical speed, airspeed, and altimeter as well as the ILS indicator, with craftiness and know-how to outguess the vagaries of wind and the ILS beam's bends and scallops.

The second way is the Flight Director (FD), which is an instrument to use while hand flying. It "thinks" and does the anticipation necessary to follow an ILS for you, and it helps overcome some of the system's vagaries; all the pilot does is follow the instrument's indications, which is simple to do. The Flight Director was invented back in the 1940s but came into real prominence with the 707. It is computer driven and makes hand flying a lot easier.

The third method is to have the automatic pilot do it all. It's directed by the same computers as the FD, and normal procedure is for the autopilot to fly the airplane and the pilot to monitor its action by watching the FD. Automatic landings are the way to go; the autopilot relieves the pilot of the manual labor of flying, which requires very high concentration on a few instruments, and allows the pilot to monitor the approach, double-check altitude, think about what to do if an abort has to be made, and a host of other things. I remember my first automatic landings. I was amazed at how relaxed I was even when making an approach to a 100-foot ceiling. I felt as though I had time to act and that I was well aware of everything going on; whereas when hand flying an approach, I was concentrating strongly, almost mesmerized by the group of instruments concerned with the approach, and not giving the attention to cross-checking I really should have simply because I was too damn busy.

One might ask, why bother having a FD if the autopilot will fly the airplane so well? Well, for one thing, if the autopilot fails and it's necessary to take over by hand, the FD makes it a lot easier than the old basic way. Pilots also like to hand fly from time to time to "keep their hands in."

The modern airplane is flown mostly on autopilot, and airlines encourage—in some cases demand—that pilots use the autopilot for all flying after takeoff through and including landing. At least they did in the first flush of the new airplanes, but this has been modified to some extent after experience with the airplanes.

A point not to overlook is the fact the computers, hence the navigation information and autopilot, must be programmed by the pilots through the CDU to the FMS, and then switches must be flipped to turn the FD and autopilot on and to set them up to follow the FMS's commands. Actually, there is more than one autopilot, as most airplanes have two and some three. Programming for navigation includes route selection, or creating a route along which the autopilot will direct the airplane. The pilots can see the route and their progress on a CRT map display. Programming includes information so the autopilot will descend when desired and cross certain points at certain altitudes. All great stuff, if the programming has been done correctly, or the computer doesn't have a hiccup as computers will have from time to time. Because of the computers and programming, "wise" people like to say that the pilot has become a systems manager. This expression grates on my sensibilities, because whether you're pushing buttons or moving old-fashioned controls, you'd better have a lot of flying knowledge, background and judgment—which makes you a pilot, not a systems manager. The computer for all its miscellany is just another tool for the trade.

The problem at the present is that the interrelationship between crew and computer for programming, reading CRTs, and responding to warning lights and sounds hasn't been satisfactorily defined—with the result that sometimes crew work load and distraction are formidable. There is also an unanswered philosophical question of how much basic awareness and command should be taken from the pilot and given to the computer. Some aircraft seem to have done this to an extreme, and others in less drastic fashion. Personally, I like the statement attributed to John I. Miller, test pilot and chief of McDonnell-Douglas MD-11 flight operations—that's the latest McDonnell-Douglas long-range wide-body airplane, the big offspring of the DC-10.

Miller said, "Computers should never prevent a pilot from doing anything. They should certainly discourage him from doing certain things, and they should prevent him from inadvertent excursions, *but should not deny him access to his full control authority.*" (Emphasis mine.)

The latest Airbus aircraft are probably the most-computerized airplanes of the lot. Their controls hark back to the joystick of aviation's early days—with a great difference. The joystick they have, which is about 10 inches tall and mounted near the captain's left windowsill—the first officer's right—is not connected directly to any controls; rather, the stick "talks" to computers via electrical wires (hence the phrase "fly by wire"). Pull back to raise the nose, and you send a signal to a computer that digests what you've asked for and compares it with the airplane's flight condition in relation to stall, high speed limits, or other factors and then raises the nose the amount it considers a proper discretionary response.

The computer also takes over responsibility for certain flying basics that all pilots are accustomed to as part of flying. For instance, when you bank an airplane in order to turn, the nose wants to go down, so the pilot instinctively pulls back on the wheel to keep the nose up as the plane banks into a turn. Not so when flying with the Airbus stick-computer; the system automatically does the pulling back, essentially taking from the pilot a feel for flying that is part of the basics. The stick-computer combination also sets trim automatically, coordinates the turn, and holds the bank attitude, as well as a few other things not directly tied to basic flying.

The computer will not allow the pilot to manage controls so as to stall the airplane or exceed maximum allowable speeds and G forces in combination with bank angles. This may sound good: the computer keeps those dumb pilots from making mistakes. But does it really? Does this take away a feeling of awareness of the flight condition, authority, and command, leaving the pilot a little miffed and confused as to who's doing what? Long arguments can result from asking these questions, which aren't confined to airplanes and computers but embrace the wider aspects of our lives: how much thinking and doing should the computer be allowed to do in relation to people's judgment? An answer to this question is seriously needed in aviation.

In July 1990, in Miami, I flew the Airbus 320 simulator, which was my first experience with the side stick. I liked its location and action and found it easy to get used to; on first takeoff, I was hardly airborne before feeling perfectly at home with the side stick.

But the glass airplanes are not perfect, and all have areas you question. One problem with present design may well be that much of it has been created with military aircraft philosophy. Military systems are great stuff for shooting down other airplanes, and for precision bombing, but airline flying is much different. The airline pilot isn't a pumped-up young person sitting on a parachute and able to "punch out" when all goes ape. NASA is working on the human factors in computerized airplane design, but NASA, with only 7 percent of it's 1992 budget devoted to aeronautics, has its head in space and is slow to get things done for the airplane side of its responsibility.

Many computer design types, who are nonpilots, seem to think computers can do it all. In their heart of hearts, computer systems designers seem to believe pilots could just as well stay home. Considering that the computer-human relationship is still in its infancy and far from being perfected, the present aircraft are probably aircraft of a transition period. In some future time we're going to have great airline aircraft with an

AIRBUS A320 COCKPIT. Note the side sticks on the left and right that take the place of control wheels. (*Courtesy of Airbus Industrie*)

unconfused relationship between the chips and the pilot, but the pilot will never sit back and let George do it if only for the simple reason that computers, even computer systems with redundancy, will fail, if rarely. I fly gliders, and our club has as members some high-powered computer experts from the Boston-Cambridge silicon area, and they keep assuring me, over rainy day, coffee-consuming bull sessions, that computers should not be talked of as "if" they might fail; they assure me that the phrase should be "when" they fail, as surely they will at some time. Pilots tell me of computers doing strange things. One pilot recalled ATC calling and saying, "You're 6 miles to the right of course." A quick check by the pilot showed the FMS indicating the airplane right on course. Back to raw data though, and, yes, ATC was correct; they were 6 miles off course. No explanation except computer discrepancy—the usual strange things computers occasionally do in your home or workplace. So backup and monitoring through raw data are still very necessary, which demonstrates that the computer in an airplane hasn't *replaced* the old ways but *added* to them.

Certainly computers have great advantages and are helpful, but they're still a long way from flying "solo." The reliability isn't as yet sufficient to guide an instrument approach through mountainous terrain, or any low approach, unless verified with definite fixes over VORs, ILSs, marker beacons, or similar units. Computer software is not perfect; way down in the software's lines of code, which could be as many as a million, there may be an unknown error lurking, ready to do harm, because it is impossible to test software completely—it simply isn't practical. It's worth remembering that the first interplanetary U.S. spacecraft, Mariner 1, was lost because a minus sign was left out of the software.

But we're talking about what's out there flying today. Our present AVTECH glass cockpit airplanes—what are they like?

Entering an AVTECH (glass) cockpit is a little like entering a modern art museum. The various colors, pleasing to the eye, that make up the lines—some solid, some dashed—on the CRTs look more like an abstract work of art by Mondrian or Davis than the traditional airplane's instruments. The atmosphere is pleasant and creates an immediate "gee whiz" reaction. Switches and annunciators are scattered among the system's lights and diagrams; the few old-fashioned instruments used as backup are set off to one side. Landing gear and flap levers are located, much as in older aircraft, on the right side ahead of the throttles.

At first glance the cockpit seems less cluttered—one manufacturer even brags, in advertisements, that it has done away with many instruments, but this is an illusion because the CRT that takes the place of many instruments actually has all those instruments crammed onto its face. The CRT displays the artificial horizon, airspeed, different kinds of altitude, vertical speed, heading, and a profusion of status information. However, there is a bothersome technique problem about the CRT in that the eye sees and focuses in a cone of small angle, like a narrow beam of light illuminating a spot on the wall. Things outside that area do not appear as sharp. Look at the date under Wednesday on a wall calendar about 3 feet away, for instance. If you stare at it without moving your eyeball, Wednesday's date will look sharp, but Tuesday's and Thursday's are unclear and Friday and Monday impossible to read. You have to scan, move the eyeball side to side, to distinguish with precision dates other than Wednesday's. It's the same with the CRT, except that you must scan up and down in addition for items above and below, as well as those side to side.

One might say that scanning the CRT requires small eye movement, but there's another phenomenon that indicates it's easier to scan across a slightly larger distance. I first experienced this in the 747. It had larger instruments, and the altitude for approach, for one example, was on the right side of the instrument, which, while not a CRT, was about that size. During an instrument approach I found my eyes did not include the altitude in their focus cone and required me to scan right to see it, but in scanning, my eyes automatically went to the altimeter outside the new, "all-inclusive," instrument. It seemed easier to see something a little farther from my usual focus than close to it. It told me that big instruments weren't an improvement; they were just bigger with room for other information, which could create clutter. Feeling this might just be a personal appraisal, I asked a number of 747 pilots if they had the same experience, and almost everyone had—though the realization was often a surprise to them.

If you really want to get esoteric, there's also a psychological factor in having two different kinds of information mingled together. In this case, there is information used to fly the airplane, such as the artificial horizon and Flight Director, but scattered around on the instrument face, additionally, is status information—what autopilot and navigation modes are set, for example. The point is that one likes to use instruments of flying in a flowing fashion, to scan with all thoughts on flying; moving eyes from artificial horizon to heading, for example, should be an uninterrupted *mental* path, but if a status annunciation is close by the eye, one's mind stops, disengaging from the thought of flying and moving to a different mental focus in order to digest what something that has nothing to do with flying is saying. Does this mean a microsecond readjustment of thought, or perhaps even more important, does the mind become used to the idea it's just status information of a lower order of importance than flying? Does this increase the chance of status information going unnoticed? With the status annunciator outside the flight instruments located with other, old-style annunciators, the pilot, at a convenient moment in scan, looks at it to ensure that the status of everything is proper. Does the crowded CRT cause a subconscious downgrading of the importance of some information? This is a good, contentious question that some research should attempt to answer.

A designer can crowd a mass of information on a CRT—the amount of information is only limited by computer software. This seems to have given the "look what I can do" people a chance to put all sorts of nifty ideas into practice on instruments, which immediately poses the question of whether or not all this is necessary.

While the instrument panel of today may *appear* less cluttered than in the days before computers, a glance down to the pedestal below reveals added items: a keyboard with 68 keys to program the FMS, which is the performance heart of the airplane (actually, not one keyboard, but two; one each for captain and copilot).

In looking back to older aircraft, flying essentially the same tasks, my feeling is that it may have been a lot easier. I may have had to store more in my head—minimum altitude, speed desired, and other things that are now marked on the instrument face—but is that necessarily better or worse than the modern method? And to what degree? A NASA report on the impact of cockpit automation tends to substantiate thinking that the older airplanes are less work than the modern glass cockpit aircraft. Actually the fact that the modern AVTECH airplanes are more work is now generally accepted by psychologists exploring this area.

I'd love to see a research project done by NASA or a university like MIT in which a group of experienced line pilots plus designers, engineers, and human factors experts would go over the complex instruments, new autopilot functions, and flight management systems. Taking each individual item in turn, the study would ask the question, "Is this really necessary—does it help, hinder, or add work?" then toss out the unneeded and see if the airplane would be easier to operate, with less chance for error. In other words by simplifying the operations, with less to program or manage, the chance for error is reduced. To establish what we mean, the proper group should inspect each portion of flight—from start-up, through taxi, takeoff, climb, cruise, descent, landing, taxi in, and parking plus the unexpected changes required by ATC and weather. The group should then design and install computer systems to fit *those* needs, no more, leaving out the tricky stuff and keeping it simple to the task. Perhaps this kind of scrutiny already has been done, but if so, it hasn't shown up in the new airplanes yet.

The airplane has many warning systems that act as reminders so pilots will not forget important things. These systems sound like good safety backups, but they raise questions: Does the mind, knowing there is a reminder, feel it doesn't *have* to remember because there will be a reminder? Can the fact of the reminder—or remembering to look at the reminder—desensitize the mind, discouraging it from doing its own remembering? These too, are good questions that need answering.

Once we had no reminders to tell us the altitude cleared to; when ATC said, "Climb to 8000," the number went in your head, and you were well aware that 8000 was what you were aiming for. The sense of its importance was strong. It went into the copilot's consciousness, also, because procedure required the copilot to call out, in this case at 7000 feet, "One thousand to go." Now when ATC says, "Cleared to 8000," one of the pilots twists the knob on a gadget, which registers 8000 feet, then goes back to other tasks, knowing the autopilot will automatically level the airplane off at 8000 feet. The gadget has a light that comes on as the airplane approaches the target altitude; if the altitude is missed, then a tone is heard 250 feet after the proper altitude, which seems a bit weird because the little light showing that you're approaching the altitude can be missed. Shouldn't the tone sound before, not *after,* the altitude? If you miss 8000 feet and climb through it, that's called an "altitude bust." NASA's ASRS tells us that the warning devices and automatic pilots haven't reduced altitude busts—there still are just as many. Is this reminder part of a set-it-and-forget-it mentality, a creator of a kind of complacency? Has the work load increased so the crew is busy enough to miss a tone warning or not notice that the autopilot failed to capture and level off at 8000?

Other items fall in this category, such as the vertical speed indicator showing a rate of descent by a needle on the CRT. But full scale of the instrument is only 2000 feet per minute; if the rate is more than that, then the needle's color changes from green to amber. Rates in excess of 2000 feet per minute are encountered on every flight. Does a color change always register with a pilot busy scanning all instruments? A picture of the location of the needle is important in order to get an idea if the airplane is climbing or descending, and how much. A large vertical speed needle displacement immediately catches a pilot's eye, warning of possible trouble in the flight path; the old-fashioned "steam gauge" vertical speed dial had that. Does a needle's color change catch the pilot's attention as well? Or is it too subtle?

As your eyes wander above the instrument panel to the glare shield, just under the windshield, you see the complex array of controls for autopilots—altitude, airspeed, climb and descent, heading, ILS, autoland and others—30 in all on a Boeing 767. This array is called the Mode Control Panel.

Nothing is more dramatic in the new airplane than the autoflight system, which does a multitude of tasks. Its job isn't just to keep the airplane straight

BOEING 767 cockpit. Note the control wheels rather than the side sticks in the Airbus. (*Courtesy of the Boeing Company*)

and level; now it does all kinds of tricks programmed through the Mode Control Panel, above the instrument panel, or the FMS below it: follows a course, climbs and descends and decides when to do so, controls speed, levels off at the proper altitude, and lands and stops the airplane.

The various modes can segregate the pilot's flying; he or she can hand fly, for instance, while the autothrottles manage power. This means the pilot can make a planned descent during which the autothrottle is putting on or removing power without being certain of precise amounts or trends. Indian Air Lines 1990 crash in an Airbus 320 was a case of the power not being applied in time when the airplane was leveling off near the ground. The pilots were blamed for improperly using the system, but I cannot help wondering what would have happened if they'd been flying an old-fashioned airplane without all this gadgetry. If they'd been handling the power themselves, would the accident have happened? The answer has to be no because the pilots would have been aware of power requirements and would have managed the power needs through hands-on throttles. The Airbus answer was to add safeguards to counter crew "overconfidence" as Airbus put it. The safeguard is an additional warning—a "voice" that says, "speed, speed," if the energy of the aircraft gets too low. This adds another warning on top of dozens of others.

When autothrottle is in use on the Airbus, the throttle levers sit motionless, something that pilots have complained about. In Boeing airplanes, the throttle levers move even when controlled automatically. But in checking the levers' position and movement pilots, at a glance, can have an idea of what's going on, and they like this.

Basic flying—using the wheel, rudder pedals, and throttles—links pilot and aircraft dynamics, the movement of one control interacting with others. But autothrottles in the new aircraft remove one of the three cues and destroy total pilot knowledge and sense of what the airplane will do in the immediate future. Autothrottle is akin to an automobile cruise control; it's useful on an open highway, but when you turn off the highway into traffic on a narrow, undulating country road, you shut it off because you want the use of the accelerator (throttle) along with brakes and steering for total command. The feel of interrelationship between controls is necessary. If total autocontrol is being used—autopilot and autothrottles—then the pilot monitors all as a unit and can keep tabs on what's going on, but to have the pilot fly the airplane, while autothrottles manage power, as many procedures require or recommend, is a hazardous way of doing things.

Autopilots aren't used until the airplane is airborne, generally at a minimum altitude of 1000 feet, but pilots are advised to use autothrottle from start of takeoff. At 1000 feet the autopilot is engaged; the pilot turns knobs to effect climb, resets an airspeed bug, selects an altitude for level off, pushes a different autothrottle button for climb power, and engages the navigation mode for the autopilot to follow FMS commands. Too much at this critical time? At times it seems so, but it's probably a matter of crew procedure and coordination. Such coordination may be done well, but between flying, ATC communication, and ATC requests for course and altitude changes, one crew member may not know what the other is doing or has done.

Exploring the airplane further you find a panel overhead with a large assortment of lights, switches, and controls devoted to airplane systems—hydraulic, electrical, fuel, pressurization, air-conditioning, pneumatics, ice and rain protection, flight controls, emergency, and others, along with a few dozen lights that vary from warning to annunciation. It's a busy area. Next comes the pedestal, that area between the pilots where throttles, spoilers, and flap controls live, along with radio and radar tuning. Most interesting and imposing are the two CDUs used to program the FMS. FMS controls and informs pilots of navigation, automatic radio tuning, display on instruments of where you're going, guidance commands laterally, speed, altitude and thrust, and a long list of performance parameters that run from best economy speed to approach reference data—a powerful and imposing bank of computer capability. Its CRT has a dozen lines for data with extra pages available if there's too much for page 1—and there are many, many pages.

An additional item with a cluster of buttons to push and written messages to read is now being added to cockpits. It is called ACARS, for Airinc Communications Addressing and Reporting System. The idea is to cut down on radio communication and do some pilot chores automatically; previously, pilots reported to their company, by radio, the clock time away from the gate, time off the ground, time on touchdown after flight, and time in at the gate. ACARS does this automatically through a radio network that receives and directs messages to the airline dispatch office. How does ACARS know when the airplane has departed or arrived? With information created by electrical contact when the cabin door is closed, the landing gear tilted after takeoff, and the reverse sequence for landing and parking at the jet-way gate. The unit will also send position, weather, delay, maintenance, diversion, and other reports—all automatically. The crew can also originate messages by typing them on the unit and then pushing a button to send them off. Transmission like this, from airplanes to ground, is called "down link"; from ground to airplane it's "up link." The ACARS space for writing is small, so the weather radar screen is used to display up to 12 lines of ACARS. This usage may be delayed if the radar is being used for ducking thunderstorms, which should have a higher priority than receiving a company message, but this has yet to be sorted out.

ACARS is good stuff that cuts down the possibility of a misunderstood voice message. There's a plan for ATC clearances to come via ACARS, so that pilots can read them again, with less chance for error. Actually, some of this is being done now especially on long-range flights, and will be universal soon—an excellent advance. It is visualized that the pilot will see the ATC message, digest it, and then, if it's acceptable, push a button and send it into the FMS, which will direct the autopilot to fly the route and altitude ATC demands.

It all sounds good, but the fear with devices, as always, is that they will be used too much, keeping the crew busy typing messages or receiving them. Down link promises well if it's realized from the start that discipline is required for its use; otherwise it becomes an added distraction that increases work load and the time one crew member spends head down with the device instead of head up looking for traffic or scanning instruments and airplane condition. Future up link will activate a cockpit paper printer, spitting out hard copy. Some systems do now. Will tearing off and reading copy create more work and distraction for pilots? Might a flight engineer be useful for this? How about a flying secretary? And, of course, the system will need a warning light and/or sound to alert the crew of a message and of any malfunction in the ACARS system. As cockpit room is always limited, I'll bet there's head scratching going on right now over the question: "Where do we put the darned thing?"

Attention must also be given to the airplane and its health, making certain that engines and systems are functioning properly. Computers do much of this. Let's consider the systems—electric, hydraulic, pneumatics, engines, air-conditioning, pressurization, and others. When something goes wrong, a message comes up on CRTs in beautiful color, telling the pilots what went wrong and the automatic corrections made to cope with the problem; if a generator fails, the CRT says so and then displays a message saying what the automatic system has done—reduced the electrical load and removed heat from galleys and coffeemakers—along with other things of a more important nature, for example. Some messages instruct the pilots to accomplish a task.

Different manufacturers do these things in different ways, depending on the firm's philosophy. Boeing believes in telling the pilots what's going on but doesn't load them with multitudinous information that may be superfluous. Problems are announced on a CRT in the middle of the panel. This is called EICAS for Engine Indication and Crew Alerting System. EICAS for Boeing 767-type aircraft can display 230 different messages about anything from access doors (a door isn't closed securely) to a wheel well fire. Airbus tends to display schematic diagrams of the system involved, and if a generator goes out, the CRT instantly displays a diagram of the electrical system with the failure emphasized and what's been done; the system contains 12 pages of diagrams. CRT's display screen only holds so much information, so the CRT, like a book, has pages, which are turned by pressing a control switch (a key, as on a typewriter) or appear automatically. Some 400 aircraft systems messages are possible. Whose system is best? Each has its pluses and minuses, and arguing pro and con is salesman's stuff.

To get the pilot's attention should something fail, both aural and visual signals "shout" or light up so the pilots will note and investigate. Many warnings are both visual and aural. Following is a typical list of aural signal types from Airbus: continuous repetitive chime, single chime, cavalry charge, click, cricket, intermittent buzzer, continuous buzzer, C chord, and synthetic voice. If you're a poor musician, as I am, how do you know a C chord? The cavalry charge is also a provocative item.

In addition there are lights and CRT-written notices of many colors for various degrees of warning. A list of colors used: red, amber, green, white, blue, magenta, and cyan. The alerts are announced according to their importance. A typical description: *red warning,* situation needing immediate action; *amber warning,* abnormal situation needing crew awareness; and *caution warning,* amber light or CRT message, monitoring. Failures come in different classes too: *independent* denotes an isolated piece of equipment, *secondary* is loss of equipment or system resulting from primary failure, and *primary* announces failure of equipment or system that could affect other systems.

Warning gadgetry isn't any guarantee of an oversight prevention; there have been two dramatic accidents in recent years when an airplane crashed because the takeoff flaps had not been extended. The NTSB reports blame the pilots for not extending the flaps. But both airplanes were equipped with a warning device to alert the pilot, by sound, if the takeoff flaps were not down at start of takeoff. In both instances the device failed to work. The NTSB mentioned this but merely put it down in the list of contributing causes. It's a difficult thing to judge, but when the airplane was built and certified by FAA, it was recognized pilots might forget to put the flaps down; consequently a warning system to cover this possible human error was designed and installed. When flaps were overlooked, however, and the warning system failed, the pilots got the blame. But shouldn't the warning system's failure at least share the blame?

It seems to me that warnings in aircraft—beyond a certain few—are admissions of design failure, admissions that the design and perhaps systems are too complicated and the only cure is more warnings to the crew. This relieves designer, manufacturer, operator, and FAA of responsibility for problems, loading it on the pilots instead. An old saw in aviation goes: "If you can't cure the problem, say you did by adding a page to the manual or a warning light, whistle, or bell."

All this indicates that automation doesn't relieve pilots of the need for attention to what's going on in the mechanical end of the airplane. No matter the double-talk or learned dissertations of manufacturer's engineers, pilots, and salespeople, the simple truth is that dropping the flight engineer has put a greater burden on the pilots. The economic "gain" by dumping the flight engineer is difficult to assess from the viewpoint of accidents; who is to say that the two caused by trying to take off without takeoff flaps extended might not have been prevented if there'd been a flight engineer who noticed and called attention to flaps not being extended. Or other accidents in which mechanical problems were a factor: might they have been prevented if a flight engineer had been there to relieve the pilot's attention on mechanical things so their major attention could have been on flying the airplane? And who has evaluated incidents of airplanes *with a flight engineer* in which major mechanical failures occurred but the flight made it safely or with minimum loss of life? No one we've heard of—if such has been done, the results have been kept from the public.

The things that could go wrong, and the procedures to use for combating them, are considerable and add to pilot concerns. Combating these possible failures requires too many steps and procedures to remember, so pilots have lengthy checklists aside from the normal checklists; these are called the abnormal checklist, or sometimes; nonnormal checklist. They encompass many things: for example, engine fire or electrical smoke or fire. Engine fire would read like this: pilot reads item on left; the other pilot accomplishes it and responds as indicated:

THRUST LEVER _____CLOSE. Disengage autothrottle if on.
FUEL CONTROL SWITCH _____CUTOFF.
ENGINE FIRE SWITCH _____PULL. If engine fire warning light remains illuminated:
ENGINE FIRE SWITCH _____ROTATE. Rotate switch to stop and hold for 1 second. After 30 seconds, if engine fire warning light remains illuminated:
ENGINE FIRE SWITCH_____ROTATE TO REMAINING BOTTLE. Rotate to the stop and hold for 1 second.

There are about 20 different nonnormal items that have checklists.

Much of this will be on the EICAS, maybe someday all of it rather than a hand-held list. Once the flight engineer read these and took care of some items while the pilots busied themselves doing other things. Now it's one pilot reading and the other acting on the items.

I'm not particularly trying to reinstate the flight engineer, but I am trying to make the case that the F/E's demise was judged on old principles of economy without thought of working the flight engineer into the modern airplane with provision and procedures to fit. By provision I mean computers and instruments created with the thought a flight engineer would be on board. Is the flight engineer needed? An FAA Fact Sheet of October 1989 about a project for researching Aircraft Command in Emergency Situations had an interesting opening paragraph with a potent sentence: "The evolution toward a two-man cockpit crew creates a tight manpower situation in an emergency."

So FAA, in an honest technical appraisal divorced from political Washington, said what the political policy part of FAA wouldn't admit. But willy-nilly the flight engineer is long gone, without much doubt never to be seen again. Let's hope the eventual computer information and automatic action will safely cover the loss. It is provocative, however, to think how useful the flight engineer might have become if his or her task were designed and expanded using today's technology. But why cogitate on a deceased horse?

There is a lot to be learned and remembered as pilots go through school on new airplanes. Much of this may never come into play; certain failures are rare enough that a pilot may fly through a long career and never experience them or, for many years, never hear a particular and perhaps unusual aural warning and therefore not recognize it when it does sound off.

One fine day I was comfortably settled in at 35,000 feet on a 747, with all going well, when suddenly we all became conscious of a horn blowing, although not loud. The crew members all looked at each other: "What the hell's that?" Nothing seemed wrong.

"Maybe somebody wants to pass us," a crew member remarked trying to be funny. But one of us pulled up from memory that a horn had something to do with pressurization, and sure enough, our cabin altitude had slowly sneaked above 10,000 feet, the trigger point to set off the horn. The problem was minor and quickly corrected. Pressurization loss is so rare an event that most of us never had the problem—certainly none of us on board that day—and the horn warning had long since drifted way back in our minds. In today's advanced aircraft we'd have quickly looked to the EICAS, and it would have displayed a message saying something like, "pressurization."

But these CRT messages are mostly for what might be termed "routine" problems with the generator, hydraulic pump, fuel pump, and so on. On rare occasions, however, compounded or unusual problems develop that automation or procedures don't cover; when these happen, the crew has to analyze, diagnose, and decide what to do. And this isn't easy because in-depth knowledge of the systems isn't taught. Schooling, for the most part, is on a basis of what the industry calls "need to know."

"If this red light comes on, push this button, and the problem's taken care of" is typical school information. But then some pilot asks, "What happens when I push the button; what's behind it?"

"You don't really need to know—you can't do anything about it anyway."

There might not even be an instructor involved; the instruction might simply be the student sitting in a cubicle watching a VCR tape. I've suffered through some of these VCR tapes, and they're a sure cure for insomnia. There's no mention nor is there any explanation of the system's use and philosophy—only a pointing up of the gadgetry, with little information about where it's used in the sequence of events, its degree of importance, or when to be careful of what. And a big vacuum exists in the fact one cannot ask a VCR questions and get answers.

For the most part, the manuals pilots are given to study and keep for reference are abominably written, difficult to interpret, and poorly organized. Nor do the manuals dig into systems so you really get to know them. This was true when I checked out in the 747 and I felt a need to know more about the airplane than the manual described. Fortunately, I had a friend in maintenance, and he "appropriated" a 747 maintenance handbook for me, from which I learned a lot more about the airplane. I frequently referred to it through the years and still have it. I also have pilot manuals for our latest aircraft, and they haven't improved a bit.

The need-to-know teaching method saves time and money; to teach more would require a lengthy school with periodic reviews necessary. It's a matter of economics: pilots receive pay for attending school because school has kept them from remunerative flying. And, in fairness, pilots themselves are reluctant to sit in school for long periods. In the DC-3, DC-4, and Connie days the airplane was studied in detail until pilots complained that they didn't have to know, for instance, "the air pressure in the nosewheel tire." Economics and the pilot complaints have shortened training time and hence limited in-depth knowledge, but perhaps the pendulum has swung too far in the direction of simplification.

"The computer knows" seems to be the answer, but computers are not perfect. In the Boeing 767 Lauda crash in Thailand, which seems to have resulted from an unusual in-flight activation of a thrust reverser that affected the flight characteristics of the airplane, one action of the crew in this desperate situation was to go digging in a document trying to learn what was wrong—clearly, the computers with their CRTs had run out of brains.

This error in the present form of education was apparent 50 years ago to the writer, philosopher, and pioneer pilot Antoine de Saint-Exupéry, as he wrote, "Today people receive instruction, but they are no longer educated."

Little has changed.

The problem, of course, comes in the rare case when more than one failure occurs, or "nonroutine" failures as in the United Air Lines, Sioux City,

Iowa, DC-10 crash, July 19, 1989, when an engine structural failure cut the three hydraulic lines that activate the flight controls, making the aircraft a floundering, helpless vehicle. There were no procedures or checklists to cover it. Crew ingenuity gave a modicum of control, but not enough to prevent a catastrophic crash landing. This occurrence was out of the "routine" failure spectrum. The DC-10 could not be included in the "modern glass cockpit" category, but the failure of redundancy, procedures, and some automatic features make the point that not all failures are a kind that can be anticipated. When the data is in the computers, your chances are excellent because of systems backups by more than one computer. You're not in trouble because a computer fails—others instantly take over the task. The serious problem arises when the computer's programs don't know how to handle the odd happenings, and this is compounded if the pilot's education on the airplane is restricted so he or she doesn't have sufficient know-how to understand what's going on and how to cope with it. As airplanes become more dependent on computer-driven functions and pilots know less about the innards of the systems, this problem will be more serious. It deserves serious research and attention.

Now let's address the advanced technology airplane in relation to its flying and navigation. Computers not only help navigate and fly but they do it more efficiently. How? One way is to maintain the best center of gravity position. An airplane gets better mileage with the center of gravity (CG) as far aft as possible. A computer can inspect the weight distribution as it changes with fuel burn, decide where it should be, and then direct fuel movement fore or aft to put the CG right at the optimum position—that's one way to save money. While the pilots could conceivably do this, it would be a big addition to their work load and even then would not be as precise as a computer can manage it. This CG management is one way to save money and increase the airplane's range.

The computer systems also react to turbulence—air bumps. When a computer-managed airplane encounters turbulence, the smart system causes the control surfaces to move in a way that reduces strain on the wings. If strain can be reduced, the airplane can be built with lighter structure, which makes it more economical.

Part of an airplane's design is to make it stable enough that pilots can fly it easily and without undue effort that would result in fatigue. But an airplane less stable can be designed differently, with smaller surfaces like fin and rudder and stabilizer. Computers allow this design, which gives better and more economical performance. The computer does the flying and isn't bothered by fatigue as a pilot would be who'd have to concentrate intensely and move controls constantly—which would be impossible, especially considering all the other tasks that require attention. This method of a computer flying the airplane is generally referred to as "control augmentation" and is quite common. The weird-looking stealth aircraft, F-117 and B-2, would be unmanageable by old-fashioned direct pilot to control; computers fly them.

Another gain in efficiency is through the FMS, which does a lot of the planning pilots once did either with hand-held circular slide rules or crusty old rules of thumb. Example: we're at 39,000 feet approaching our destination; when is the best time to begin descent, and what speed during descent is most economical? The FMS computers figure this to a gnat's eyebrow and tell when to start down. ATC, however, is often a counter to this efficiency: the pilot has to be cleared to make that descent. If ATC cannot allow it because of traffic, or requests the airplane to start down earlier, then the economics are shattered and rules of thumb are followed. But many times the system works and certainly is better than rough estimates.

Another saving is learning the answers to the questions, What's the best altitude to fly on a certain route segment, and with the prevailing winds, what's the best speed to use? This calculation is a snap for the computer. The FMS has a multitude of quick answers to help pilots, too many to enumerate here, but suffice to say the FMS and its computers have given flexibility and fast response to flight operations.

Navigation planning is also easier on these airplanes. Say we're going from San Francisco to Atlanta; before takeoff we type in "KSFO" and then "KATL," and the computer loads all the courses and distances and on its colorful CRT shows the airplane's progress—the navigation radio stations are tuned in automatically. Really neat stuff.

The FMS is programmed before takeoff with airplane weights, fuel, and routes. This input requires considerable time by the crew and careful double-checking. Once in flight the computers, aside from steering the airplane, tell of fuel used and remaining, time to destination, and many other things we had to figure with circular slide rulers. To list all the possibilities within the FMS would result in this being an airplane manual and course of instruction; suffice to say the computer has been a major advance. In simple form pilots seldom have to refer to maps or scratch figures on paper, and the day may come when they no longer even carry maps and charts.

But these computer systems are complicated. The FMS's 68 keys and many pages of data give ample opportunity for human error. The systems' performance also must be under suspicion; they need monitoring to see they're doing the right thing, doing what they were programmed to do.

The major problem is the human: is the data typed into the CDU correct? Good airline procedure requires cross-checking by both crew members and precise policy as to who does the programming. These procedures work in normal operation but tend to break down when the unusual occurs. Say you're in flight, busy descending, and ATC suddenly requires a route change. In an instant all the slick FMS programming is nullified. The pilot flying must look down to the CDU and reprogram; pilot number two is busy responding to radio calls or looking out the windshield for traffic or, perhaps, checking some aircraft system that's showing an irregularity. The number two pilot doesn't get a chance to watch and double-check as pilot number one reprograms the FMS. If the second crew member is able to check, this person, then, is also looking down at the CDU to watch what the programming crew member is typing in. Then both are heads down looking in, but no one is looking out!

There are times when simply flying the airplane is the answer. A quick change in runway, an overshoot procedure, or ATC demands when close to the ground may best be handled by "clicking off," as it's called, which means pressing a button on the control wheel that shuts off all the fancy stuff and gives the airplane back to the pilot to fly the old-fashioned way. The tendency to reach down and "fly out" by reprogramming the FMS when close to the ground is dangerous. A captain told me of a missed approach he had to make in which ATC gave clearance to climb out on a course different from the normal missed approach programmed in the FMS. Both pilots reached down and started pushing buttons to reprogram until one said, "Jesus! We're only 800 feet, with our heads down playing with buttons!" The captain quickly "clicked off" and flew manually. Something like this is a delicate situation, difficult to spell out in procedure, dependent on pilot judgment, and potentially very dangerous indeed.

The computerized airplane with its Flight Management System is designed to reduce pilot work load, but it periodically does the opposite and increases it. This is a point worth enlargement.

The NASA report *Human Factors of Advanced Technology ("Glass Cockpit") Transport Aircraft* tells an interesting tale. This article reported on a three-year study of airline crews flying advanced technology aircraft—the ones that are computerized. It was authored by Earl L. Wiener of the University of Miami. He's a pilot, although not an airline pilot, and a master in the business of pilots and psychology. Recognized as being a realist, he attended ground schools, rode on many flights in the jump seat, and questioned 201 volunteer pilots, who were given anonymity so they would speak freely. An impressive study by the RAF (Royal Air Force) Institute of Aviation Medicine using an extensive questionnaire that was answered by 1372 pilots reported much the same answers Weiner's NASA report revealed.

The conclusions were not sharply defined; pilots praised the new aircraft, and pilots criticized them. A few comments, while not unanimous, were sufficient to be of concern:

- "The flight engineer is missed." A few said they liked just two in the

cockpit.
- "Training concentrated too much on the CDU and FMS and not enough on the airplane."
- "Even after flying the airplane for a year surprises on how things worked were not unusual." (Which shows the deficiencies in training.)
- "In the busy time below 10,000 feet—the area of highest collision hazard—there is too much FMS programming going on because of ATC demands such as sudden runway changes, and this often results in both pilots being heads down and no one looking out."
- "The computers and automation increase work load"—but one heard equal comments that work load was reduced.

There was the fairly unanimous opinion that en route, cruising at altitude, the computers relieved work load; "That's when I sleep," one pilot remarked. Below 10,000 feet, however, when departing or arriving, subject to traffic, runway selection, preparing for instrument landing, and more, the consensus seems to be that the computer aircraft has increased work load. A trite expression has circulated for years to the effect that flying was "hours of boredom intermingled with moments of stark terror." The terror is largely gone, so to fit modern times the expression might be modified to "hours of boredom intermingled with periods of frantic action." The fact that things get very busy is borne out by orders to flight crews by some major airlines not to program the FMS map function—not to set up routes—when below 10,000 feet. The general impression is that pilots like the automated airplanes but still feel development is needed in computer software and the gadgetry of buttons, as well as development in procedures and crew coordination.

An interesting part of the investigation involved questioning pilots who returned to older-style aircraft after computer aircraft experience; some said they loved the new and would like to fly them, while others said they were glad to get back to older styles with uncomplicated flying and a third crew member—the flight engineer.

My experience in the 767-type aircraft and Airbus is limited; I got a feel for them in simulators and in the case of the 757/767 some air time and lengthy study of both airplanes' systems while doing a project for Boeing. To really know the way it is, I'd need many hours of actual time in the aircraft, so I have to fall back on conversations with pilots who do fly them—sessions of questions, as well as documents like the previously mentioned NASA report by Wiener—and 37 years of airline flying, of which many were spent evaluating new ideas and airplanes. For part of this time I was chief pilot for TWA and was able to learn a lot about pilots, how to talk to them and dig out information and understand their reactions. There's a rapport between pilots who've "been there," so they almost talk in a kind of shorthand, or code, knowing that when one tells another of some airplane matter or function—how it works or what it provides—the listening pilot automatically places it in the milieu of flying that includes day and night, good weather and bad, when tired or apprehensive of ATC so not only the function, device, or airplane registers but how it would fit in a flier's world. I have the benefit of my experience, and my son, captain for a major airline, has had extensive experience in the glass airplanes. From his first solo at age 15, he grew in aviation, listening to long sessions between me and other pilots, soaking in the atmosphere as he developed his own flying character. So we can talk and understand each other, and he is now able to impart to me what it's like out there in his age. And I talk and question many pilots, both young and old, from various airlines. So I'm comfortable with the input.

Summation: pilots generally like the new aircraft, but they also admit to errors of serious nature when certain modes were not recognized or set properly—throttles have shut down power when not expected, speeds have been in error, altitudes were busted. These and other items make it clear that the new airplanes are still subject to human error, especially when ATC, communication, weather, and mechanical problems overload the cockpit. Procedures break down and the redundancy of two crew members falters. This is serious stuff because the redundancy of two people, one checking the other, is a basic in the world of aviation safety. With this breakdown, however, the double check is missing, and in effect, one has a single-pilot operation except it involves two pilots working in different directions. It's obvious that more effort is needed to simplify the computer aircraft. Wouldn't it be a good thought, as an example, if designers, human factors people, and operators looked at the Mode Control Panel with it's 30 buttons, switches, and display windows and said, "Let's reduce those to 15"? (And one would hope they wouldn't make the 15 remaining more complicated.)

The FMS and other computer systems can also fail or give false results so that it's necessary for pilots to monitor what they are doing. Computer people will tell you this isn't necessary, but it is, and the aircraft designers should make this monitoring by the pilots as simple as glancing at one or two instruments. As we stand today, the computerization has not removed the necessity for old methods being on hand, ready to use—a fact that, in itself, says we've added to, not reduced, the work load.

There's much good in the new airplanes—their safety record is excellent and we'd never want to go back to older ways—but the human factor relationship has fallen behind technology, and this gap increases the potential for accidents. So does the matter of monitoring the systems for their errors, either because they've failed or been programmed improperly. These aren't simply matters as new aircraft are developed; the original glass cockpit airplanes need retrofitting as well. Research is needed with strong leadership behind it, not FAA's snaillike pace, or NASA with its preoccupation with space, but a strong force to shake those administrations up, and the industry as well, to get such research and development going before the accident potential becomes a shocking reality.

The accident rate of airline flying is good, but it has remained essentially the same for 15 years. Your chances of getting killed are slim, but even with the accident rate remaining the same, the increase in air traffic in the future will mean more flights, hence more accidents, even with that same rate. The public doesn't seem to think about accident rates as it reads the newspaper or watches TV and hears of another accident, but if the number of accidents increases, then the public becomes outraged, and air transport suffers. So the accident rate must be improved, and doing the things we've discussed is a good direction to proceed in—but the need is urgent.

17 | PSYCHOLOGISTS, CRM, AND REMAKING THE PILOT

F

rom those early days when ATC wasn't necessary and instrument flight was uncommon, the industry has advanced to provide reliable and safe high-speed transportation to millions of people in big sophisticated airplanes that fly in almost all weather conditions.

The advancement has been impressive, but many aspects of it have been turbulent and solutions to its problems elusive. Too often when problems have been impossible to solve or when better solutions have been too damaging economically, they have been handed off to pilots, who must then follow rules and procedures that add work, stress, and distraction.

The industry's increasing demands on the human have been made without much consideration as to whether or not they are too heavy and the results counterproductive. The pilot's task and the situations he or she encounters, often unrelated to one another, require unforgiving concentration. It is inevitable that errors occur; what is amazing is that they so seldom result in disaster—a credit to successful training, superior equipment, and the dedication of crew members who realize their serious responsibility.

The system—including ATC, aircraft design, weather dissemination, and a mass of Federal Aviation Regulations that often seem to have been written speciously, and always in difficult-to-comprehend legalese—sanctimoniously removes executives, regulators, and nonflying people from blame. All this needs an objective look and overhaul to recreate simplicity and unburden the human. Progress in this direction is hampered by bureaucratic bungling, the clamoring of economic influences, and paralyzing controversy between adherents of opposing technologies.

The industry, meanwhile, has found a way to reduce the chance of human error, a way that makes the airline executive and regulatory hierarchy feel that something is being done. This answer is an attempt to fine-tune pilots, to mold them so they'll work faultlessly in the difficult environment, to bring on the psychologists and create a thing called CRM—Cockpit Resource Management. It started in the 1970s as a result of NASA human factors work, although Captain Bob Mudge of Delta Airlines was working with the concept as far back as 1947. Its introduction created instant response; it was, by comparison with other things, simple to put in action, and it gave the industry a new buzzword and FAA something to expound on and command. The idea spread like wildfire.

Psychological testing was old stuff that pilots never much liked. Tests to determine if pilots were suited for the job were given in the mid 1940s to active pilots and in one case was part of the cause for a pilot strike. This pretty much put a stop to testing active pilots; testing is now confined to the interview routine of pilot applicants.

CRM, however, isn't quite that same thing, although the shadow of it lurks in the background. As CRM is used to date its goals are not to test but to teach crews—pilots, flight engineers, and cabin attendants—to work together and use the resources of their knowledge, analytical ability, acumen, and observation in team fashion to the benefit of all. This is a good thing.

CRM surged into popularity like a new fashion, and every airline rushed to introduce CRM programs in the late 1980s. It was an exciting time for psychologists as airlines took them on as consultants. Wondering just what went on in these programs, I asked three major airlines to allow me to take part in their classes, which they kindly did. The courses varied in length from three hours to three days. It was immediately evident that the psychologists who had been hired to work for the airlines had quickly assumed the leadership role; you had the feeling the airlines had become subservient to them.

Psychologists work in a perplexing way: they carry the aura of their extensive education and impressive degrees well in front for all to see; although they are supposed to be experts at communicating, their conversation is generally spiked with big words that are frequently unintelligible to the audience. Ask why lovebirds act as they do, snuggling together because neither can stand being separated from the other, and the psychologist's answer will be something like, "It is a dysfunctional relationship of pathological enmeshment."

I discovered a lot of this in CRM, in discussions of heuristics, impersonal conflict negotiations, Maslow's hierarchy of needs, and others. Heuristics, incidentally, was explained as "human biases which affect the decision-making process by allowing shortcuts to the selection of the solution." Some pilots' reaction was, "What the hell has this to do with flying?" More curious minds reacted as though they'd been transported back to their school days taking Psych 1.

The paradox is that psychologists also like to explain things in idiot simple and condescending ways that border on insult to persons of normal intelligence. One class I sat through played the same games people play at Tupperware parties; for example, with six sitting around a table, one person whispers a statement in the next person's ear, that person whispers it to the next person, and so on to the last person, who tells aloud what he or she has heard. And as anyone knows, the message has changed appreciably—often humorously—from the way it started. To play this game with grown-up pilots who have spent many hours hearing messages misinterpreted on the radio is an insulting waste of time. The airline instructor whose CRM class was only three hours long covered the problem by simply saying, "You all know how radio messages get screwed up," and then went on to make his points about communications, which were interesting. For example, errors in transmitting a message result from mumbling, an accent, ambiguousness, hostility, a poor choice of words, and a distraction while forming the message (frequent while flying). Errors in receiving are caused by poor hearing, too much information too fast, hostility, poor radio reception, and timing. Most interesting was a list of factors affecting communication in percentage of importance: words used, 7 percent; tone, 38 percent; and body language, 55 percent.

But, of course, body language isn't possible between people separated by great distance, as is a pilot in an airplane talking to some unseen person on the ground. So there goes 55 percent of effective communication, a percentage that has to be made up by some other, as yet undefined, technique. But the point to be made is that the short class registered all this just as well as the one doing the time-consuming Tupperware party caper.

Nevertheless, CRM classes are not only sessions of psychological mumbo-jumbo but honest attempts to show how crews fail because of poor understanding and lack of assertiveness, leadership, and exchange of information. The courses always emphasize past accidents, reviewing emblematic incidents to clearly demonstrate how poor crew resource management caused the accident.

People tend to judge any event by the sphere within which they live. It's difficult to be completely objective; a person's knowledge, background, and interests are the paramount factors in the way that person thinks. Psychologists aren't any different; their worldview concerning human actions or lack of them shape the key points talked about when it comes to evaluating accidents. It is fine to awaken crew members to the importance of certain human interrelationships, but it does a disservice, too, by tending to submerge the complex systems factors that make the human foul up to begin with.

The notorious Air Florida accident at Washington, D.C., during the winter of 1982, when a snow-laden Boeing 737 slammed into the 14th Street Bridge, is invariably discussed in CRM sessions. It's quickly pointed out that the basic cause of the accident was the copilot remarking on the engine instrument's irregular readings and the captain not responding to abort the takeoff, which is what CRM people say the copilot was trying to coax the captain to do. Almost any pilot listening to the tape would say that was not the case but rather that the crew members were trying to analyze what was going on. To further substantiate this is the fact the copilot was well-known to be an assertive individual who would have said loud and clear if he'd thought they should abort. Being pushed by ATC to hurry the takeoff because a landing aircraft was right behind them, being faced with a runway with snow falling on it, which would make for questionable braking action, and knowing the general point made in the industry around the V_1 controversy that it's better to keep going than try to stop would make any pilot doubtful about aborting. The NTSB said, after analysis, that an abort was possible even if the runway had been slippery. How was a pilot to know that? No way from training, no way was there any runway coefficient information given the pilot; a typical NTSB after-the-fact, pedantic, unrealistic piece of laboratory-developed information.

Accidents are a result of many factors; in this one, they included improper deicing on the ground before takeoff, affecting the aircraft's wings and engine probes, which must be clear for proper engine instrument indication; a long traffic delay taxiing under conditions of sticking precipitation; the sensitivity of Boeing 737 aircraft to ice and the resulting nose pitch-up with even a small amount of ice on the leading edge flaps, or slats; the crew not using engine anti-icing. This last item is one that always bothers me because, technically, they could have believed engine anti-ice was unnecessary, depending on how they interpreted the airplane manual. The manual says: "Engine icing may occur when the following conditions exist *simultaneously:* The ambient temperature is below 8°C (46.4°F). Visible moisture such as fog, rain or *wet* snow is present. Fog is considered visible moisture when it limits visibility to one mile or less. Snow is wet when the ambient temperature is *1°C (30°F or above)*" (emphasis mine).

Fog was not reported, and the temperature was 24°F, so if you're going to nitpick about it, engine deicing heat wasn't required. I'll be the first to admit most pilots would have used engine anti-ice under the conditions that day, but who knows how the airplane's manual specifications, as written, may have influenced the pilots? So judging this accident as a psychological problem between captain and copilot is not accurate nor does it place sufficient blame on other important factors.

Some CRM courses broke the students into teams and had them review certain flights or accidents. After team study in closeted rooms they revealed how they had decided the incident or accident could have been avoided by better teamwork, which is useful dialogue. The teams were scored on their decisions, which injected an element of competition that is sometimes used in CRM training. To this observer, it's difficult to understand how competition in the cockpit would be of use; on the contrary, it can be a detriment.

CRM instructors made good points about communication, identifying standard speech patterns, mentioning the pressures to talk too fast, noting that longer messages are more often wrong, and identifying other irregularities that cause messages to be missed.

Sitting, listening to all this, I wondered what efforts were being made to reduce the need for so much communication. What efforts were being made to lower the pressure of crowded ATC systems that demand fast talk, talk tumbling from a dozen aircraft like water over rocks in a fast-moving stream. And I wondered: would CRM training retard the urgency for new and better ways to communicate?

CRM's lessons about assertiveness—stressing that the copilot and crew members shouldn't be afraid to speak up and voice their opinions, to inject their thinking—are a good thing; if a crew member is afraid to bring something to a captain's attention, they lose the value of double-checking and redundancy. I always appreciated crew members who would speak right up and point out something I'd missed or mention an item they'd noticed had gone awry.

CRM really started, without title or formal recognition, many years ago, and I remember my first lesson as a copilot. One of my earliest trips was with Captain Lloyd Olson, naturally called Ole. The airplane was a DC-2. Ole was a quiet man, one today we'd call laid-back; I doubt he would have shown emotion if the wings fell off. The trip went smoothly, and he was patient with my fumbling, helpful with a short, no-words-wasted remark when needed. Between Pittsburgh and Chicago I suspect he had decided it was time for a lesson on my status as copilot and to show me what CRM calls "assertiveness."

We were flying through a pleasant evening sky, passing Akron, Ohio. Ole had the airplane on autopilot and sat with his right foot perched on the pedestal, the other on the floor, left arm vertical from the armrest, cupped hand holding his chin—a model of relaxation as he gazed out the windshield at sky and ground. I wasn't so calm; we were running low on fuel in the right tank, and it was time to shift to the full left tank. The gauge was on zero, and I glanced at Ole—not a flicker of concern. My eyes went to the fuel pressure gauge, which would go down as soon as the last of the fuel came from the tank, after which a red light would go on, followed by the engine stopping. I was timid about saying anything. Some captains would consider such a reminder as treading on their territory, challenging their awareness and skill.

I watched the pressure gauge needle as it flickered and started down. A quick glance at Ole—nothing. I squirmed as the needle hit zero, and the red light popped on. To heck with Ole, what was the matter with him? I reached down, changed the fuel valve to the full tank, and pumped the hand wobble pump to bring back pressure. The engine ran on. Ole took his hand away from his chin and looked over at me. Now I'd catch it. "I wondered," he said calmly, "when you'd get around to changing that tank."

He put his chin back in his hand and resumed studying the sky and ground. But he'd taught me a lot in that moment, changed my self-image from that of a nervous new boy to feeling that I was part of the crew, useful, able to do things expected of me. It was hands-on CRM, as they'd say today. Ole flew his career to retirement, loved and respected by all who flew with him. I was especially inspired, when I checked out as captain, to be given one of my check rides by Ole.

But there are also negative sides to assertiveness that I heard little reference to, such as the judgment needed by crew members to know when they are helping and when they are being a hindrance. At briefing, I always made it clear to crew members that if they noticed anything unsafe, or saw me forget a safety item, to sound off strongly, but I cautioned them not to heckle me on other matters unless their suggestion could be made at a time free of pressure and high activity. A captain manages a flight with a certain flow of operation in mind, an internal step-by-step program to manage things. CRM says the captain should brief the crew how this program of flight management will be done, but sometimes there isn't time. Or the requirements may change quickly with events. If a crew member injects an idea, the captain has to break her or his chain of thought and interrupt concentration, listen to what's being said, analyze it, accept or reject the suggestion, and if time allows, explain the rejection. Tricky stuff, but important, yet I did not hear it addressed in the CRM classes. I felt the concept should have been explained, taught, or at least the problem addressed. After one course I remarked to the instructors that I felt the concept of "assertiveness" had come across as a "beat-up-on-the-captain" session. A captain who overheard my remark immediately agreed with the observation. In one case, there were captains who had CRM training six months previously (CRM is not a one-shot deal but a continuing thing with periodic refresher sessions), and the instructor asked how CRM had changed things on the line. "One thing I noticed," a captain responded, "is that copilots talk a hell of a lot more." Had they been taught too much assertiveness and no discretion in its use?

There was evidence that, in CRM, psychology had superseded good airline operational methods and that the airline hadn't really checked if the psychologists, in their flying innocence, hadn't suggested things that were not good operational practice. This was hazardous in that newly hired copilots might get an idea that what went on in CRM was always the way the airline should operate.

Take the topic of effective assertion, for example. In the slide representing this were the headings of a crew member's progress during an emergency: opening, expressing concern, stating the problem, proposing a solution, and achieving agreement.

A theoretical situation was set up to demonstrate: the airplane is charging down the runway on takeoff, and the second officer—flight engineer—notes a hydraulic failure. That's the *opening*. Now he *expresses concern:* "We've got a problem." Next, *stating the problem:* "Hydraulic failure." This is followed by *proposing a solution:* "Abort!" *Achieving agreement* was never discussed because there were three senior captains in the class, and on announcement of abort, they came right out of their chairs in protest. The person making the abort decision should be the captain because he or she has, or should have, all the information. The second officer, sitting back away from instruments and windshield, doesn't know what the speed is, how much runway remains, if it's slick or dry, or other equally important factors. The captain has to take all these factors into account before deciding to abort—and one of them is the fact more accidents and incidents have occurred because of aborting than continuing the takeoff.

Thinking back to my own flying and the good second officers I flew with, I mused over what action they would have taken in a similar situation. I could hear someone like Bushy (S. C. Bushy, but always called Bushy), an excellent crew member, calling out: "Hydraulic failure—you've lost nosewheel steering." and whatever else the failure had affected. His calling out these effects would give me important information to add to the other elements I had in my mind for use in judging whether or not I'd abort the takeoff. *That's* good crew teamwork—not someone jumping the chain of command with uninformed and questionable judgment.

Another negative aspect of assertiveness may be caused either by the captain or copilot, especially in our modern computerized aircraft. It starts with procedures, which are the backbone of flight operations. Procedures, in simple form, tell who does what, when, and how. Good procedures make the flow of work smooth, prevent the crew from overlooking important items, and make possible operation of computerized aircraft by two people. An added important aspect of procedures concerns big airlines with thousands of crew members: a captain and copilot may meet for the first time just before their first flight together; if the airline's procedures are good and the discipline to use them strong, the crew will operate without a hitch.

CRM, I felt, did not emphasize procedures enough. The two, CRM and procedures, are so closely interrelated that I expected the courses to stress this constantly, but they didn't. The need for procedure discipline should be an airline's constant goal—each crew member should do his or her tasks so the others know what's going on and to make sure everything has been covered. If a captain, for example, programs the FMS while the copilot is busy answering radio calls, and doesn't tell the copilot what's been done, then the copilot is out of the loop. Similarly, copilots sometimes take it on themselves to program the FMS, or tune radios, or do other things without the captain knowing about it. Then situational awareness breaks down and the accident potential increases.

An important part of CRM, sometimes emphasized, sometimes skipped over, is that if an abnormal situation not covered by procedures occurs and the captain is forced to improvise, or do things out of the ordinary, the captain should keep the copilot informed of his or her thoughts and actions if time allows.

Another accident often discussed is the Northwest DC-9 at Detroit in 1986. The airplane didn't climb after liftoff because the takeoff flaps had not been extended. The NTSB's key findings were that the crew didn't extend the flaps and slots and that the crew had failed to read the taxi part of the checklist. Ninth on the list of NTSB's findings was the fact the takeoff warning system didn't work; the NTSB called it "inoperative."

In NTSB's recommendations there were numerous requests for investigation and improvement in the airplane's warning system. Equal emphasis was given to the matter of checklists, better CRM training, and standard procedures. Never mentioned was the appropriateness of a taxi checklist. Checklists are read in sections; before starting, taxi, before takeoff, after takeoff, and so on. The taxi portion, which includes the very important check on flap extension, is done while the airplane is taxiing out through a maze of taxiways, during a time when radio chatter from the tower is often constant, when radio messages from the company about last minute weight changes and such are directed to the aircraft, and while the pilots are trying to find their way to the runway through the labyrinth of taxiways. Detroit is notorious for confusing taxiways, and this flight, because of a recent runway change, was under a constant bombardment of radio calls. On December 3, 1990, a runway incursion accident between a DC-9 and Boeing 727 occurred at Detroit, and the NTSB's report included: "The complex intersection of taxiway Oscar-4 and runways 09/27 and 3C/21C was a recognized danger area with a strong potential for runway incursion and was nevertheless inadequately marked." The flight we're talking about took off on runway 3C.

The taxi checklist is frequently interrupted by all this action; it is hoped the crew will finish it after the interruptions. It's a stupid time to be reading checklists. Why is it done? To save time. Properly, these important items should be covered just before takeoff; ideally, the airplane should stop before takeoff position so the crew can read a checklist that covers the killer items. But to do it this way would consume time—at a point when the tower and the long line behind you are creating an atmosphere of pressure, pushing you to hurry. Stopping as I've suggested would materially hold up the show. Is this part of the economics of trying to crowd more airplanes into the overcrowded system? NTSB never mentioned this aspect at all nor have I ever heard the taxi checklist considered as a safety item. Yet numerous aircraft have crashed trying to take off without flaps, obviously not having read the taxi checklist, or having skipped an item because of interruptions, or having responded affirmatively to the flaps being down although they haven't been checked because of other distractions.

An interesting point suggested by a copilot during one of the classes was the possibility that the crew thought it had read the checklist but in fact was thinking of having read it during the previous takeoff. Crews—especially commuter crews—may make many stops in a flight pattern; they can be tired from night flying or accumulated fatigue, so events run together in their minds, and one leg of the flight may be confused with others. This was an intriguing thought, and I asked a number of pilots from various airlines if they really thought this could happen. The response was a firm yes. NTSB and CRM haven't talked about this to my knowledge. But either way, the taxi checklist should be abolished.

Habit patterns do not seem to get any attention in CRM, yet they are important. Many pilots have a personal checklist they go through even though normal checklists are also read. In my own case, when the tower said, "Cleared for takeoff," there were a few killer items I quickly checked as the throttles were advanced; a look over my shoulder to see the fuel valves were set properly, then flap settings, spoiler handle down, stabilizer set in the green, and the directional heading in agreement with the runway heading. It only took a few seconds and became such a habit that takeoff was impossible without going thorough the ritual first. It was almost a superstition. It's still with me, and when I start the throttle up on the simple Cessna 170 my son and I own, I still check for fuel on, stabilizer set, and other items. This isn't to take the place of the checklist in any way but is simply a habitual double check. When my son was 16 years old and learning to fly, I instilled this in him, and he tells me it's still a habit pattern he goes through before takeoff on the airline.

Perhaps CRM people, and airline people, think such emphasis might degrade the standard checklists, but I believe they're missing a good bet. Most of my friends, now retired after 30 years or more without accident, will agree that they had such systems—perhaps a throw back to the days we flew before checklists were introduced. I'm told by responsible psychologists that people can be taught habit patterns. Why not pilots? I would guess the airlines are afraid pilots would then stop using checklists. But this point—habit *after* checklist—can be made part of the education.

CRM stressed the need for briefings between pilots to make certain of the method of doing things. What will the procedure be after takeoff while following ATC's clearances or if an engine fails? According to CRM, a briefing should be done between the captain and the cabin team to tell what kind of flight it will be, what's expected in an emergency, and other items each airline spells out.

Certainly the idea of briefing is excellent, but it doesn't tally with reality. As previously explained, changing cabin teams more than once during a day frequently means that there is a lack of time for briefing. And pilot briefing before each takeoff has a psychological hiccup in that it gets to be old hat, especially if you have five takeoffs a day and go through a litany of what's to be done if an engine fails before each takeoff. This situation frequently is covered by the captain calling out, "Standard briefing."

The crew should know the proper emergency action through training and procedure, and it should not be any more necessary to review on each takeoff than to say aloud, "I pull the wheel back to go up!" The briefing that *is* important is a spoken review of the routings and altitudes ATC has cleared the flight so all agree it is correctly understood. Clearances are generally different for each departure.

The matter of briefing hasn't really been addressed in depth as to what's needed and what is mumbling repetition that actually lessens its impact. So often these things sound good and holy in a classroom or on paper but aren't functional in the real world.

How do we sum up CRM? Is it good, or is it bad? There's no doubt that it has value; whether or not it is achieving its objectives is a difficult question to answer because airline accidents are so few it is impossible to say, "See, the accident rate has decreased since CRM." There are so few accidents that the reasons for a blip on the increase or decrease curve are almost impossible to determine.

An evaluation of CRM's value is attempted by the psychologists using scientific research methods—largely by asking questions of participants and then carefully tabulating the answers and making postulations in fancy terms. While most scientific people are honestly attempting to find true answers, some of the questions asked crew members require that you answer yes or no. I filled out these questionnaires after each CRM class, and in all cases I didn't feel I could properly respond to a question because I was forced to answer by checking off either "agree" or "disagree," when I really felt a sentence or two was necessary to respond properly.

People within the airlines responsible for training have latched onto CRM with much enthusiasm and passed it on to crew members in amounts that seem excessive. Captain Alfred Haynes of the United Air Lines Sioux City DC-10 crash was loud in his praises of CRM and wrote in the *Air Line Pilot,* ALPA's journal, " I am convinced that CRM played a very important part in our landing at Sioux City with any chance of survival." I respect the captain's thoughts, but I'll wager a man of his long experience—he was almost ready to retire, and since has—would have reached down into that experience and handled the situation to the same conclusion even without CRM training.

The LOFT (line-oriented flight training), mentioned previously, which is a simulated airline flight fraught with problems artificially created, is considered part of CRM. The analysis of a LOFT flight can certainly show how the crew worked together. But with FAA's penchant for creating rules to be enforced with subsequent penalties if rules are broken or performances are not up to its standards, CRM-LOFT may become something one passes or fails. If so, it seems the value of it as a means of improving skills will suffer. A few pilots I interviewed feel that the concentration on LOFT has reduced simulator time they once used in their annual simulator sessions to try maneuvers and things that had been perplexing them but were impossible to try on line flights. LOFT has robbed them of this opportunity as simulator time is limited and expensive. The marriage of CRM, procedures, and techniques can be very effective in a LOFT exercise. But it needs to be packaged so pilots realize CRM is simply one aspect of flight management. I fear that without proper prioritization CRM may be overemphasized and detract from the basics of procedure, techniques, and flying the airplane.

CRM is now an industry standard: all crew members get it, including the cabin team; ATC controllers are getting CRM, mechanics too, and each day the list grows of airline employees who will get CRM training.

My hope is that CRM will become more practical, that it will show people how to get along together and do so in a practical fashion. I'd like to see the psychologists become servants of the airline-training people, with the airline-training people not awed by psychologists' fancy and obtuse talk. I'd like to see the airline say to the psychologist, "We've got some captains who are egotistical, overbearing, and nonconformist. What do we do about it?" And then get some earthy, practical advice. A list could be developed on the failings and needs of the crew members so the psychologists could advise the airline supervisors and training people. But it should be understood that the airline folks are dominant and the psychologists are working as consultants for them, not the other way around.

How well is CRM working? Talk to the adherents, and you'll hear that it's the salvation for human factor errors. Ask pilots who have lived under it a year or more, and a typical answer will be something like, "Oh, it was interesting, but it's sorta died down—things haven't changed much."

In the years ahead, CRM will doubtless be streamlined and better taught. My hope is that it will not be used in an attempt to remake the pilot into a superhuman in order to fit the more-complicated aircraft and the ATC system. It makes more sense to concentrate on reducing aircraft and airways system complexity as the way to lessen chances for human error. We can benefit from CRM, but it should not be considered the primary way to cure human factor errors.

18 | ARE PILOTS OVERPAID PRIMA DONNAS?

In the back of a pilot's mind
lurks a disturbing aura of uncertainty that is present all the time
to some degree. It is related to job security, not the fear of
flying.

Airline pilots live in a goldfish bowl, under the constant scrutiny
of FAA and their company. Every word spoken on the radio is
taperecorded by ATC; the conversation in the cockpit between crew
members goes on a cockpit voice recorder (CVR); a crash-proof flight
data recorder—the FDR—provides a transcript of how the airplane is
being flown in great detail; ATC observes, with radar, the exact
movement of the airplane, ready to catch any deviations laterally or vertically
that may be passed on to FAA for legal action. The next step planned is a
cockpit video camera recording what is on the CRTs to see if they, or the
pilots, have made any errors. A pilot's job is placed in jeopardy by physical
exams twice a year; exams can end a career instantly. When you go in for
a physical—to specified FAA doctors—you fill out a long form that includes
permission to get your files from any doctor you've seen as well as records
of past traffic violations of serious nature. Drug tests, which pilots fear only
because of possible error, may be sprung on them any time.

How well a pilot can fly is inspected under a magnifying glass in
proficiency checks on simulators and aircraft at least twice a year; an FAA
inspector may climb on board a scheduled flight any time to check
performance, bringing instant anxiety to the crew. Many pilots feel the
presence of an FAA inspector in the cockpit creates such nervousness in the
crew that it may degrade safety.

The rules and demands of performance plus required knowledge of

216

aircraft, airways, and procedures are so voluminous there is ample opportunity for the nitpicker to fault the pilot; and pilots will tell you, with accuracy, that it's impossible to fly without breaking some rule. Pilots lead the way in knowing what living under Big Brother's watchful eye really feels like. A single misstep, an innocent infraction of a rule, an irregular wiggle on a cardiogram, and the job is finished. When psychologists talk of stress, they refer to stressors as the cause; pilots have stressors like poor dogs have fleas, and many are generated by the FAA.

Going to work for an airline is like getting married; your company is your airline for life—with no divorce provisions because if your airline fires you it's almost impossible to go to work for another. You get your seniority number the day you start to work, and after a few years you accumulate enough so that your choice of position and location is enhanced. Your seniority number applies to one airline, and you can't take it with you. Should you be unusual and move to another airline, your buildup of seniority starts all over, from the bottom.

Before we go further we'd best get a point or two straightened out about seniority. Airline seniority systems are not like the U.S. Congress, where length of service automatically puts one in position of authority.

Seniority governs how quickly you become captain, whether or not you fly desired equipment, where you are domiciled, and if you get a desired choice of flights. The important point is that it does not make you captain or allow you to check out on new airplanes automatically; it only gives you a chance to try. Example: when the Boeing 747 was introduced, I had the enviable seniority number of one. As the expression goes, I could bid on heaven. Well, I bid to fly the 747 and got the bid. What that did was give me the opportunity to try to qualify on the airplane; it was still necessary to pass a three-week ground school—passing grade 80 percent—and then undergo much flight training in simulator and airplane, doing all normal flight procedures and emergencies of every conceivable nature. Next came an oral examination on the aircraft by an FAA inspector, and after that a 2½ hour check flight by an FAA inspector, again doing normal and emergency procedures. Before I could command an actual flight, however, I had to make a round trip, New York–London, with a TWA check pilot. After his approval I was then qualified to be captain in charge and fly scheduled flights. So all seniority did was give me a chance to qualify and then fly the airplane.

First officers—copilots—can bid to fly different equipment (the bigger the more pay), but they too must pass school and checks almost as extensive as the captain's. A first officer sits in that position until seniority is enough to get a captain bid.

When copilots' seniority reaches the point where they can make captain, they go through a very extensive period of training and testing. What if they fail? In most cases they are fired. A very few exceptional cases have been allowed to remain flying as copilot, but this is rare. If pilots fail to check out on a new airplane, the chances are they will be given early retirement or released. In some cases they may be allowed to return to the equipment they had been flying, but from then on they're performing under extra surveillance, and a cloud hangs over them.

So don't suppose that seniority allows old incompetent pilots to fly—it's hogwash. I can remember the preseniority days when pilots were picked by their superiors for a captain's spot. Great unfairness occurred when a quiet, competent pilot sat as copilot while a buddy club cousin of the chief pilot with fewer years of service was advanced ahead of him. While it didn't happen often, it was often enough to cause rancor. Seniority has proved to be a fair system, although it is damned by those who don't get what they want. And certain unfairness and harm has occurred with airline mergers and the consequent impossible job of merging two seniority lists. No matter the effort, someone always gets hurt.

Airlines aren't anxious to hire "old" pilots over the age of 40—even 35 casts a shadow. The reason for job loss carries a stigma, and no one will take you because of it, although recent laws concerning job discrimination and age have changed this picture somewhat. If busting a physical was the reason, then it's all over: no license, no chance for flying again. Sometimes a physical fault may be accepted, such as certain heart problems or high blood pressure corrected by surgery, diet and health program, or medicine, but only after a long period of meeting difficult FAA test requirements. These are rare cases. Most pilots, unfortunately, are not trained for any other occupation, so at 45, to pick a not uncommon age, having three children, wife, house, and mortgage and no job prospects is grim stuff. Most pilots carry loss-of-license insurance to ensure a lump sum of money should they fail physically; it is expensive insurance, and the cost and remuneration change with age. The older you are, the less you get. At 45 you pay $1260 per year for a $105,000 lump sum, which will not keep you and your family for life but hopefully will suffice while you're trying to learn some other business. At age 55 the lump sum payment is down to $20,000. Pilots have often been criticized for having other business on the side, and a small percentage do, but it's part of that insecurity and an attempt to prepare should job disaster strike for physical or any other reason.

Pilots live from one six-month period to another. January, let's say, is physical time; you start fretting about it a month ahead, begin a fresh exercise program, and cut down on food. Once you pass the physical, a cloud lifts, and life relaxes until May when the next physical, scheduled for June, begins to cast its shadow. The physical aspect has made pilots health conscious, with concern for regular exercise and good diet, but follow-through isn't always possible because decent restaurants aren't open all night. Hot dogs from a coin machine in a fluorescent-lighted passageway often become an evening meal during a stop.

The incidence of smoking has dropped until today a pilot who smokes is a rarity. In DC-3 days, it seemed, most all smoked. I remember putting a pack of Camels on the windshield ledge at the start of an overnight flight; come morning and arrival, they'd all be gone. Gradually most pilots quit—I did in 1947—and now cockpits are almost all smoke free. Like most reformed smokers I developed an antipathy for smoking and finally wouldn't allow smoking in the cockpit. I got some flack about this but soon found that my copilot or flight engineer was a nonsmoker anyway. What happened was the word got out that Buck didn't allow smoking in the cockpit, so smokers didn't bid flights on which I was captain, but nonsmokers did. Benefit to all.

Then there's the recurrent training. You go to the company training center, take two days of ground school reviewing airplane systems and hijack and emergency procedures—generally ho-hum stuff, much the same as last time. Then follow three days in the simulator for the not ho-hum stuff, doing instrument approaches with and without emergencies—failed engine, hydraulic system, or electrical system or other trying situations. There will be a LOFT (line-oriented flight training), which is simulated flight with an entire crew. This flight, however, will have many irregularities that test how the crew members act and the captain commands. A CAM recorder films the flight, and when the LOFT is over, the videotape is run for the crew to watch as an instructor critiques performance and techniques. It's an excellent procedure and not supposed to be a check, but crew members are still uptight, wanting to look good and not build any doubts in the instructor-check person's mind about their ability. The final simulator session is a proficiency check of much that you've been doing with multiple emergencies and a number of low approaches of different types. You must do it without making errors that have accident potential. If such an error is made, then you do it over and stay for retraining. If you fail, the pressure is heavy; it's as though you've fallen in a deep hole difficult to claw your way out of. The instructors watch closely; you pressure yourself to be perfect—it's a tense, trying time, and you have to fly better than during the first check. So checks bother people, some more than others. A scattering of pilots enjoy these sessions; others dread them. Recently a young captain, obviously at a most enviable age and peak of ability, told me he actually had stomach trouble and couldn't eat properly for days before his checks.

Checks generally come twice a year, although a new system that allows for only one yearly check, but closer line observation, is evolving. This is explained in lofty terms as a better way—it even has a name: "advanced qualification program" (AQP)—but you have to wonder if the genesis isn't economic, so that airlines will only have to pay for one training session a year rather than two.

Line checks are accomplished on regular line flights with a supervisor pilot, generally called a "check pilot," riding along to observe your performance with a crew. This is scheduled once a year. There is also the possibility an FAA air carrier inspector may climb aboard any day. The inspector rides in the cockpit observing, frequently taking notes in a little book, which makes you wonder, "What the hell's he writing?" Once we had trouble with FAA inspectors who rode your flight, shook hands, said, "nice flight," and departed, only to be heard from two weeks later. A letter might arrive criticizing some action or even requesting a hearing. Strong protests from ALPA got this stopped, and all in all, FAA inspectors are now quite open and friendly. I always made it a practice, however, when a check was over and the good-bye handshake in progress, to say, "If there was anything you didn't like, I'd like to hear about it now."

Do many pilots bust checks? No. The failure rate is low because pilots are good and keep up on things with extra review of limitations, procedures, and manuals, especially when scheduled for the annual or semiannual session. In early years there was a great buddy club atmosphere about instrument checks, as they were called. The airline was smaller, everyone knew everyone, and the company had its list of who was good and who was weak. Checks, with a good friend doing the checking, might be a joyride over your house or golf course, some steep turns, a few unusual maneuvers, and an instrument approach with one engine shut down—all most jovial. As the number of pilots increased, the close-knit club approach no longer worked, and companies tightened up. The simulator was developed with no other purpose in life than training and checking, so the buddy club, easy check went the way of the dodo bird. Now it is all business. FAA also entered the process, approving training and checking programs, which tightened up methods and curriculums, and frequently FAA inspectors are observers on simulator checks. Today the training and checking is serious, professional, and of a quality that doesn't allow inadequate pilots to slip by.

Of course the complexity of regulations and aircraft operation has reached a point where the pilot is unsure of what he or she may be overlooking, and that, in turn, creates a nervous uncertainty. For the pedantic instructor or checker it's become a field day. So while few fail checks, no one anticipates them with joy.

Mergers and the cruel impersonal takeovers have added to problems not only of seniority but of job security. Pilots flying airlines decimated by debt and run by entrepreneurs with little concern for individuals have extra concerns about their company being alive the next day.

W. H. Gunn is a unique individual; a Ph.D. in psychology as well as a retired airline pilot of over 35 years experience, he authored a paper, "Airline Deregulation: Impact on Human Factors," delivered before the International Association of Aviation Psychologists, at Ohio State University in April 1991. His learned research revealed that a pilot flying for one of the shaky financial airlines works under a feeling of despair that increases irritability and anger, decreases attention, and escalates accident proneness from 50 to 90 percent over that of pilots flying for stable airlines. The pilots flying these airlines, with their reduced salaries, pensions, and morale, deserve credit for keeping their accident record on a level with the others.

But what kind of lives do airline pilots live? The public gets most of its impressions from statements released by airline companies during labor disputes or from pilots who have failed to get an airline job and secretly envy those holding one. The impression given is that airline pilots only work 75 hours a month and are paid $200,000 per year. Well, that isn't quite right.

The average pilot's salary is $80,772 per year (1992), and a pilot works a bit over 80 *flying* hours per month. If you're interested in such things, the so-called average pilot is 42.9 years old and has been with the company 14 years. Pilot minimum pay was established by a now famous decision of the National Labor Board, Decision 83, which was also incorporated into the Civil Aeronautics Act of 1938. This was precipitated by a threatened nationwide pilots' strike in 1933 when an NRA code proposed a $250 minimum monthly pay—and 140 flying hours for the same period. Prior to that, airmail pilots were making about $1000 per month. Pilots today can thank David L. Behncke and his Air Line Pilots Association for minimum working conditions and pay under law—even though the process of deregulation and the takeover airlines' financial manipulations have served, at least in part, to destroy such things.

Working 80 hours a month sounds like a pretty soft job, but let's first realize that figure reflects just the hours spent flying, from the time the airplane leaves the gate until it arrives at the destination. It doesn't count the 1 or 2 hours at the office before flight or the half hour after flight; it doesn't count the time waiting around at intermediate stops or training or the proficiency checks and getting to and from them, which may mean "deadheading," the day before, from Boston to Atlanta. It doesn't count the time spent in the correspondence home study courses many companies require or the time to get physical exams. It is reasonably calculated that pilots work an hour on the ground for each flown, so that's 160 hours a month, or about 40 a week. Now let's look at what kind of hours.

Pilots don't fly every day but rather in sequences from 3 days on duty to perhaps 12 for international flights. Some schedules are such that a pilot is home every night, but this is rare. The sequences are the various flights flown when on the job. In the parlance they're called "lines of time," and they change monthly. Bid sheets are distributed toward the end of one month for the next month's lines of time; they are in a package of paper that lists each line, with days of the month flown, layover points, and time of day or night the pilots operate. Pilots study these bid sheets the way horse players study the racing forms, looking for the lines that will fit personal plans, like being home for a child's birthday. The lines are scrutinized for bad flights, ones that drag through the midnight to 6:00 A.M. period, flights with decent layover times, and a number of other things that include pay time, especially if a previous month has come up short on hourly pay; then the pilot will look for a line that allows making up some of that shortage. Once decided, the pilot bids on the lines most desired, generally handing in a sheet of paper with his or her list, although some airlines provide for computer bidding so a pilot can do it from home, if that home has a computer and modem.

What a pilot is finally given depends on seniority. If you're number 1 on the list, you pick the one line most desirable, bid that, and get it, but if you're number 50 at your base you put down 50 choices picked after lengthy, agonizing study of the bid sheets. You may get lucky and come up with your first choice; more likely it'll be some number in the 40s. You bid for vacation slots in the same manner.

It sounds complicated, and it is. In early days the airline ran by a first in, first out basis; you came in and went to the bottom of the pilot list. Pilots were used from the top of the list, and you moved up until you were on the top and first to go out—on any trip that was next. With this system, all was uncertain, including when you'd fly next, where, and for how long. There was also sneaky finagling, resulting in names moved up or down on the sly, especially if a romantic relationship existed between scheduler and pilot. Gradually, to correct these and other abuses, the line of time was created.

Let's look at a typical line of time a pilot may get:

First day: Leave Boston 3:25 P.M.; make stops at Atlanta and Ontario, California, and arrive San Diego 9:51 P.M. Pacific time—51 minutes after midnight your time. Fifty-three minutes on ground in Atlanta, 42 minutes at Ontario.

Second day: Leave San Diego 8:28 P.M. Pacific time—11:28 P.M. yours. Stop at Los Angeles for 1 hour 47 minutes; then fly to Cincinnati arriving at 6:01 A.M. your time (Eastern).

Third day: Leave Cincinnati at 6:49 P.M. after 12 hours 48 minutes *daytime rest;* arrive San Francisco 8:45 P.M. Pacific time—11:45 P.M. yours.

Fourth day: Leave San Francisco 3:25 P.M. Pacific time; stop at Atlanta for 1 hour 2 minutes; go to Boston, home, arriving at 2:10 the next morning. Then you're off for 4 days.

It is easy to see that flying is not a 9:00 to 5:00 job with weekends off. Pilots work 12 to 15 days a month. That sounds pretty nice, but we should remember that at the end of a flying day the pilot isn't home but rather in a motel or hotel a long way from home, missing family and a bit lonesome. Flying to attractive places soon palls and becomes routine. Dinner may be eaten with the other pilot and flight engineer, but after that the program is the motel or hotel room with a washed-out color TV, a book, or an attempt at sleep.

Sleep is often difficult. It may be time to sleep for tomorrow's flight, but you're across the continent, with 3 hours' time difference from home, and your body says it isn't time to go to bed. The FAA's regulations on flight duty time aren't realistic because they don't consider time of day or layover time. The regulations are complicated but generally call for maximums of 8 flying hours in a day, 30 in a week, 100 a month, and 1000 per year. Rest periods are required by FAA after flying 8 hours, but they are somewhat unrealistic and have exceptions within the regulations. Nine hours' rest is required for less than 8 hours' flying, and 10 hours if flying over 8 hours but not over 9 hours, and 11 hours' rest if flying over 9 hours.

The key point to think about in flight time limitations is that they are referred to as "scheduled" flight times; if weather and ATC delays make for longer flight times, the 8 hours can be stretched. A pilot may fly for 2 hours, stop and then be held for 3 hours waiting weather, then fly another 2 hours, wait again for a few hours, and so on, so the 8 hours flying may stretch into an all-night, hanging-around-drinking-coffee-and-getting-tired flight but still be legal. The rules have all sorts of iffy paragraphs and are often difficult to interpret. Example:

> A flight crew member is not considered to be scheduled for flight time in excess of flight time limitations if the flights to which he is assigned are scheduled and normally terminate within the limitations, but due to circumstances beyond the control of the air carrier (such as adverse weather conditions), are not at the time of departure expected to reach their destination within the scheduled time.

Translated it means a pilot cannot fly over 8 *scheduled* hours, but if weather, ATC delays, and such cause the flight to be more than 8 hours, it's okay.

One large problem concerning pilot working hours and rest is that no one has been able to develop a test to decide when a person is tired physiologically, so the determination of what limitations should be are not objective but a combination of guesswork, labor negotiations, and tradition. Eight hours in a day, for example, goes way back to ALPA's beginning and pre–World War II days when Behncke and others argued, successfully, that 8 hours was a normal worker's day and should be that for pilots. Deep down, FAA's attitude is that flight time limitations are a matter of contract between pilots and their companies; I actually had a deputy FAA administrator tell me that once when I complained about time and duty regulations. The companies make some attempts but they are inconsistent and unrealistic; flights on international routes, for example, have longer time limits because you just can't fly some of the distances in 8 hours, which doesn't have a thing to do with objectively judging fatigue. The regulations are often developed as compromises between the airlines arguing economics on one side and pilots thinking of fatigue on the other.

Pilots aren't like night workers, who have a chance to become accustomed to sleeping days; pilots may fly all night one day, half-day and half-night the next, all day the next, then all night again. Most times sleeping in the day results in only a nap because the body's normal rhythm isn't set for a solid 8 hours, so you wake after a few hours. Sleeping in the daytime has other frustrations: hotel maids make up rooms close by and call to each other in the halls, vacuums run, doors slam, and all the activity of the day does its best to make your sleep difficult. Hotels also have a way of putting airline crews in the least desirable rooms because they're getting a reduced rate, and after a period of seeing you come and go, hotels treat you less like guests and more like relatives. Your room is likely to be next to an elevator or over the alley where garbage is picked up and deliveries made.

So here we are, wide awake at 1:00 P.M. when we wanted to sleep until at least 4:00, when it's time to get dressed, have something to eat, and go to the airport for an all-night flight. You try to sleep, toss and turn, "spin in the sheets" as it's called, and finally arise angry. So you get 5, maybe 6 hours sleep during a layover and take off legally rested but physically fatigued.

That would be on a domestic flight; international flights can compound the problem. You fly a nonstop flight that departs New York at 7:30 P.M. to Paris, arriving 7:30 A.M. Paris time (2:30 A.M. home time). You go to town and crawl into bed at 10:00 A.M., but sometimes later after having to sit around the lobby for a couple of hours until the room is made up because the outbound crew just vacated the room and the maids are slow. You flop into bed tired and sleepy, but before dropping off be certain to set the travel alarm for 3:00 in the afternoon because if you take too long a nap you'll never be able to go to bed early that night—which you have to do as there will be an early morning crew call the next day. So you get up at 3:00, take a long walk through Paris—always a good, relaxed time—then have dinner and go to bed. The call in the morning will be at 5:30 A.M. for your flight to Tel Aviv. You fall asleep praying that nothing wakes you because you're actually going to bed at 4:00 in the afternoon home time and your body thinks it's just for a nap. Chances are you'll be awake part of the time, tossing and turning. Finally it's time to sleep back home. Your body responds as you sink into deep slumber; unfortunately this is just before crew call, and in a moment it seems—5:30 A.M.—the phone rings. Back home it's just past midnight. You feel very draggy, speak little, and maintain yourself in a suspended state until finally, after a ride to the airport, flight plans, weather check, and all, you get on the airplane, into the air, and then have some coffee and breakfast served by a most welcome hostess, as my airline called the attendants.

So Geneva, Rome, Athens, and Tel Aviv, arriving at 5:00 P.M. Tel Aviv time—it's only 10:00 A.M. back home. Here we go again: loaf around, then eat dinner, and go to bed early evening in Tel Aviv—it's afternoon back home. Try to sleep because the call will be at 5:00 A.M.—10:00 the previous evening at home! Same problem: fight restless sleep because of that time change. Brrrring, it's 5:00 A.M. again; you stagger around, wait for breakfast after reaching the field—although the hotel, being very civilized, has coffee in the lobby. Athens, Rome, and Paris, arriving there noon Paris time. Change clothes, have lunch, and then fall in bed ready for the first good sleep since leaving home. Crew call for the flight home the next day is late enough so you can go to bed a bit later. Screwed up? You bet, and the time lag doesn't go away quickly, so the first day or so at home has a zombie feeling about it as your internal clock attempts to settle down. There's no special trick for handling jet lag; experienced pilots are subject to it just as much as first time tourists.

Senior pilots bid the best-paying flights, generally. The best-paying flights are often the most exhausting, with long nights across oceans. So the oldest pilots take the maximum beating. Some European airlines have flights that crowhop around the short distances of Europe for the day and wind up back home at night, so a pilot can be home every night to sleep in his or her own bed. They've set up the pay system so flying these flights doesn't reduce the pay; hence the "old" pilots don't yo-yo their bodies through time changes and night duty. Nothing like that exists in the United States.

I suppose it's necessary to briefly refer to the people who smirk, nudge, and hint for juicy tales of hanky-panky on layovers. But if there once were reasons for the nudges and winks, they're gone now. Nowadays the cabin team—as it is referred to—rarely stops overnight at the same town as the cockpit crew on domestic flights. The cabin attendants have their own lines of time because of working agreements different from the pilots', and some companies deliberately keep cabin crews and cockpit apart for unspoken, unwritten reasons.

A day of domestic flying with many stops may have two or three changes of cabin crew. Pilots sometimes hardly know who's back there; taxiing out from St. Louis, a female attendant sticks her head in the cockpit and says, "I'm Jane. I'm A line—I'll come up later about coffee." "A line" means she's head of the cabin team. Aside from the coffee or meal and a brief stop in the cockpit, that's all the communication pilots will have with Jane and her cohorts. This isn't particularly good because proper rapport and briefing with the cabin crew is accomplished in fleeting fashion, with quick reference to when it might be turbulent, how bad, and whether or not crew members can keep serving when it gets rough—and what the signal will be to indicate if they should sit down and fasten their seat belts. Occasionally there are benefits. A pilot told me of sometimes getting a new cabin team who had just come from where it was now flying back to. Having just flown the route, the cabin team knew about the turbulence and could brief the pilots on how it would be!

Cabin crews are an important part of safety, and many accident reports have recounted their heroic, lifesaving acts since air transport began. Nellie Granger was in TWA's second group of young women hired. On April 7, 1936, she was hostess on a DC-2 that crashed in the Pennsylvania mountains. Nellie was thrown clear of the airplane and uninjured. Two passengers survived, a man and a woman, both badly injured. Nellie covered them with blankets, made them as comfortable as possible, struggled across the snow-covered mountain for 11 miles before finding help, and then insisted on returning to the crash site, showing rescuers the way. She was only a 100-pound slip of a girl—one of the first heroines from the ranks of the cabin attendants.

Having sufficient time for the captain to brief the cabin team on how he or she runs things and what to expect is important, but with cabin crew changes done on a quickie basis, this isn't always as thorough as would be best. When I flew international—DC-4s to 747s—we had the same cabin crew for most of the round-trip. Sometimes the crew's lines of time and ours coincided. And I've also flown New York–Paris trips with the same cabin team for a couple of months. We got to know each other and how we operated; before each flight I'd have a briefing reviewing emergency procedures, discussing what weather to expect (when there might be turbulence so meal service could be juggled to do it during a smooth period), and outlining our flight plan and any other useful information. It paid off when we had a bomb threat out of Paris and the cabin team performed magnificently.

The women flying now are generally older; many married with families. They're interested in rest on layovers, not whooping it up. The jet created a much faster pace, so getting rest is a necessity. I suppose there are "friendly" relations somewhere and in some places, but I'm sure no more than in the office of your insurance broker or bank. Whether you're a cabin attendant or pilot, flying for an airline is serious stuff, and the cheap Hollywood image is false. I respect and admire the people doing their jobs in the back end of the airplane.

The question is bound to come up concerning pilots and drinking. It's not a serious problem. The FARs say no drinking less than 8 hours before flight—and many airlines make that 12 hours under their own rules. Pilots stick to this because the cost of breaking the rule is too severe—probably the loss of their jobs. Yes, there have been alcoholic pilots, but they are soon discovered and reported, generally by other crew members. Once this was automatic dismissal, but the modern approach is to attempt rehabilitation in which the companies take an active part. The ALPA members of each airline have a Professional Standards Committee that is quick to learn of drinking problems or any other out-of-line behavior, and it goes right to the offender and works to straighten him or her out. Nothing impresses people more than to have their peers bring improper behavior to their attention. The FAA put in place a drug-testing program a few years ago, and pilots were given surprise tests. The positive results were infinitesimal, so much so that little is heard of the program now. The old-time vision of pilots "drinking it up" doesn't apply today. Pilots respect their jobs and realize their responsibility too much to risk either.

How about those luxurious four days a pilot has off between trips? Getting home for pilots isn't like returning from the office at 6:30; pilots arrive any hour day or night. The beating from jet lag, crazy hours, poor sleep, irregular meals, and tensions of the job don't always have you arriving home cheery and bright, ready to go dancing or coach Little League. No, you're tired and want to shed that uniform that is dirty and smells of the airplane, push the flight bag under your desk, take a shower, and relax. The first night home, I found, was one of good sleep, but the second night was often restless with unexplained wakefulness and a period of turning and tossing. Was this the leftover effect of confused time zones and mixed-up day and night flights? Who knows, but for sure it takes a couple of days to feel reasonably back on schedule. The desire for loafing and sleeping is strong, but you soon discover that doing good hard physical work or exercise will get you back to normal quicker than will lolling around.

One of the days off is always spent going through the mail, paying bills, taking care of chores. Clever helpmates don't meet you at the door on your return with a string of problems like a backed up septic tank, your son's bad school grades, or a dented fender, but, if clever, reveal them at favorable times when you're rested. I suppose female pilots get problems tossed at them by husbands when they return—well, welcome to the club. An airline pilot's life isn't easy on marriage; the mate left at home while you're off flying has to take on many responsibilities alone, some that cannot wait for your return to be decided on. Children don't wait for your return to get sick. It takes two understanding people and often sacrifice to keep a marriage together, and pilot divorce rates seem above average.

There are pluses, too. One is that when you're home you're really home all day. You're there when the kids get home from school or able to do things during the week that daily commuters can only do on crowded weekends. The privileges of free transportation allow the family easier and more frequent travel. This isn't as good as it might sound, though, because the free passes are subject to space; you don't make reservations and have confirmed seats but rather go to the airport, bag, baggage, and family, and then hope there are empty seats to accommodate you and your gang. If not, you sit around and wait for the next flight and hope it has space. Flying like this can have its trying moments.

The stress of the job never leaves you, and while enjoying your home and family, unspoken thoughts and concerns slip across your mind to disturb the day: recurrent training coming up, the time for your physical, that small slip on leveling off at altitude—only 200 feet but was it reported to FAA and would it act on it? The job never leaves you. Of course many jobs are like that, but it isn't a job that all find great, and the startling fact is that of the pilots joining ALPA and starting a career as line pilots 60 percent fall by the wayside before reaching mandated retirement age. Medical deficiency accounts for 30 percent; the rest are due to normal or accidental deaths (very few deaths are the result of an airline accident), failure of proficiency, or just plain being fed up. I was hired in a group of eight, but only two of us—Roger Don Rae and I—hung in until age 60 retirement; that's a real life example of how it goes.

Being an airline pilot isn't the cushy high-paying job a large part of the public—and especially airline executives—believe. It has stress, uncertainty, heavy responsibility, and physical demands few realize or understand. Prima donnas? I don't think so.

19 | AND NOW

More than 60 years have passed since that open biplane. This book shows, by guiding the reader through those decades, how the pilot has been burdened with more tasks, greater responsibility, and the necessity for diversified knowledge that includes science, law, and psychology. A broad base of intelligence like that is generally envisioned as something cultivated and reflected upon in studious solitude, but a pilot is frequently called on to use it immediately and unexpectedly during flight, without the luxury of time for contemplation.

The job has become one of stress that comes in various forms, from immediate concern for a low fuel supply and worsening weather causing growing ATC delays, to obtuse FAA regulations or nagging worry about a slight pain that comes and goes in one's chest.

The broad scope of the job invites opportunity for human error—pilot error. While a specific mistake may appear as a simple error, such as not extending the flaps before takeoff, the root causes are not simple, and there is always an underlying reason, of important and large dimension, why the flaps were overlooked. One charge we make here is that the large dimension is not sufficiently tracked down and remedied. All accidents are the culmination of more than one failure, and we charge that the published and promulgated results focus mostly on one cause—pilot error. While the reports may mention contributing causes, there is little follow-up aimed at exorcising them.

What has industry and government done to relieve the pilot of at least part of the entwined mass of demands? Essentially nothing. In fact the industry has added to rather than reduced the work load and mental stress.

Of course pilots have been aided by better-flying airplanes, in which navigation is simple and position is never in doubt; the cockpit has advanced from a cold and noisy place that leaked during bad weather to a comfortable, quiet, shirtsleeve workplace. But such advances are not what we're talking about; technology has progressed, but human factors—and I'm getting to hate those two words—have not. The fact that reducing demands on the human will reduce chances for human error has not been addressed with the intensity and honesty it deserves—which may be the most important thing said in this book.

Two paramount factors can be highlighted as reasons we are where we are: false economies and ponderous bureaucracy.

Economy, for example, requires the jamming of airplanes into airports and airways beyond their safe capacity. No matter how lofty the exclamations are made to deny this, it is so. Witness the constant reduction of separation margins to get more airplanes on a runway within a short time. The addition of flights and resulting confusion following deregulation has only aggravated the situation. The result is that ATC has assumed top priority in flight operations, pushing judgment and flight management down into a lower category.

In 1947 President Harry Truman created a Special Board of Inquiry on Air Safety headed by the chairman of the Civil Aeronautics Board, James M. Landis, and leaders of NASA (then NACA—National Advisory Committee for Aeronautics), CAA, ATA (Air Transport Association), and ALPA, for whom I took part as an alternate member. Many recommendations resulted, and one related to airport crowding. Recommendation number 40: *"The airlines should undertake to coordinate their operation so as to schedule fewer planes into congested airports at the busiest hours of the day."*

The report further charged Congress to adopt legislation that would require dispersal of operations at congested locations. Little beyond lip service has ever been given in the ensuing 44 years to correct this problem, which is economic in nature.

Economics caused the demise of the position of flight engineer, as discussed. The manufacturers, anxious to make their aircraft attractive to airlines by offering lower operating costs, found eliminating a crew member one way to do so. Strong claims that it is just as safe, or even safer, were advanced—the pros and cons of which are discussed in this book. But before dropping this crew member there was no exploration made to discover how a third crew member, developed from the flight engineer, could perform duties such as monitoring for errors made in the complex, fast-moving, and sometimes confusing environment in and out of the airplane and managing communications, weather gathering, and aircraft systems problems. I am not pleading for or against the third crew member, but I do claim unbiased study might have shown sufficient value to justify this position for reducing pilot pressures and chances for error—and perhaps even economic gain in maintenance advice and troubleshooting.

Manufacturers do everything possible to make safe aircraft—strong, reliable, and able to combat the elements—but when they reach the cockpit, the safety aspect becomes blurred by technology's weak points and the demands it places on the human, demands often unrealistic and unreasonable in the light of a human's fallibility.

FAA is the organization that everyone, at one time or another, points at as the culprit responsible for all problems. Many times FAA *is* to blame. It is slow to move, and when it does, it grasps at quick, shallow regulations to deal with problems of an immediate nature. All this blame, however, is not always valid; FAA does numerous things well. The problem is that it's too big, with too many diversified tasks: running ATC; making rules and regulations; doing research; certifying aircraft, crew members, mechanics, and traffic controllers; and monitoring airline operation for safe practices. FAA is involved in international affairs, checks airports, rides herd on all matters in a mass of regulations, keeps the airways' facilities working, investigates accidents or takes part in their investigation—and there are probably more duties I've failed to mention. With such a mass of work under one administrator, things don't get done in good time, if at all.

Back to Truman's Special Board of Inquiry. Item number 23: "Research agencies, industry and government should make every possible effort to stimulate the development of an adequate aircraft collision warning indicator."

Interestingly the Air Transport Association said in testimony at that time that it had a continuing project for the past 1½ years and estimated it would take another 1 to 3 years to solve the problem. Well, 40 years later the first collision warning device, TCAS, was finally installed in a few aircraft and mandated as required by FAA. There are problems with TCAS; it isn't perfect, and the industry awaits improved models.

There are many other things that have taken too long to accomplish, as discussed in the cases of airways' modernization and airport detection radar. The problem seems to be that aviation does not have a high authority that makes FAA accountable. Why wasn't someone there to see that collision warning devices didn't take 40 years to develop—to question the slowness and demand, with authority, that it be done?

NTSB investigates accidents and then makes recommendations to FAA, but many recommendations are never implemented. Why haven't we an authority that asks why not and can follow through to see they are accomplished? For one thing NTSB and FAA both work for the same boss, the Department of Transportation. The NTSB is supposed to be independent and report only to Congress, but its placement in government under Transportation makes that claim suspect at least. The Department of Transportation reports to the president and is responsible to Congress, both of whom only seem to become involved if there's a newsworthy problem. Unfortunately, any problem soon loses its immediacy when other events supersede it in the public's eye. Congress has, on occasion, forced a rule, like requiring ground proximity warning devices on airline aircraft. But such action focuses on one item, while the real need is constant surveillance of the entire spectrum of aviation that falls within government purview; and an operational law, put in place by Congress, creates the fear that Congress's knee-jerk action may create a worse problem.

The organization of aviation in government needs serious overhauling, with FAA redefined and perhaps split up; removing ATC to a separate organization is one change frequently suggested. Above all, however, the government agency charged with safety and progress needs to be monitored by a stern system of accounting.

But safety must not be viewed as government's task alone; it is industry's responsibility also, perhaps even more than government's. The success of the airline industry, and thus the airplane manufacturers, depends on the safety of air travel, both from the viewpoint of public acceptance and the ugly effects of liability and from the airline's responsibility to the public for its safety. It is difficult , therefore, to understand the industry's willingness to accept unsafe practices for economic benefit—encouraging the crowding of ATC, as an example.

This book's objective is not to scare people or to say flying is unsafe—it isn't; by any measure, it is the safest way to travel. But the potential for danger is real because one slip can create catastrophe; two airline airplanes, for example, carrying 200 people each, could collide in midair—a terrible thought. The chances of that happening are infinitesimal, but the potential is there, lurking in the shadows. The task is to be ever alert and neutralize the dangers that risk turning potential into reality.

We've asked, "pilot error, whose fault?" and our answer must be that we're all at fault. Not enough attention has been given to reducing the openings for error by lessening the demands and stress on the pilots, by lessening the possibility that a moment's distraction or forgetfulness will extract a terrible price. Unless this reduction is given proper attention, pilots will continue to make that occasional mistake. CRM, though of benefit, will not cure the problem nor will adding another regulation, or adding a bell, whistle, light, or other warning device to the plethora already aboard an aircraft, or adding rules to the already-stuffed rule books.

From the simple beginning of an instrument flight with no radio or ATC the pilot's job has increased in size, complexity, and responsibility. Each era has asked for more exacting, faultless performance. Modern technology both in aircraft and ATC systems has not reduced the work load; in fact, they have added things to it. ATC and the glass cockpit have added a problem little talked of or investigated: how much pilot judgment have they removed? The fact is that pilot judgment, despite smug computer and cockpit designers, remains an essential quality; only a pilot can judge a thunderstorm and the action to take against it, or the flight's condition regarding fuel, weather, and alternate landing site, or how to handle a compound, unplanned emergency. Yet the modern system erodes this judgment, suggesting the computer, dispatcher, and ATC controller can direct what a flight should do. This is a fallacious and dangerous concept.

The focus has been on technical development, but no forceful, organized effort has been made to lessen the pilot's burden, which, in turn, will reduce the chance for pilot error.

Our plea, then, is to develop and then implement real ways to reduce rather than add to the pilot's burden, to simplify the pilot's job rather than complicate it, to respect, finally, that pilot judgment will always be needed—and to make room for it.

SELECTED BIBLIOGRAPHY

ACCIDENT REPORTS

National Transportation Safety Board, Washington, D.C.
Trans World Airlines, B707, Atlantic City, New Jersey, July 26, 1969;
World Airways, Douglas DC-8, King Cove, Alaska, September 8, 1973;
Pan American, B707, Pago Pago, American Samoa, January 30, 1974;
Air New England, De Havilland DHC-6-300, Hyannis, Massachusetts, June 17, 1979;
Redcoat Air Cargo, Bristol Britannia, Billerica, Massachusetts, February 16, 1980;
Air Florida, B737, Washington, D.C., January 13, 1982;
World Airways, DC-10, Boston, Massachusetts, January 23, 1982;
Scandinavian Airlines System, DC-10, JFK Airport, February 28, 1984;
Delta, L-1011, Dallas–Fort Worth Airport, August 2, 1985;
Northwest Airlines, DC-9, Detroit, Michigan, August 16, 1987;
Delta B727, Dallas–Fort Worth Airport, August 31, 1988;
Eastern Airlines and Epps Air Service, Atlanta, Georgia, January 18, 1990;
Northwest Air Lines Flights 1482 and 299, DC-9 and B727, Detroit, Michigan, December 3, 1990.

Report by the Ministerio de Transportes y Communicationes, Madrid, Spain.
KLM Royal Dutch Airlines, B747, and Pan American Airways B747, at Tenerife, Spain, March 27, 1977.

OTHER SOURCES

Airbus Industrie. *A320 Flight Crew Operating Manual.*
Aircraft Command in Emergency Situations. FAA Fact Sheet, Atlantic City International Airport, New Jersey, 1989.
Answers and Explanations for FAA Instrument Rating Question Book, Batavia, Ohio: Sporty's Academy, 1988.
Aviation Weather Services. Seattle: FAA-ASA Publications, May 1990.

Beaty, David. *The Human Factors in Aircraft Accidents*. London: Secker and Warburg, 1969.

Billings, Charles E. *Human-centered Aircraft Automation: A Concept and Guidelines*. Moffett Field, California, NASA, August 1991.

Billings, Charles E., and E. S. Cheaney. *Information Transfer Problems in the Aviation System*. Moffett Field, California, NASA Technical Paper # 1875, 1981.

The Boeing Airplane Company, Seattle, Washington.
Preliminary 707 Operations Manual, November 1957.

The Boeing Company, Seattle, Washington.
Jet Transport Performance Methods, 6th Edition, May 1969.
Operations Manual 767, May 1982.

Brown, Joe A.
Thunderstorm Characteristics and Flight Procedures. Kansas City, Missouri: Trans World Airlines, September 1945.
Wind Factor Effect on Descent Rate. Kansas City, Missouri: Trans World Airlines, March 1966.
Wind Shear Effects on Air Speed. Kansas City, Missouri: Trans World Airlines, 1961.

Business and Aviation Safety. Journals of 1990 and 1991.

Chandler, Jerome Greer. *Fire and Rain*. Austin: Texas Monthly Press, 1986.

Connelly, Mark E. *Report: A Study of Techniques to Compensate for Severe Wind Shears and Thunderstorms in Landing*. Massachusetts Institute of Technology, Cambridge, September 1981.

Davies, D. P. *Handling the Big Jets*. Surrey, England, Air Registration Board, April 1970.

Edwards, David C. *Pilot*. Ames: Iowa State University Press, 1990.

FAA Historical Fact Book, 1926–1971. Washington, D.C., 1974.

Federal Aviation Regulations, Parts 23, 25, 61, 91, 121, 135, and *Air Traffic Control Data—United States*. Washington, D.C. Current as of 1993.

Fujita, T. Theodore
DFW Microburst. The University of Chicago, 1986.
The Downburst. The University of Chicago, 1985.

Halaby, Najeeb E. *Cross Winds*. Garden City, New York: Doubleday and Company, 1978.

Helmreich, R.L., T.R. Chidester, H.C. Foushee, and S.E. Gregorich. "How Effective Is Cockpit Resource Management Training?" *Flight Safety Foundation Digest*, May 1990.

Hopkins, George E. *Flying the Line*. Washington, D.C., Air Line Pilots Association, 1982.

Huff, Darrwell. *The Strategy of Taking Tests*. New York: Appleton, Century, Crofts, 1961.

Human Factors Digest, vols. 1 and 2. Montreal, Canada, International Civil Aviation Organization, 1989.

Instrument Rating Question Book. Washington, D.C.: FAA. Reprinted by Sporty's Academy, Inc., 1988.

Jet Aircraft Loss Data. Wichita, Kansas, Aviation Data Service, 1991.

Karman, Theodore Von. *Aerodynamics.* New York: McGraw-Hill Book Co., 1957.

Kent, Richard J., Jr. *Safe, Separated and Soaring.* Washington, D.C.: FAA, 1980.

Komons, Nick A.
Bonfires to Beacons. Washington, D.C.: FAA, 1978.
The Cutting Crash. Washington, D.C.: FAA, 1984.
The Third Man. Washington, D.C.: FAA, 1987.

NASA Aviation Safety Reporting System. Quarterly reports 3, 6, 8, 9, 10, 12, 14. Moffett Field, California, 1977–1983.

Owens, Charles A. *Flight Operations.* London: Granada, 1982.

Pilot Attitude to Flight Deck Automation. Farnborough, Hants, England, Royal Air Force Institute of Aviation Medicine, 1991.

Porter, Richard F. *A Review of In-Flight Emergencies in the ASRS Data Base.* Moffett Field, California, NASA, May 1981.

Preston, Edmund. *Troubled Passage.* Washington, D.C.: FAA, 1987.

Report to the President of the United States by the President's Special Board of Inquiry on Air Safety. Washington, D.C., December 29, 1947.

Rochester, Stuart I. *Take Off at Mid-Century.* Washington, D.C.: FAA, 1976.

Soderlind, Captain Paul A. *Jet Turbulence Penetration,* Flight Standards Bulletin 8-63. Minneapolis, Minnesota, Northwest Airlines, 1963.

Solberg, Carl. *Conquest of the Skies.* Boston: Little, Brown and Company, 1979.

Trans World Airlines, Kansas City, Missouri.
Boeing 747 Flight Handbook, 1975
Constellation Crew Operating Manual, Models 049, 749-749A, 1049, 1049G, September 1956.
Emergency Procedures Handbook, 1986.
Pilot's Manual: Lockheed Constellation, Model 49-25, July 1946.
TWA Maintenance Handbook, 747, 1969.

Weiner, Earl L. *Human Factors of Advanced Technology ("Glass Cockpit") Transport Aircraft.* Moffett Field, California, NASA Report 177528, June 1989.

Weiner, Earl L., and David C. Nagel, eds. *Human Factors in Aviation.* New York: Academic Press, 1988.

Wilson, John R. M. *Turbulence Aloft.* Washington, D.C.: FAA 1979.